WOMEN EMPOWERMENT AND GLOBALISATION:

A Modern Perspective

WOMEN EMPOWERMENT AND GLOBALISATION:
A Modern Perspective

Dr. Amrit Prasad

SWASTIK

SWASTIK PUBLICATIONS

DELHI-110094 (INDIA)

SWASTIK PUBLICATIONS
31 Gali No. 1, A Block, Pocket 5, CRP Water Tank,
Sonia Vihar, Delhi-110094
Cell: 9968482939, 9899462604
e-mail: swastik_books@yahoo.com

**Women Empowerment and Globalisation:
A Modern Perspective**

First Published 2012

ISBN:- 978-93-81084-17-5

PRINTED IN INDIA

Published by Indra Mani Pandey for Swastik Publications, Delhi and Printed at Asian Offset Press, Delhi-53

Preface

The empowerment of women is a broadly endorsed strategy for solving a host of difficult problems, from child poverty to gender violence to international development. The author offers thoughtful critiques of the notion of empowerment based on their studies in twenty countries in all regions of the world. The comparative introduction places concepts of empowerment in the context of models of the market and of community, showing how contradictions in these models as they are enacted on the ground provide both spaces and constraints for women.

The chapters consider opportunities for women in the context of globalization, resurgent nationalism and politicized religion and cultures of masculinity. They show how initiatives at national or global levels are transformed by local cultures and power structures, and demonstrate the fruitfulness of tensions between universal values of human rights and contextualized understandings. This landmark, multi-disciplinary analysis will be an essential addition to the fields of Political Science, Women's Studies, Economics, Sociology, International Development, Environmental Studies.

There have been increased economic opportunities for women but also mounting threats. In the present global reshaping of labour, studies have shown that, as a company adopts labour casualisation, the higher is the number of women employed and the greater is their vulnerability to exploitative conditions. Labour flexibility has also led to job insecurities for men, resulting in the erosion of their masculinity. To what extent, however, has this led to increased gender violence and strengthened patriarchy?

While the developmentalist and corporatist state, because of its links with capital, has been unable to qualitatively improve working conditions for women, global and local pressures have led it to make concessions to women, particularly in the passing of laws to improve and protect the position of women. In a sense, these laws have not really threatened the economic and political base of the State and of those in power and are thus tolerated. Today, however, the issue of women, at least at the level of rhetoric, can no longer be discounted.

Nonetheless, these laws, while helpful, have not genuinely transformed unequal gender relations nor have they led to more democratic processes and structures in society. Women do not want market democracy but genuine democracy. The call of the Women's Agenda for Change in 1999 for more accountability and democracy will not be accepted by the State.

It is thus important for the women's movement to link up with other social movements and for the wider democratic social and political movement to seriously incorporate women's concerns. However, we must be able to present alternatives to the present trends of commoditisation, individualism and materialism as well as the forces of conservatism if we, indeed, want to engage with globalisation on equal terms and in the context of our own interests.

It is our attempt to focus on women and for changing status after globilisation.

Author

CONTENTS

1

Introduction

Globalisation the growing integration of economies and societies around the world is a complex process that is variously affecting different regions, countries and areas and their populations. To some, globalisation is an inevitable, technologically driven process that is increasing economic and political relations between people of different countries and areas. For them, it is seen not only as a natural phenomenon, but also as something good for the world. To others, there is a much deeper concern about the related challenges and possible risks associated with the globalisation process. It is widely perceived that the process produces both "winners and losers". The complex and contradictory impacts of globalisation are notably marked in the situation of women:

- In many countries in the ESCAP region, the global pursuit of profit has enhanced employment opportunities for women, where previously they had not existed. Employment has facilitated some degree of economic independence for many women. This, in turn has generated the self–esteem that comes from such independence.
- The migration of women in search of better employment opportunities has helped to ease the problem of poverty in many cases and meet the labour needs of a number of countries in the region. More remittances are generated for the home economy and there is also a greater possibility of technology transfer and enhanced skills formation.
- Globalisation has also contributed to the creation of new associations of women and the strengthening of their networks

to offer mutual support and resources. The global social movement of human rights, in affirming women's equality, have provided women's groups in the region with international standards to rise against adverse national or local codes. Instantaneous communications have facilitated the formation of alliances and coalitions, lessened isolation for women in remote or secluded areas, allowed for rapid mobilisation over issues and provided support on a global basis.

- In several countries in the region, new information and communications technology (ICT) have improved the access of women to health, microcredit and employment opportunities. Access to ICT among rural women in recent years has been enabling them to participate in economic development through entrepreneurship and small–scale businesses.

However, globalisation has further reinforced many existing gender inequalities:

- The traditional sexual division of labour (the location of women in employment to which they are regarded as inherently suited, for example, the caring professions or textiles industries) has been furthered through the addition of new locations and forms of work (services industry, tourism, work in free trade and export process zones). What remains constant is the low economic value accorded to work performed primarily by women in conditions of exploitation, no job security and violations of human rights.
- The shift to more knowledge intensive production has not uniformly impacted women. New jobs have been created but women increasingly have to contend with vulnerable forms of employment. These range between technological redundancy, the casualisation/informalisation of labour, as well as the health and safety hazards associated with new technology. This is especially severe in transition economies where women had the protection of the socialist state system; the opening up of the market to foreign capital has meant a loss of these rights.
- One major impact of the recent financial crisis, an unintended impact of globalisation, was the rapid increase in unemployment as hundreds of small and large firms across the region were

forced to close their doors. Women were the first workers to be laid off–both because the industries in which they predominate (*e.g.* garments) were those most affected by the crisis and because women were less unionised and therefore easier to sack. The unemployment situation was aggravated by increasing numbers of returning migrant labourers, many of whom were women, who were being expelled by countries which were experiencing their own unemployment problems. Moreover, cuts in public social sector expenditure, that came in the aftermath of the crisis, brought even more hardships, especially for women who have primary responsibility for care of the family.

- Perhaps the most critical of the impacts of globalisation on women is the worsening situation of violence against women. One aspect of this deserves urgent attention the trafficking of women and girls.
- This monograph offers an analysis of the issues facing women in Asia and the Pacific region, particularly in the context of globalisation and social development. It also suggests some policy options that could be pursued in order to address the challenges women face.
- The structure of this monograph reflects, first, the core goals of social development and, second, the social risks and global opportunities that challenge the realisation of these goals. Given the focus of this study, these risks and opportunities will be examined in gender terms.
- A substantial portion of the material in the chapters have been drawn from the Theme Study of the fifty–eight session of the Economic and Social Commission for Asia and the Pacific entitled "Sustainable social development in a period of rapid globalisation: challenges, opportunities and policy options" (United Nations, 2002).

POVERTY AND SOCIAL EQUITY

Widespread poverty and excessive inequality remain the principal challenges in the globalisation process that has been under way during the last two decades. Even as economies and Governments adjust in order to give a larger role to markets and a smaller role to the State in development, the importance of public action to deal with poverty and vulnerability has increased. It is for this reason that the World Summit for Social Development in 1995 called upon countries to reduce substantially overall poverty and to eradicate extreme poverty.

These goals were re–emphasised in a time–bound and measurable framework by the United Nations as core Millennium development goals. These tasks are indeed daunting in the ESCAP region, where in 1998, an estimated 800 million people, or 67 per cent of the world's poor, were living below the international poverty line of $1 per day per capita at 1993 prices.

Defining and Measuring Poverty

There is currently broad agreement that the multiple dimensions of poverty cannot be adequately explained or addressed by definitions and measurements based only on income or consumption. The income–consumption approach to poverty fails to show the human development outcomes.In gender terms, moreover, the use of the household as the unit of analysis in poverty measurement, cannot adequately describe women's well–being or lack thereof as a result of intra household inequalities in resource distribution.

As some researchers have shown, gender inequality is not necessarily correlated with household poverty. Women can be deprived in rich households, and increases in household incomes can co–exist with greater inequality in terms of a woman's well-being. Poverty is a deprivation of essential assets and opportunities to which every human male and female should be entitled. Everyone should have access to basic education and primary health services. Poor households have the right to sustain themselves by their labour and be reasonably rewarded, as well as have some protection from external shocks. These rights and entitlements are understood as "endowments" that people have in any society.

Beyond income and basic services, individuals as well as societies are also poor and tend to remain so if they are not empowered to participate in making the decisions that shape their lives. Poverty is thus better measured in terms of basic education, healthcare, nutrition, water and sanitation, as well as income, employment and wages. In addition, the poor may not have acquired essential assets because they live in remote or resource–poor areas; or because they are vulnerable on account of gender, age, health, living environment or occupation.

They may be denied access to assets because they belong to an ethnic minority or a community considered socially inferior, or simply because they are female or have a disability. At a broader level, poverty may stem from situations where gross inequality of assets persists because of vested interests and entrenched power structures. Finally, essential assets may not be available to the poor because of the lack of political will, inadequate governance and inappropriate public policies and programmes. The entitlements and capabilities framework of Amartya Sen (1990) provides a more useful approach to understanding poverty, as it emphasises the whole range of means, not just income, available to achieve human capabilities.

These means may include personal security and community participation as well as the Human Develcpment Indicators such as literacy, longevity and access to income. Sen's concept of well–being in the form of choice over capabilities is achieved through a combination of entitlements and endowments. Viewed in this way, poverty and deprivation are a result of entitlement failure, rather than scarcity per se. Furthermore, what is implicit in this approach is the idea of human agency to exercise choice over different combinations of capabilities. The Human Poverty Indicators of UNDP, which are built on Sen's framework, is useful to monitor and compare experiences of human poverty over time.

These indicators, together with the Gender Development Index, provide the basis for comparing the gendered experiences of well–being and deprivation, including within the household. They also help in for the understanding the magnitude of differences in actual well–being between men and women.

Risk and vulnerability to poverty, especially in the context of rapid globalisation, have received renewed attention in recent years. Vulnerability to poverty is an important dimension of poverty and deprivation, but it is also a cause of deprivation. Many individuals, households and population groups, while not currently "in poverty", are vulnerable to events that could easily push them into poverty: a bad harvest, a lost job, an unexpected expense, an illness and an economic downturn. Vulnerability may also be seen as determined by the options available to households and individuals to make a living, the risks they face and their ability to handle such risk.

Recognising this worldwide situation of poverty and vulnerability, the World Summit for Social Development set as one of its core goals and commitments the eradication of extreme poverty and the reduction of overall poverty.

These commitments, however, were not matched with a clear definition of poverty nor appropriate indicators for measuring progress. In September 2000, the United Nations Millennium Summit took these commitments a step further in adopting a set of time bound and measurable targets to reduce extreme income poverty as well as some major aspects of human poverty. These include the following:

(a) Between 1990 and 2015, halve the proportion of people whose income is less than $ 1 a day;

(b) Between 1990 and 2015, halve the proportion of people who suffer from hunger;

(c) By 2015, ensure that children everywhere, boys and girls alike, will be able to complete a full course of primary schooling;

(d) Eliminate gender disparity in primary and secondary education, preferably by 2005, and to all levels of education no later than 2015;

(e) Reduce by two thirds, between 1990 and 2015, the under–five mortality rate;

(f) Reduce by three quarters, between 1990 and 2015, the maternal mortality ratio;

(g) Have halted by 2015 and begun to reverse the prevalence of malaria and other major diseases;

(h) Halve by 2015 the proportion of people without sustainable access to safe drinking water;

(i) By 2020, achieve a significant improvement in the lives of at least 100 million slum dwellers.

Poverty Trends in the ESCAP Region

In the ESCAP region as a whole, poverty, as measured by income/consumption standards, was declining in the 1990s. By subregion, poverty reduction in East Asia and the Pacific, including China, was quite significant (27.6 per cent of the population to 15.3 per cent) in the 1990s. However, poverty reduction has been slow in South Asia (reducing the incidence of poverty from 44.0 per cent of the population to 40 per cent) and the incidence of poverty has risen in Central Asia (from 1.6 per cent of the population to 5.1 per cent).

The sharp reduction in the incidence of poverty in East Asia and the Pacific as a whole, as well as in China in particular, has meant that the number of people classified as "income poor" in these countries has also fallen quite substantially during the 1990s. However, in South Asia, which is characterised by a large population and a high incidence of poverty, the smaller reduction in poverty incidence has not helped to prevent an increase in the number of income poor. The largest number of poor people is in South Asia, particularly in India. Moreover, between 1996 and 1998, during which time East Asia was afflicted by the 1997/98 financial crisis, poverty rose marginally in the whole of East Asia and significantly in China, resulting in an increase in the number of income poor in those countries. Currently, nearly 800 million people, two thirds of the world's poor, live in the Asian and Pacific region.

TABLE: INCIDENCE OF EXTREME POVERTY BY SUBREGIONS, 1990–1998

	Percentage of population living below $1.08 a day (1993 purchasing power parity) Poverty rate (percentage below $1.08)				
	1987	**1990**	**1993**	**1996**	**1998**
East Asia	26.6	27.6	25.2	14.9	15.3
Excluding Chin	22.9	18.5	15.9	10.0	11.3
Eastern Europe and Central Asia	0.2	1.6	4.0	5.1	5.1
South Asia	44.9	44.0	42.4	42.3	4.0
Asia snd the Pacific		34.3			25.6

Source: ESCAP based on World Bank, World Development Report 2000/2001.

TABLE: PERCENTAGE OF POPULATION BELOW NATIONAL POVERTY LINES IN SELECTED COUNTRIES, 1990–2000

Country	1990	1991	1992	1993	1994	1995	1996	1997	1998	1999	2000
Bangladesh	47.8	..	42.7	..	..	..	36.0	..	..	..	34.0
Cambodia	..	..	..	..	39.0	..	..	36.1	..	35.9	..
China	9.4	..	..		–	7.1	6.7	5.4	4.6	3.7	..
India	38.9	..	..	..	36.0	..	..	..	..	26.1	..
Indonesia	15.1	..	..	13.7	..	..	11.3	..	..	18.2	..
Kazakhstan	..	..	..	..	..	..	34.6	43.0	43.4	34.5	31.8
Kyrgyzstan	..	..	..	40.0	..	..	..	51.0	..	..	..
Malaysia	17.1	..	..	13.4	..	9.6	..	6.8	..	8.1	..
Mongolia	..	..	17.0	24.0	..	36.3	..	..	35.6	..	..
Nepal	41.4	..	..	..	..	..	42.0	..	..	..	38.0
Pakistan	..	22.1	..	22.4	29.3	..	..	31.0	..	32.6	33.5
Philippines	..	45.2	..	..	40.2	..	..	..	43.0	..	..
Republic of Korea	8.4	..	..	8.2	..	..	7.0	..	..	..	..
Sri Lanka	..	33.0	..	..	..	..	39.2	..	..	..	..
Thiland	27.2	..	23.2	..	16.3	–	11.4	..	13.0	15.9	..
Vite Nam	..	..	..	58.2	..	..	..	..	37.4	..	32.0

Source: ESCAP, 2001, Manila, World Bank, 2001;

Note: Poverty estimates are based on country specific poverty lines, expressed in national currencies. Many countries have more than one such poverty line, and efforts have been made to put consistent time series data on the incidence of poverty.

a. (1989)

b. (1988)

c. (1985)

It shows that poverty was declining in Bangladesh, Cambodia, China, India, Malaysia, the Republic of Korea and Viet Nam. Poverty has increased, however, in eight countries, especially in Indonesia, the Philippines and Thailand after 1997. Trends in the incidence of poverty, as revealed by the country specific data, tally with the idea that during the 1990s, which were the years of rapid globalisation, the advances registered in the "war against poverty" in a few countries in the Asia and Pacific region have either been weakened or partially reversed.

Gender Equity

Equity is also about the distribution of opportunities for participation in social and economic life, which is in turn influenced by the distribution of power at various levels: between rich and poor people, men and women, different regions and ethnic groups, to name but a few dimensions. Equity reflects poverty which, as emphasised previously, is more than low incomes and social indicators. Equity is about access to social benefits as well as about the inability to exercise basic human and political rights. Inequity is about the absence of dignity, deprivation in knowledge and communication, environmental impoverishment and the violation of rights.

The term "feminisation of poverty" was first coined in 1978 to describe trends in the United States, where it was argued that two thirds of the poor over the age of 16 were women. Similar claims over the years have been made for countries in the ESCAP region. ADB and UNDP have also described poverty as having "a women's face": of 1.3 billion people in the world living in poverty, 70 per cent are women, two thirds of the poor in Asia are women. IFAD (1992: 22) found that between the period 1965–1970 and the mid 1980s, the number of rural women living in poverty increased by 48 per cent, while the number of rural men living in poverty increased by 30 per cent in the same period. At the same time, there has been a general perception of an increasing incidence of female headship of households on a global scale and an association of this trend with the "feminisation of poverty". The "feminisation of poverty" concept has become influential in the foundation of development policy and in practices, such as, in targeting of subsidies, for example. The concept implies that:

(a) Women have a higher incidence of poverty then men;
(b) Women's poverty is more severe that than of men;
(c) There is a trend towards greater poverty among women, particularly associated with rising rates of female headship of household.

However, there are limitations to the full acceptance of this concept based on the following:

(a) There is a lack of systematic sex–disaggregated data on expenditure and consumption;
(b) Empirical studies show conflicting conclusions;
(c) The use of the household as the unit of analysis in poverty measurement does not provide a good predictor of women's well–being because of intra–household inequalities in resource distribution and other institutional biases (recent empirical studies show conflicting conclusions.

Using various indicators such as the Human Development Index, Human Poverty Indicator and the Gender Development Index, researchers have shown that the relationship between women and men, in most countries in this region, is characterised by glaring inequalities.

Women tend to fare poorly in relative terms compared with men, even at the household level. Moreover, the gender based inequality is evident not only in the lack of opportunities for women to develop skills and talents, but also in more fundamental areas such as nutrition, health and survival.

In terms of equity as well, there is a gender disparity in the distribution of opportunities for participation in social and economic life. In many Asian countries, one effect of gender inequality is the remarkably low ratio of females to males. While the worldwide ratio of women to men is 98.5:100, in the Asian region it is 95.7:100. India had 32 million "missing women" in 1986, and China had a somewhat higher estimate of 36 million missing women during the same period. Female infanticide, the neglect of female children and son preference are some of the practices that have led to the excess female mortality and the low ratio of females to males in these countries. However, there are also more subtle and widespread practices that have aggravated the plight of women.

The persistence of extremely high levels of gender inequality and female deprivation, and the emerging feminisation in agriculture are among the most serious social and economic problems in the region. There is also mounting evidence that gender inequality does not decline with economic growth. For example, South Asian countries have achieved an annual economic growth rate of about 6 per cent over the last two decades. However, South Asia as a region lags behind second to last in the world with respect to social indicators and it suffers from very low levels in other measures of gender related indicators, namely, the Gender Development Index and the Gender Empowerment Index.

Structural adjustment and globalisation are also having effects on women in the region and their roles as producers, mothers, household managers and community organisers. The implications have been typically negative in terms of reduced real incomes and standard of living for most women, along with a greater burden of unpaid work.

One very important area, where negative impacts in gender terms deserve special attention is that of food security. It is a critical issue throughout the countries of South Asia as well as in China and Indonesia and several other parts of the region. Structural adjustment programmes and their attendant processes, emphasis on the export of primary commodities along with cuts in food and other subsidies, the commercialisation of agriculture, *etc.* have led to increase in food prices and declining food security, especially in peasant households. It is widely acknowledged in many Asian societies, that when household per capita access to food declines, women and girls face disproportionately excessive cuts in their food consumption. Perhaps the most critical of the issues related to women's poverty is the many forms of violence against women. One aspect of this deserves urgent attention the trafficking of women and girls. During the past decade, this form of trafficking has become an issue of growing concern in this region, especially in South–East Asia. It has been conservatively estimated that at least 200,000 to 225,000 women and children from South–East Asia are trafficked annually, a figure representing nearly one third of the global trafficking trade.

Women and girls who are victims of this international trade are at an increased risk of further violence, as well as unwanted pregnancy and sexually transmitted infection, including infection with the human immunodeficiency virus (HIV) which cause the acquired immunodeficiency syndrome (AIDS) (IOM 2000). Two Millennium Declaration targets that specifically address gender inequality concerns are:

(a) Eliminate gender disparity in primary and secondary education, preferably by 2005, and at all levels of education no later than 2015;

(b) Reduce by three quarters, between 1990 and 2015, the maternal mortality ratio.

The primary indicator to monitor progress in meeting these targets is the ratio of females to males in primary, secondary and tertiary education. The secondary indicators are (a) the ratio of literate females to males among youth 15 to 24 years old (b) the share of women in wage employment in the non–agricultural sector and (c) the proportion of seats held by women in the national parliament.

In view of the data available, it is unlikely that the region as a whole would achieve the Millennium Declaration target of eliminating gender disparities in primary and secondary education. This is particularly so for Bangladesh, Cambodia, India, the Lao People's Democratic Republic, Nepal, Pakistan, Papua New Guinea and Solomon Islands. In terms of tertiary level education, a number of countries in North and Central Asia show a ratio of women to men higher than 100 per cent; in South Asia, the male to female ratio was generally lower.

As for the secondary indicator, female youth literacy, the overall male and female figures showed nearly universal female youth literacy in South–East Asia, East and North–East Asia, and North and Central Asia; however, the rates in South Asia, were lower. Data on the share of women in wage employment in the non–agricultural sector is very limited. And on the proportion of seats held by women in national parliaments, the available data show very low rates ranging from 2 per cent in Solomon Islands to 26 per cent in Turkmenistan. The targeted rates should, however, be close to 50 per cent.

TABLE: GENDER EQUALITY AND EMPOWER WOMEN

Country By subregion	Ratio of literate female to male 15–24 years old		Share of women in wage employment in the non agricultural sector		Seats in parliament held by women (as % of total)
	1990	1999	1999	1992	2000
East and North–East Asia					
China	94	97	39	21	21.8
Democratic people's republic or Korea				20	20.1
Hong Kong. China	101	101	42x		
Japan			39x		<10
Macao, China					
Mongolia	78	87		4	7.9
Republic of Korea	100	100	39x		3.7
North and Central Asia					
Amerce	100	100			3
Azerbaijan					12
Zeorgia					7
Kazakhstan					11
Kyrgyzstan					
Rusian Federation	100	100			6
Tajikistan	100	100			
Turkmenistan					
Uzbekistan	95	97			7
South and South–West Asia					
Afghanistan					
Bangladesh	59	65		10	9.1
Bhutan				0	2
India	74	81	15x	7	8.9
Islamic					

Republic of Iran	89	95		3	4.9
Maldives	100	101			6.3
Nepal	41	54			6.4
Pakistan	51	61	8x	1	2
Sri Lanka	98	99	44x	5	4.9
Turkey	91	95	10x	2	4
South–East Asia					
Brunei Darussalam	101	101			
Combodia	40	55			
Indonesia	97	99	38x	12	8.2
Lao Peoples Democratic Republic	52	69		9	21.2
Malaysia	99	100	36x	8	103
Myanmar	96	99			
Philippines	100	100	40	11	12.9
Singapore	100	100	44x	4	4.3
Thailand	99	99	45x	4	4.3
Viet Nam	99	100		19	26.0
Pacific					
American Samoa					
Australia					
Cook Islands			47x		22.4
Fiji	99	100	31x	4	107
French Polynesia					
Guam					
Kiribati					
Marshall Islands					0
Micronesia (Federated States of)					0
Nauru					0
New Caledonia					
New Zealand			48x		29.2
Niue					1
Northern Mariana Island					
Palau					0
Papua New Guinea	83	88		0	
Samoa	100	101		4	8.2
Solomon Islands				0	2
Tonga					0
Tuvalu					0
Vanuatu					0

a/World Bank, World Development Indicators 2001.

b/UNIFEM 2000.

c/1992 figures from United Nations Development Programme, Human Development Report 1994.

d/Figures as of January 2000 (United Nations Development Fund for Women, 2000, p. 77)

The other Millennium Declaration target on gender inequality is to reduce by three quarters, between 1990 and 2015, the maternal mortality ratio. The primary recommended indicator is the maternal mortality ratio and the secondary indicator is the proportion of births attended by skilled health personnel. In many the countries in the region, the percentage of births attended by skilled health personnel was below 50 per cent. The rates were particularly low in countries with high maternal mortality ratios, for example in South Asian countries.

For many developing countries in the region, it appears that the prospects of meeting this Millennium Declaration target is very slim, unless countries seriously intensify their efforts to provide skilled care at birth to 90 per cent of women by 2015.

TABLE: MATERNAL HEALTH

Country By subregion	Maternal mortality ratio per 1,000 live births		Proportion of britiss attended by skilled health personnel (% of total)	
	1990	1999/2000	1999–1992	2000
East and North–East Asia	60	30		67
China	35			100x
Democratic people's republic or Korea				
Hong Kong. China		3	100	
Japan				100x
Macao, China				
Mongolia	150	58	100	93
Republic of Korea	20	8	95	98x
North and Central Asia				
Amerce	29			97
Azerbaijan	43	15		100
Zeorgia	22			

Kazakhstan	80	22		98
Kyrgyzstan	80	26		98
Rusian Federation	74	50		99
Tajikistan	120	20		79
Turkmenistan	65	33		96
Uzbekistan	60	22		98
South and South–West Asia				
Afghanistan		165		8x
Bangladesh	600	61	7	13
Bhutan	500	80	16	15x
India	440	41	44	34x
Islamic Republic of Iran	130		78	86
Maldives	390	60	55	90x
Nepal	830	75	8	9
Pakistan	200	90	40	19
Sri Lanka	60	15	85	94x
Turkey	55		77	81
South–East Asia				
Brunei Darussalam	22			98x
Combodia	590	100		
Indonesia	450	42	47	34
Lao Peoples Democratic Republic	660	93	47	56
Malaysia	39	8		14x
Myanmar	230	77	94	96
Philippines	208	31		56
Singapore	9	3		100x
Thailand	44	28	71	71x
Viet Nam	160	37	95	77
Pacific				
American Samoa				
Australia				
Cook Islands	30	26		99x
Fiji	31	18		
French Polynesia			98	
Guam				
Kiribati	225	53		72x
Marshall Islands		63		97
Micronesia (Federated States of)	561	20		90x
Nauru		25		
New Caledonia				

New Zealand				95x
Niue				99x
Northern Mariana Island				
Palau				99x
Papua New Guinea	390	58		53
Samoa	70	21	52	76x
Solomon Islands	550	22	85	85x
Tonga	160	18		92x
Tuvalu		40		100x
Vanuatu	68	37		79x

Trends in the Economic Participation of Women

Some indication of the gender dimensions in the economic participation is available from Table. This gives the female labour force participation rates in 1997, which can be said to be the "peak" year in terms of feminisation of work the continuing increases in the female share of employment in the region, as well as the proportionate change since 1985. It is evident that for most countries of the region the period between 1985 and 1997 witnessed a massive increase in the labour force participation of women. This process was most marked in the Southeast Asian region which was also the most dynamic in terms of exporting.

Throughout Asia, as a consequence, the gap between male and female labour force participation rates narrowed, suggesting that the recent period has been one in which at least in terms of quantitative involvement the gender gap has been narrowing. Among the 4 countries registering declines in labour force participation of women the percentage change is small ranging from –1.5 (Papua New Guinea) to –5.0 (India).

The declines in Fiji, Laos and Nepal should not made too much of, given the problems of data collection in these countries and the well known problems associated with the underreporting of women's work. Despite the growing involvement of women in recognised economic activity in Asia, they have continued to remain dominant in unpaid household work, as also shown in Table.

The very low share of female unpaid workers to the total in Pakistan is likely to be because of the lack of recognition of women's work, especially given the very low overt work participation rates for women in that country. The point that growing responsibility for paid economic activity does not necessarily reduce the burden of unpaid work for women is of course well–known by now, and has been reiterated many times. But the sheer fact that women continue to be the dominant suppliers of unpaid family labour is likely to be of growing significance given the current reliance on adjustment policies which shift more economic activity onto unpaid family labour, as will be discussed.

TABLE: LABOUR FORCE PARTICIPATION RATES OF WOMEN IN ASIA AND THE PACIFIC

Country	Labour force participation rate (age 15+) per cent in 1997	Per cent change since 1985	As share (%) of male rate in 1997	Female unpaid family workers as % of total
Bangladesh	44.4	7.8	77.2	71
China	55.7	13.8	87.3	n.a
Fiji	22.7	2.5	41.7	21
India	29.0	-5.1	50.3	n.a
Indonesia	37.9	16.9	66.9	71
Lao People's Democratic Republic	44.7	-5.1	86.9	n.a
Malaysia	30.5	16.9	60.6	71
Nepal	37.9	-1.7	69.6	61
Pakistan	20.8	23.3	40.3	33
Papua New Guinea	42.5	-1.5	76.9	n.a
Philippines	31.4	14.3	60.8	56
Republic of Korea	41.2	29.4	70.1	89
Singapore	39.4	20.5	64.8	75
Sri Lanka	30.5	51.3	55.4	53
Thailand	55.5	12.0	86.3	69
Viet Nam	49.4	11.2	93.9	n.a

Table shows the shift in employment patterns in three of the "typical" economies of the region, where the growth of export orientation in both production and employment meant that women wage workers came to dominate in the Export Processing Zones (EPZs) and even became much more significant in other non–EPZ manufacturing activity. In this period women workers were frequently the main contributors to household income, rather than subsidiary workers working for supplementary earnings, and this dominant material contribution in the households reflected also their substantial contribution to the aggregate national economies.

Table: Share of women in employment in EPZs and non-EPZ manufacturing (per cent)

Country	Year	Whole economy	EPZs	Other manufacturing
Malaysia	1980	33.4	75.0	35.6
Malaysia	1980	35.5	53.5	47.2
Philippines	1980	37.1	74.0	41.0
Philippines	1994	36.5	73.9	45.2
Republic of Korea	1987	40.4	77.0	41.7
Republic of Korea	1990	40.8	70.1	42.1

Source: Susan jokes (1999)

This pattern is made even clearer in Table, which shows the ratio of female employment to total employment in all sectors of the economy taken together. As is evident, the countries of the East and South–East Asian region show very high shares of female employment over the 1990s. (The ratios given are the average of the years for which data were available in the period 1990–1997.) The female share of total employment was over 30 per cent, and reached almost 46 per cent in Thailand.

Table: Female share of total employment in the 1980s (per cent)

Country of area	Percentage of total employment
Bangladesh	38.7
Hong Kong	37.8
India	14.8
Indonesia	38.1
Malaysia	34.5

Pakistan	13.2
Philippines	34.8
Republic of Kòrea	40.5
Sri Lanka	31.6
Thailand	45.9

Source: ILO 1998

Note: The number relate to the average of years for which data were available over the 1980s.

India and Pakistan show relatively low rates, which are even slightly lower than the average for developing countries. However, even here, it is worth noting that the 1990s witnessed an increase in the female share of manufacturing employment alone. Meanwhile, the two South Asian countries in which export oriented production has been or has become more important Sri Lanka and Bangladesh show female shares in total employment which are comparable to the South–East Asian countries. This trend towards feminisation of employment in Asian countries resulted from employers' needs for cheaper and more "flexible" sources of labour, and was also strongly associated with the moves towards casualisation of labour, shift to part–time work or piecerate contracts, and insistence on greater freedom for hiring and firing over the economic cycle.

All these aspects of what is now described as "labour market flexibility" became necessary once external competitiveness became the significant goal of domestic policy makers and defined the contours within which domestic and foreign employers in these economies operated. Feminisation of work was also encouraged by the widespread conviction among employers in Southeast Asia that female employees are more tractable and subservient to managerial authority, less prone to organise into unions, more willing to accept lower wages because of their own lower reservation and aspiration wages, and easier to dismiss using lifecycle criteria such as marriage and childbirth.

This was made more relevant because of technological changes which encouraged the use of labour which could be replaced at periodic intervals. There are three main macro economic factors which were widely seen as creating or contributing to these changes in work relations including the tendency towards feminisation:

(a) The liberalisation of trade, emphasis on export production and greater international mobility of capital created a new regional division of labour, which in turn led to the need for employers to achieve quick responses to uncertain markets. This necessarily required more flexibility in the labour market as well, and the more flexible contracts and lower wages under which women workers were typically employed rendered them more attractive than their male counterparts.

(b) Technological changes allowed for a stratification of the work force into a small group of highly skilled and highly paid workers, and a large pool of low to medium skilled workers whose chances of upward mobility were low and whose possibilities of on the job training and learning by doing were far more restricted than before. This meant that there was less need for long term implicit contracts between employer and employee. In fact, frequent replacement of workers was not only less of a problem but was even seen to be desirable in certain types of activities (such as in the electronics sector) which create high worker burnout. Recent technological changes have also facilitated decentralisation even of very modern manufacturing work, through the miniaturisation and modularisation of products and processes, which reinforces these tendencies.

(c) Organisational changes in production were closely related to the above two features. There was a very substantial increase in subcontracting, in the growth of ancillary small scale units, and in home based manufacturing production, which is effectively at the bottom of a complex production chain. Just–In–Time organisational methods, which at one time were spreading rapidly from Japan to the newer exporting industries in Southeast Asia, further strengthened these tendencies. The revival and expansion of putting out arrangements in the 1990s, which essentially involved homebased women workers, throughout Southeast Asia and parts of South Asia, was evidence of this.

This was the received wisdom at least until the crash of mid 1997, which dramatically altered both the potential for continued economic activity at the same rate, as well the conditions of employment in the region. When the export industries in some countries started to slow down from the middle of 1995, it became evident that continued growth of employment in these export oriented industries could not be the same engine of expansion that they had served as over the previous decade. It also became clear, therefore, that there could be some setback to the feminisation of employment that had been occurring, since the export industries had become the most important employers of women at the margin. Indeed, the very features which had made women workers more attractive to employers the flexibility of hiring and firing and the more casual, non–unionised nature of labour contracts are precisely those which are likely to render them to be the first to lose their jobs in any recessionary phase. But it now turns out that even the earlier assessment of the feminisation of work had been based on what was perhaps an overoptimistic expectation of expansion in female employment. Table presents some information on trends in aggregate manufacturing employment and female employment in this sector over the 1990s in some of the more important East and South–East Asian economies: Hong Kong, China; Indonesia; Malaysia; the Republic of Korea; Singapore and Thailand.

TABLE: TRENDS IN MANUFACTURING EMPLOYMENT AND SHARE OF WOMEN WORKERS

Year	Total manufacturing employment, 000s	Women employed in manufacturing, 000s	Share of women workers, per cent
Indonesia			
1990	7,693	3,483	45
1991	7,946	3,536	44
1992	7,948	3,661	47
1993	8,784	4,165	47
1994	10,127	4,323	43
1995	10,840	4,920	45
1996	10,773	4,895	45

Republic of Korea			
1992	4,828	1,931	40
1993	4,652	1,785	38
1994	4,695	1,765	38
1995	4,773	1,756	37
1996	4,677	1,716	36
1997	4,474	1,594	35
Malaysia			
1992	1,637	767	47
1993	1,723	766	44
1995	1,781	761	43
1996	1,912	797	42
1997	2003	807	40
Thailand			
1990	3,133	1,564	50
1991	3,465	1,748	50
1992	3,600	1,719	48
1993	3,961	1,929	49
1994	3,851	1,912	49
1995	4,377	2,172	49
1996	4,334	2,065	48
Singapore			
1991	423	189	44
1992	434	191	44
1993	429	182	42
1994	422	175	41
1995	408	152	37
1996	406	171	42
1997	414	166	40
Honk Kong. China			
1990	751	314	42
1991	717	292	41
1992	650	255	39
1993	594	225	38
1994	563	202	36
1995	535	197	37
1996	482	177	37
1997	444	160	36

Source: International labour office, Yearbock of labour statistics various issues.

Table does not indicate a clear picture of continuous employment in manufacturing industry over the decade even before the period of crisis. In several of these economies–Hong Kong, the Republic of Korea and Singapore aggregate manufacturing employment over the 1990s actually declined as their economies matured towards a greater reliance on the service sector. Only in Indonesia, Malaysia and Thailand was there a definite upward trend in such employment. The second is that, while it shows that female employment in manufacturing was important, the trend over the 1990s, even before the crash, was not necessarily upward.

In most of the economies described in table, there is a definite tendency towards a decline in the share of women workers in total manufacturing employment over the latter part of the 1990s. In Hong Kong and the Republic of Korea, the decline in female employment in manufacturing was even sharper than that in aggregate employment; indeed, in the Republic of Korea, the share of women's employment in total manufacturing employment declined from 40 per cent to 35 per cent in the five years between 1992 and 1997. Similarly, even in the countries in which aggregate manufacturing employment increased over the period 1990–1997, the female share had a tendency to stabilise or even fall.

Thus, in Indonesia the share of women workers in all manufacturing sector workers increased from an admittedly high 45 per cent to as much as 47 per cent by 1993, and then fell to 44 per cent by 1997. In Malaysia the decline in female share was even sharper than in the Republic of Korea: from 47 per cent in 1992 to only 40 per cent in 1997. A slight decline is evident even in Thailand, where the ratio moves from 50 per cent at the beginning of the decade to 48 per cent by 1996 and 1997. Evidence from table suggests that the process of feminisation of work really peaked somewhere in the early 1990s, and that thereafter the process was not only less marked, but may even have begun to peter out. This is interesting because it refers very clearly to the period before the effects of the financial crisis began to make themselves felt on real economic activity.

Despite the growing involvement of women in recognised economic activity in Asia, they have continued to remain dominant in unpaid household work, as also shown in table. The very low share of female unpaid workers to the total in Pakistan is likely to be because of the lack of recognition of women's work, especially given the very low overt work participation rates for women in that country. The point that growing responsibility for paid economic activity does not necessarily reduce the burden of unpaid work for women is of course well–known by now, and has been reiterated many times.

But the sheer fact that women continue to be the dominant suppliers of unpaid family labour is likely to be of growing significance given the current reliance on adjustment policies which shift more economic activity onto unpaid family labour, as will be discussed below.

This is an important issue that clearly requires further investigation. The reversal of the process of feminisation of work has already been observed in other parts of the developing world (notably in Latin America) were it has been found to be associated with either one of two conditions: an overall decline in employment opportunities because of recession or structural adjustment measures, or a shift in the nature of the new employment generation towards more skilled or lucrative activities.

In the East Asian case, until 1996 at least neither of these conditions would have been so important, except to some extent the second factor (shift towards more skilled jobs) in certain economies like that of the Republic of Korea and Singapore. Another relates to the relative cost of hiring women workers, and the relation to perceived other advantages.

It is obvious that one of the important reasons for preferring women workers in many export–related activities in particular, has been the lower reservation and offer wages of women. Table presents evidence on this for selected Asian economies. It shows that women workers' wages have been consistently and significantly lower than male wages in the aggregate. The differentials are particularly sharp in the case of the Republic of Korea, Malaysia and Singapore, where the average female wages are just above half those paid to male workers.

TABLE: FEMALE WAGES AS PERCENTAGE OF MALE WAGES

Economy	Percentage
Bangladesh	71.7
Honk Kong, China	65.9
Republic of Korea	52.3
Malaysia	57.9
Philippines	84.0
Singapore	57.1
Sri Lanka	87.8
Thailand	63.8

Source: ILO 1998.

To some extent this reflects differences in the types of jobs for which women are used, which are typically at the lower skill and lower wage end of the employment spectrum. But it also reflects the general tendency for gender discrimination in pay, whereby women are paid less even for similar or identical jobs. This feature, which was quite marked in East Asia, is precisely the feature which tends to be rendered less potent as more and more women are drawn into employment. As women become an established part of the paid work force, and even the dominant part in certain sectors (as in textiles, ready made garments and consumer electronics of East Asia) it becomes more difficult to exercise the traditional type of gender discrimination at work. Not only its there an upward pressure on their wages, but there are other pressures for legislation which would improve their overall conditions of work.

While this is fundamentally desirable and necessary, such action could reduce the relative attractiveness of women workers for those employers concerned with export profitability. The rise in wages also tends to have the same effect. It is worth noting that the female wage as a proportion of the male wage has been rising in most parts of East and South–East Asia in the 1990s up to 1997, including in Malaysia (from 49 to 57 per cent between 1990 and 1995), the Republic of Korea (from 50 to 56 per cent between 1990 and 1997), Thailand (from 63 to 68 per cent between 1991 and 1995 and Singapore (from 54 to 60 per cent between 1990 and 1997). Hong

Kong is the only economy in the region for which there is a decline in this ratio, from 69 to 61 per cent between 1990 and 1997. Thailand registered the highest ratio of female to male wages.

What this narrowing of the wages gap has meant is that women became less cheap as labour in exporting industry. Over this period (1995) there have been several moves towards protecting the interests of women workers, for example in terms of slightly better maternity benefits and some improvement in the nature of contracts. In the Republic of Korea, a law which allowed women to be fired once they got married was repealed in the early in the 1990s. Legislation in other countries in the region has allowed for a modicum of benefits which were previously denied mainly to women workers, to be provided.

If these improvements explain the tendency towards reduced employment of women, then it raises certain crucial questions which will become increasingly important in the near future. How is it possible to ensure a minimum provision of basic rights and privileges to women workers, and to improve the conditions of their work, without simultaneously eroding their attractiveness to employers and reducing the extent of female wage employment? How can such rights and basic labour standards be assured in the coming phase, in which heightened export competition is likely to be combined with a phase of aggregate employment contraction, as the full force of the current adjustment measures is felt in the real economies?

These are already pressing concerns, as is evident from the growth of unemployment in the region, which is bound to accelerate in the coming period. Already, over the 1990s, female open unemployment rates were much higher than those of men even in the expansionary phase, as table makes clear. But now, as the exporting industries are hit and as the general economic decline is worsened by adjustment measures that could affect workers (men as well as women) adversely, the problem is likely to become more acute.

Feminisation of the Elderly

Another demographic trend of concern is the falling fertility rates in the region, especially the wealthier Asian countries. Fourteen countries and cities in Asia have fertility rates below the 2.1 births per woman required to replace the older generations. This is more pronounced in the region's more affluent nations and cities, such as Japan, Hong Kong, China, Macau, China, Singapore, Taiwan, Province of China and the Republic of Korea where fertility rates are below 1.5 per woman, while Thailand is marginally higher at 1.8. Women in these countries are having fewer babies or no children at all because of career pressures.

Asia's fertility rate plunged from around six children per woman from 1950–1955 to 2.7 children per woman between 1995–2000. The current fertility rate in the region of 2.7 children per woman is slightly below the world average. The implications are far reaching and profound, as they affect the age structure of the population, giving rise to population ageing, labour force shortages, increased elderly dependency ratios and feminisation of the elderly population. One key impact will be on the labour force, where there will be fewer younger people to take over jobs left by the greying generation, who may have to work longer than normal before retiring. By 2050, Japan's old age population categorised as people aged 65 and above is forecast to be more than 36 per cent of the total population, up from 17 per cent in 2000. This will be three times as high as the proportion of people aged between 15–64. The proportion of the old age population will exceed that of the younger population in Singapore by 2020, 2025 in the Republic of Korea, 2035 in China and 2040 in Thailand. What this means is that countries with high social security coverage will come under pressure to provide pensions for the growing number of elderly.

The problem of care for the elderly is likely to be especially acute for older women, who constitute the majority of the elderly in virtually all low mortality populations. Because of women's greater longevity in most countries of Asia and the tendency for men to marry women younger than themselves, women are more likely than men to end their lives as widows. The implication of this is a serious gender asymmetry in the support and care of the elderly. Population ageing is also a women's issue in that the care for the elderly is still considered to be the responsibility of the family, part of a cultural value of filial piety. Women in the family or in the community have to play a major role in providing this care and support.

The onset of physical disability in old age may produce a need for support as well as for care if the individual's income depends on continued employment. Likewise, the social disabilities created by a sex based division of labour or by arbitrary rules of retirement may also create both support and care needs in old age. An important issue in formulating policy, then, is whether social norms concerning such issues as the gender based division of labour or the mandatory retirement age, create or exacerbate problems for populations as they age. The problems that elderly women face are, moreover, frequently compounded by their difficulties in obtaining sufficient income because of their limited access to pensions and rights to property.

In Asia the numbers of rural elderly are projected to increase in absolute terms. Such increases have implications for health needs and other necessary services. Many countries in the region will face an important elderly dependency ratio, which raises the issue of the possible future vulnerability of the rural elderly as a group in view of the pressures which will be placed on the family and community institutions. A large percentage of the future rural elderly will not benefit from any significant pension, health insurance or social security support which, insofar as they are being developed, are limited mostly to urban elderly. Again, the sex ratio is in favour of women, particularly in rural areas. From a rural gender perspective, distribution issues such as land property or tenure and other assets need to be examined.

Women in Development

In recent decades issue of gender equality and empowerment of women have been increasingly given particular attention national and regional development efforts. This has come about, to a large extent, as a result of the impetus given and commitments made by a succession of international meetings and conferences since the declaration of the first International Women's Year in 1975. The momentum of action in this area by Governments and NGOs has accelerated, as is evident in the reviews of progress made, most recently at the Fourth World Conference on Women, in Beijing in 1995, and the special session of the United Nations General Assembly in 2000.

The efforts in promoting and integrating the role and status of women in development have led to the following achievements, among others; greater de jure equality, closer gender parity in school enrolment ratios in many countries, increased participation in the labour market and business, better recognition of women's unpaid work and initiatives taken to quantify such work in alternative national and domestic accounting systems, and increased political participation.

Important mechanisms and institutions have been established, such as equal employment laws, revisions in inheritance, property and succession laws and other family laws to accord women equal rights in matrimonial and family affairs, national machineries to advocate and coordinate strategies and plans for women's empowerment and gender equality in the household, economy and polity, national policies and action plans to integrate women in development at all development levels, measures to prevent or penalise discrimination in employment practices and sexual harassment at places of work, and violence against women.

Gender related Development Index (GDI) values have been calculated based on three major achievements in human development, namely, a long and healthy life as measured by life expectancy at birth, knowledge as measured by the adult literacy rate and gross enrolment ratio, and a decent standard of living as measured by the estimated earned income adjusted to account for inequalities between men and women. The GDI values between 1994 and 1999 improved in 20 out of the 25 ESCAP countries for which data were available. The other five countries lost some. Among the 25 countries as a whole, the GDI increased by an average of 9.1 per cent.

In the context of globalisation, with greater political and cultural awareness there is increased expectation regarding the attainment of human rights and women's rights, among others. Globalisation has led to an unprecedented increase in women's NGOs and networking for mutual support and dialogue. These movements have catalysed women's advocacy of gender dimensions in the outcomes of international, regional, national and local forums concerning various development issues. They have also promoted the role of women in building a culture of prevention and peace. Yet many obstacles remain, blocking a fuller social participation for women because of legal and customary barriers, including family and labour laws, and deep rooted socio-cultural perceptions and practices. In many developing countries, gender disparities are still prevalent in indicators of health, literacy, education, income and employment. Women face difficulties in elections and appointment to public office, retaining guardianship rights over children, receiving fair judgement as victims of domestic and sexual violence.

The integration of women in the development process remains a key policy issue for sustaining social development. Based on studies that suggest a positive relationship between access to social services by poor women and girls, with improvements in overall family and community well-being, the empowerment of women and gender equality are integral to social policy considerations in national agendas. Public policy can encourage the decision-making roles of women, including in political leadership, and for conflict management and resolution in the globalising world, it can also support the use of international and national legal instruments and agreements towards attaining greater integration of women in development.

Promotion of Women's Rights as Human Rights

The promotion of women's rights as human rights was one of the main objectives of the Beijing Platform for Action. In that context, ratification and implementation of the Convention on the Elimination of All Forms of Discrimination against Women has become an important instrument in empowering women in the region. As of January 1999, the Convention had been ratified by over two thirds of ESCAP members and associate members. Of those, nearly one third have entered reservations for reasons of religion, culture and conflict of law. Such reservations and/or declarations effectively dilute the human rights standards set by the Convention for women in those countries and also for the region. Even where ratification has been without reservation, implementation has been slow in a number of countries, thereby allowing existing discriminatory practices against women to continue under the sanction of religious principles or cultural and customary values. Given the differences and the degree of sensitivities posed by the cultural and religious particularities of individual countries of subregions, a rights based approàch to gender equality may provide some common ground which can yield positive results. In recent years, trafficking in women has attracted a great deal of attention. It is now widely seen as one of the worst forms of the violation of women's rights as human rights. It has become a serious problem without borders, affecting countries within Asia as well as other parts of the world. Women have been trafficked for prostitution and other forms of sexual exploitation such as sex tourism and pornography, domestic workers, labourers in sweatshops and on construction sites, as beggars and brides. The increasing use of new information technologies, in particular, the Internet, presents a new dimension to the problem faced.

Poverty and economic deprivation have also subjected women to trafficking. In many instances, trafficked women are becoming victims of highly organised networks. Women victims in these situations lack legal protection and legal rights. The United Nations General Assembly, in its resolution 52/98 of 12 December 1997, emphasised the need for more concerted and sustained national, regional and international action over the alarming levels of trafficking in women and girls. The adoption of the Bangkok Accord and Plan of Action to Combat Trafficking in Women at a Regional Conference on Trafficking in Women, held at Bangkok in November 199, provided the first step forward in harnessing a regional response to the problem.

Violence against women constitutes another form of gross violation of women's rights as human rights. It has become a grave social problem, requiring urgent attention. Although the problem in the region is not new, it has so far attracted limited social recognition and legal redress owing to the complexities of patriarchal values, traditions, norms and standards. Even laws often discriminate against women and offenders go unpunished. Violence against women takes a variety of forms, including physical, mental and sexual abuse. While many countries in the region are engaged in combating violence against women in cooperation with NGOs and women's organisations, there is a need for more cooperation at the regional and subregional levels, particularly in those areas which affect women from several countries.

Promoting Greater Participation in the Decision–Making Process

Promoting the greater participation of women in the decision making process remains another major objective in several countries of the region towards the goal of empowering women. Awareness of the need for promoting the greater participation of women in the decision making process is on the rise. In several countries of the region, women have reached the highest positions of political authority. Parliamentary representation is also on the rise in several countries. Yet, women by and large still find themselves excluded from the state or government apparatus in many countries of the region. Regional experience suggests that women tend to do better in terms of participation in the decision making process when proactive policies are in place, backed up by a social consensus on the need for empowering women.

2

Key Areas of Concern

The Oxford English Dictionary defines empowerment as "to give (someone) the authority or power to do something (or) to make (someone) stronger and more confident, especially in controlling their life and claiming their rights." Literature is much divided about the term's exact meaning in theory and practice. Different disciplines vary greatly in their conceptualisations of empowerment: it may include goals like the provision of financial independence and earning/spending power, gender equality in the labour sphere, equal protection of human rights by governments and equal access to basic resources like electricity.

N. Kabeer points out that in politics, "female empowerment is often translated into clear cut official developmental goals rather than interventions that promote female empowerment on more intrinsic grounds." In other words, it is easier to promote female literacy programs than to address the reasons behind female illiteracy, a much broader and more daunting goal positioned in the sphere of social justice. It may be easier to measure to outcomes of clear cut goals, but these outcomes will disappoint for as long as set goals ignore the broad spectrum of elements that constitute women's lives. Female empowerment programs therefore need to consider the fundamental dynamics of women's contexts if they are to maximise their contribution to female empowerment.

Whilst governments and funders seek concrete outcomes, non governmental organisations (NGOs) use 'empowerment' to refer to a shift from handouts towards a more active approach which aims to cultivate sustainable independence. In the past, 'aid recipients' were cast in passive, receiving roles, but now they are 'programme participants', encouraged to capitalise on their agency. For example, programmes encourage and support people to farm their land to produce food, instead of simply handing out food, which achieves a very short term, narrow goal.

In societies where men traditionally had/have more power, they may offer resistance to female empowerment initiatives. African females are often considered subordinate position to men and in some cases African women are blatantly discriminated against due to their sex. Unfortunately, this gender inequality often manifests in the low priority of developmental goals related to women. The concept of female empowerment may be perceived (whether consciously or not) as a threat against men and the positions they hold in society. In one case, Kaler found that empowerment was perceived as "making men weaker" and "making men redundant," which led to conflict between the genders and general disapproval of the use of the female condom. Power is often not recognised as actual 'power' until it is challenged. In other words, female empowerment initiatives that challenge the status quo also highlight it and men become aware of authority they may lose. Countries, cultures, individuals and situations differ and humans and their environments change. Developing interventions that do exactly what they intended to do seems near impossible. Compromises and consensus therefore constitute a core element of female empowerment initiatives.

Consensus on Empowerment

'Empowerment' broadly refers to women's ability to make choices for her and her family. Control over resources and matters of life is often stressed in definitions, as are the dynamics and processes of decision making. Here we use Kabeer's definition of empowerment as a reference point. Empowerment is "the expansion in people's ability to make strategic life choices in a context where this was previously denied to them." This definition conceptualises empowerment as a process of change driven by choice. Available options and the ability to choose are therefore central to having power. "It is the possible inequalities in people's ability to make choices, rather than differences in the choices they make that is of importance." Note also that the ability to make choices does not automatically translate into empowerment, because all options are not of equal value. All of these complexities underpin the empowerment endeavour.

Multi–dimensional Empowerment for Multi–dimensional Lives

A combination of initiatives often most effectively empowers women. For example, the empowering effects of microfinancing as a single initiative are mediocre when social and material factors are excluded. This means that access to resources can be misleading, since it does not necessarily guarantee a correlating increase in women's options and power to choose. Without agency, available resources merely represent potential choices, not actual choices. Although research found an autonomy (agency) enhancing effect in women who worked for a wage, these effects where still significantly mediated by the social and material contexts in which their wages were earned.

Initiatives that combine resources (education, life skills, micro financing and health education) are most successful, presumably because they resonate with the multi dimensional nature of human life. An initiative called EXPRO, developed in six Ethiopian regions, significantly improved women's livelihoods through combinations of skills and entrepreneurship initiatives.

Female empowerment initiatives not only help women, but their communities, too. For example, the 'Microfinance for AIDS and Gender Equity' (Image) program against intimate partner violence (IPV) in South Africa showed that an increase in the eco–wellbeing of involved women resulted in a significant reduction in IPV and better living conditions within the community. The initiative combined a microfinancing poverty alleviation program with participatory training on domestic violence, gender and sexuality norms and HIV education and prevention. Studies furthermore show that educated women more often seek medical care, more often immunise their children and are better informed about children's nutritional requirements and sanitation practices. As a result, their children are usually healthy and attend school regularly. This fact is especially true for girl children. Female empowerment through education is also connected to a reduction in children's mortality rates, better family planning and pre and post natal health care.

Concluding Remarks

The conceptualisation of empowerment is debated and the evaluation and measurement of empowerment initiatives' outcomes even more so. Kabeer's three dimensions of choice (resources, agency and achievements) are interconnected, which means that options can only empower when a woman has enough freedom to exercise her agency. Regarding the evaluation of initiatives, achievement can only be accounted for if a reasonable guess can be made as to whose agency was involved.

Empowerment initiatives need to work from the bottom up: first address the issues at the heart of disempowered states of being. Where girl children don't attend school, their families need not only be educated about the importance of education for girls, they also need resources to fulfil the role the girl child performs in the household in order to let her go, ranging from wood and water collection, food preparation, income generation, care for younger siblings and care for HIV and AIDS affected family members. In this particular example, basic service provision and entrepreneurial programmes could alleviate much of the physical burden that falls on the girl child. Multi–faceted approaches to empowerment therefore need to be supported, advocated and implemented carefully. Contact a local NGO to find out how you can help to make a difference.

Out of the 1.3 billion poor people in the world, 70 per cent are women, the majority of whom are illiterate with no access to basic amenities like safe drinking water. Two thirds of the 130 million children worldwide who are not in school are girls.

Between 75 per cent and 80 per cent of the world's 27 million refugees are women and children. Women hold 10.5 per cent of the seats in the world's parliaments. The majority of women earn an average of about three fourths of the pay of males for the same work. In most countries, women work about twice the unpaid time that men do. One in every four households in the world is now headed by a woman. Worldwide 20 per cent to 50 per cent of women experience some degree of domestic violence during marriage. The primary victims of today's armed conflicts are civilian women and children, not soldiers, with rape becoming more evident as a weapon of war.

The Feminisation of Employment

In order to respond to increasing and intense global competition, corporations are creating various strategies to meet the challenges of their own survival. One of the major strategies deals with labour and takes three main forms: labour flexibility, the casualisation of labour and the feminisation of labour. Concretely, dual labour processes are occurring. One leads to a fragmentation of the labour process resulting in low skilled and repetitive work whereby there is a shift and/or combination of regular work with various forms of non–regular, flexible employment, *e.g.*, part–time, temporary, subcontracted and home–based workers. The other process is the upgrading of workers' skills in multitask jobs using information communication technology (ICT), resulting in an increasing demand for multiskilled workers with hardware and/or software as well as business skills. The majority of the workers in the first category are women while those in the second are men, although more and more women are now being employed in ICT led sectors.

The export boom in Southeast and East Asia in the last quarter of the 20th century was fuelled by the contribution of women in export related activities and through the remittances made by migrant women workers. In Malaysia, we know that electrical and electronic products comprise about 60 per cent of the total manufactured exports of the country with the industry generating about one third of manufacturing employment in Malaysia. Many of us forget though that the majority of those employed, particularly at the operator level, are Malay women. As noted above, this trend towards the feminisation of paid employment in Asian countries was driven by the need of employers, usually transnational corporations (TNCs), for cheaper and more flexible sources of labour. Global capitalism makes use of the existing patriarchal ideology whereby women are perceived to be more subservient to (male) managerial authority, less prone to organise or be organised into unions, more willing to accept poorer working conditions and easier to dismiss using such life cycle criteria as marriage and childbirth. However, such a process is also double edged. On the one hand, the globalisation of trade and the economy has definitely opened up economic and income opportunities for women, resulting in her improved status in the household and an increase in her position in society as well as her self esteem. It has opened up choices for women in both the manufacturing and services sectors and for those in the higher valued industries, it has also meant an increase in her skills.

A research with Maznah Mohamed and Tan Beng Hui on women electronics workers in two TNCs found that they are confident, have a great sense of pride in their company and a positive perception of themselves as part of the company in which they work. With the expansion of ICT, information processing work can now be globally distributed, leading to new modes of working, such as telework, teletrade and e–commerce. Women as offshore data entry workers, software programmers and systems analysts are finding novel employment opportunities in this digital age. In my own study of software companies in Malaysia, 30 per cent of the software personnel were women.

However, on the other hand, we know that the majority of the women workers labour under inferior working conditions and often on shifts with serious implications for their social and physical health. Those in the lower end, labour intensive consumer electronics industries suffer from health problems that include extreme fatigue and general health problems due to chemical hazards and job stress.

The current economic crisis has more serious implications for women than for men, not least because more women than men are hired in the export led industries being affected and more women than men are in the unskilled and low skilled jobs, but also because women are also strongly affected by the loss of their incomes within the household. The retrenchment data for the Malaysian electronics sector reveals that 26 per cent of the employees in this sector were retrenched during the 17 month period from January 1998 to May 1999. The majority were local workers with women comprising 65 per cent of those retrenched. Most of the retrenchment came from foreign owned companies with their workers forming 75 per cent of the total retrenched. According to Jayati Ghosh, there is a real possibility that the long march towards equality for women in the region, particularly for poor women, may be halted or even reversed by the current economic turmoil.

This is because poor women all over Asia are at the bottom of a vertical sub contracting process which squeezes profits at each level. These women, located in urban slums, in small towns, estates, rural villages as well as migrant workers, will be the most exploited as they are often low skilled, possess less formal education, are unorganised and, hence, are more vulnerable. They will not enjoy the opportunities offered to their sisters who have a command of information technology. In such a situation, those who fall by the wayside are the older production workers, both men and women. Generational gaps will occur within and across genders in terms of the new and dynamic forms of knowledge based employment.

Migration–Breakdown of the Extended Family and Kinship Network

Like globalisation, migration is not a new phenomenon. Terms like berjelai and merantau in Malaysia indicate that the notion of 'movement' is part of the local vocabulary. However, rural households were previously held together by kinship structures and reciprocal labour networks (berderau, gotong royong, bekerjasama) which ensured the cohesion of the community, including fema headed families. However, as a result of the Green Revolution, these socio-economic networks today have been replaced by cash and commodity relations, endangering these structures so crucial for social cohesion.

In rural areas, with the commercialisation of agriculture and the migration of husbands and daughters to the cities, poverty now has a female face. In indigenous communities, the taking away of their customary land to make way for the construction of dams and commercial crops has led to a denigration of the status of indigenous women who once owned land and in which the planting of 'padi' (padi pun or spirit) was related to their high status in the community. At the global level, more than 120 million migrants have left their home countries in search of greener pastures abroad, leading to a warning by the United Nations of the 'human crisis of our age.' In Asia, migration for economic reasons has denuded poor families, leaving children to fare for themselves with either their father or mother away in a foreign land. The problems faced by female migrant workers are concerns with which we need to grapple in a systematic manner. The migration of males has been a major factor leading to an increasing proportion of female maintained households, the majority of which live in extreme poverty. Thirty per cent to 35 per cent of all rural households in India, for example, are female headed households compared to 25 per cent in Cambodia, 21.4 per cent in Mongolia and 15.7 per cent in Korea. In Malaysia, there are 600,000 female headed households. The breakdown of the extended family is more clearly seen in the urban sector.

Today the nuclear family is more and more the norm, especially in the cities, where the burden is heavier for working couples who have to deal with stress both at work and in the family. Stress at work is compounded by calls for efficiency, productivity and the achievement of quotas while, at the familial level, there are daily struggles to catch up with the increasing cost of living, particularly as various public services are privatised. With women finding employment and a newfound freedom, they are asking for traditional gender relations to change. Without proper communication and with patriarchal ideology slow to change, tensions within families increase, leading to a breakdown of the family. Divorce rates are increasing, especially in the cities, and society often blames women for marriage breakdowns as they have become more aggressive in 'demanding their own space.' Will there now be a backlash for women who have struggled so long for their rights?

Better Laws, Increased Awareness, Increasing Violence against Women: A Crisis in Masculinity?

There is no doubt that there has been an increased awareness that violence against women is a crime. In fact, this awareness, coupled with reforms in the relevant laws, has been one of the successes of the women's movement at the global and national level. Yet why is it that violence against women in many countries is not decreasing despite numerous campaigns by women's groups? As noted earlier, 20 per cent to 50 per cent of women worldwide suffer some domestic violence during marriage. Let us look at other statistics.

(1) The total number of reported rape cases in Malaysia increased from 879 in 1993 to 1,323 in 1997–an increase of 50 per cent. The rape of teen age girls rose form 604 cases in 1995 to 719 in 1996. Police statistics disclose that 67 per cent of rapes in 1996 were victims below 16 years of age; 85 per cent of these rapes were committed by boyfriends, family members and neighbours.

(2) The reported cases of female domestic violence increased from 466 in 1992 to 5,799 in 1997, a 1,000 per cent increase. This number actually shot from 2,291 reported cases in 1996 to 5,799 in 1997 perhaps because of increased awareness created by the implementation of the Domestic Violence Act.

(3) Domestic abuse of women, both physical and mental, is on the rise with Bangladesh reporting an increasing trend in suicides among women.

(4) Increased cases of dowry related deaths and the harassment of young brides are reported in India, Nepal and Bangladesh.

(5) Prostitution, forced prostitution and trafficking in women and children with associated violence and harassment have become a major concern in the region.

(6) Widespread sexual violence against women in areas of armed conflict and civil unrest are reported in Laos, Cambodia and the Philippines.

(7) Women migrant workers are increasingly becoming victims of sexual violence.

How do we explain the above phenomenon? In Malaysia, despite the wide publicity given to the sexual harassment code, our own male parliamentarians made unwanted sexual innuendoes towards our female members of Parliament. Moreover, it is well known that when both the amendments to the laws on rape and the Domestic Violence Act were proposed there were loud guffaws from male MPs. Feminist accounts in the West since the 1970s have suggested that gender violence increases when men feel they are losing ground as a sex. It is also not very clear to what extent the economic crisis has led to an increase of violence against women. Indeed, today 30 per cent, or 2.5 billion members of the work force, are unemployed or underemployed. Many of these are men whose socio–cultural and symbolic role as the breadwinner in the family (in fact, this is increasingly untrue, but society still treats female labour as secondary) is increasingly being threatened. In Malaysia, 55 per cent of those retrenched during the recent crisis were men. The ability of men to 'take care of the family' is thus being chipped away, leading, to a crisis in masculinity.

From another angle, very often the transformation of unequal gender relations touches very intimate cultural and emotional knots in our personal lives, which are the hardest to acknowledge and change. For men, who are themselves exploited as workers, it means giving up years of macho masculinity and learning to say that one is sorry after beating up your wife for years. How do you treat your wife as an equal when you have always been the master of the house? For women, 'sleeping with the enemy' makes it all the more difficult to challenge such violent relationships. If globalisation is a project of modernity leading to changing female roles, patriarchal attitudes are certainly still in the premodern, if not primordial, stage. The notion of equal partnership as articulated through relations, processes and structures have yet to take root.

The Commoditisation of Women and Sexuality

The market has also affected culture, which is increasingly being commercialised and commoditised. The rise of individualism (to be different, to compete with others by having more) and consumerism actually accompany globalisation and the need for TNCs to sell their products to accumulate a greater surplus for themselves. Firms and individuals follow this trend in their pursuit of materialism and the creation of status symbols. In the same vein, sexuality and women's bodies are being commoditised as never before, from pornography, sex tourism and sex trafficking to advertisements and beauty schemes which feed on our emotional insecurities and little vanities.

Economic globalisation in the form of 'market democracy' has also created the image of the New Asian Women. She is the professional woman, entrepreneur, manageress, executive who is articulate, glamorous and assertive. This image is in every women's magazine that is avidly read by the middle class and aspiring working class women who do not have the means to buy designer clothes and skin whitening products. This icon of the fashionable and glamorous energy filled woman is sharply contrasted with the veiled Muslim woman.

Privatisation and the Rolling Back of the State

Last, but not least, let us comment briefly on privatisation, a strong arm of globalisation, and its implications for women. Under the guise of free market restructuring, the privatisation of public services has led not only to its reduced availability but often to higher prices for such services as well as basic necessities. Because women are still expected to be responsible for child care and family maintenance, they will bear the disproportionate weight of these constraints.

Women as homemakers have to balance the extra costs due to increasing charges for public utilities, education and health care as a result of cuts in public subsidies. Not only will their double burden be intensified, there will also be mounting pressure to assume multiple roles both as paid and unpaid labour, *e.g.*, taking care of the elderly, the retrenched, taking on extra work in the informal sector. Those adversely affected will be poor women who will have decreased or no access to such amenities or will have to struggle more to gain access to these services for their family.

Conclusion

There have been increased economic opportunities for women but also mounting threats. In the present global reshaping of labour, studies have shown that, as a company adopts labour casualisation, the higher is the number of women employed and the greater is their vulnerability to exploitative conditions. Labour flexibility has also led to job insecurities for men, resulting in the erosion of their masculinity. To what extent, however, has this led to increased gender violence and strengthened patriarchy? While the developmentalist and corporatist state, because of its links with capital, has been unable to qualitatively improve working conditions for women, global and local pressures have led it to make concessions to women, particularly in the passing of laws to improve and/or protect the position of women. In a sense, these laws have not really threatened the economic and political base of the State and of those in power and are thus tolerated. Today, however, the issue of women, at least at the level of rhetoric, can no longer be discounted.

Nonetheless, these laws, while helpful, have not genuinely transformed unequal gender relations nor have they led to more democratic processes and structures in society. Women do not want market democracy but genuine democracy. The call of the Women's Agenda for Change in 1999 for more accountability and democracy will not be accepted by the State.

It is thus important for the women's movement to link up with other social movements and for the wider democratic social and political movement to seriously incorporate women's concerns. However, we must be able to present alternatives to the present trends of commoditisation, individualism and materialism as well as the forces of conservatism if we, indeed, want to engage with globalisation on equal terms and in the context of our own interests.

3

Pursuits of Women Intellect and Activity in Independent India: Measures and Challenges

Indian Women has an age long history of intellectual pursuits and leadership activities. In Upnisadic period we find the name of *Gargi* who entered the debate with *Yajnavalkya* and asked serious questions regarding *'brahman vidya'*. *Mahabharata* refers name of Sulabha, a leady who stated merits and demerits of a *vāda* (reasoning) in the court of king *Janaka*. This long list which include the names of *Ghosha, Lopamudra, Madhavi, Draupadi, Kunti, Sita* and many others. There is another list of Indian women who wrote golden verses on the pages of political history of India including *Rajia Sultana, Maharani Laksmi Bai, Rani Ahalya Bai Holker, Smt. Indira Gandhi, Smt. Sonia Gandhi, Her Highness Pratibha Devi Singh Patil* and others.

The long list of 'women in literature' includes *Meera Bai, Mahadevi Verma, Mahasweta Devi etc. Kalpana Chawala, Aishwarya Rai, P.T.Usha, Sanya Mirza, Malleshwari,*....the list may include thousands of names but the motto of this chapter is not to prepare the list of distinguished Indian women . Indeed, there is another aspect of this golden coin ironically. In this post modern era Indian women continues to languish in a patriarchal society and a colossal per centage to them, largely belonging to traditional and religiously orthodox families, are deprived of even social mobility and are bound to live in a low social status. In independent India cases of atrocities and exploitation of women are on increase. According to a recent survey 20% of Indian Women think that physical violence against a women is 'an expression of love' of their husbands and 58% of male grant it as 'husband's right'.

The decade old Bill for reservation for women in both houses of Parliament and State Assemblies is still to be tabled in Parliament. According to latest census report of India (2001) in independent India women literacy rate is 39.30%, non enrolment of girl children is 29%, voting in parliament is 55%, life expectancy at birth is 59.4%, 30% of Indian Women live in below poverty line, Women representation in Lok Sabha is 7.9% of the total seats (this time this percentage is more shrinking), gradually declining sex ratio *etc.* tells the whole story of the status of women in independent India.

But there is a positive sign. A large number of Indian women are no longer prepared to accept the idea that a women's chief function is to be house wife and mother. They have begun to attach more importance to financial independence and social importance. 'Half of the nation's population and half of the opportunities' is the clarion call of modem Indian women.

This 'clarion call', indeed, is a result of women awakening, especially, during the world wide movement of feminism started during second half of the last century. There are two long term feminist goals that underlie women struggle for liberation from oppressions and discrimination in all spheres and in all levels in society. The first one is freedom from oppression from women involves not only equality but also the right of women to freedom of choice and the power to control their own lives and bodies as it is essential to ensure a sense of dignity and autonomy for every women. The second goal of feminism is to remove inequality and oppression through the creation of a more just social and economic order, nationally and internationally. This means the involvement of women in plans for national development and in local and global strategies for change.

After independence the Govt. of India has taken numerous measures and making honest endeavors to hoist the status of women and establish gender equality. The constitutional obligations as well as different plans, programs and policies have laid emphasis on women empowerment in order to bring them to the mainstream of development. Article 15 of the Indian Constitution prohibits any discrimination on the grounds of sex, while article 15(3) clarifies that this provision will not prevent the State from making any special provision for women. Article 42 of the Constitution envisages that the State shall make provision for securing just and human conditions of work and maternity relief.

Besides, the Directive Principles of State Policy also urge that the State shall direct its policy towards securing an adequate means of livelihood for women and ensuring equal pay for equal work for both men and women. The Eighth Five Year Plan intends at enabling women to function as equal partners and participants in development by extending the services to both qualitatively and quantitatively. Moreover, the plan also aims to effectively implement social legislation for women by formulating and strengthening grass root level women's group.

The Ninth Five Year Plan intends to empowering women as the agents of social change and development. Formulation of National Commission for Women and idea of setting up a National Council for Empowerment of women are encouraging steps in this direction. Moreover, the effort to formulate the National Policy for Empowerment of Women and setting up a National Resource Centre for Women are other steps taken by the Department of Women and Child Development.

The history of the efforts of women empowerment in India has a lengthy background. After independence, in the modem India, in the first five year plan (1951–56) the question of women's dignity was perceived, primarily, as a social factor. Women were perceived as beings in need of education, health and welfare service only. The third, forth and fifth plan, including the four years of plan holiday before the fifth plan, continued the same approach with declining support to the strategies of organisation building and human resource development. Some priority was accorded to women's education after the report of National Committee on women's education.

However, the planers failed to resolve the major problem of poverty, illiteracy, non–enrolment, drop out and so on that the large majority of girls and women. From the 3rd five year plan and onward the issue of population control acquired increasing priority and gradually the issue of child care and mother's health was dragged in attention. However, till this period women had not been viewed by the planners as a being in need of an independent livelihood to the point where women's decreasing work participation rate and share of employment increasing poverty and insecurity in economic sectors, in which they used to dominate earlier (agriculture, forestry, livestock, cottage industry, sericulture, fisheries *etc.*) were not even viewed as unfortunate problem of change. This process of marginalisation of the large majority of women in the economy and their consequent neglect and devaluation by the society and the state were demonstrational of gender, class and urban bias.

Year 1975 was a milestone in feminist movement when this year was declared as the 'International women year'. After that, in India, a serious exercise in policy review was taken up in between 1977 and 1980. Among this the foremost significant exercises were:

(i) The Report of the Working Group on development of village level organisations of rural Women (1977–78),

(ii) Report of the Working Group on Adult Education Program for Women (1977–78),

(iii) Report of the National Committee on the role of participation of women in agriculture and rural development (1979–80).

These exercises definitely marked a water shade in conceptualising basic problems and strategies for women's development in India. In stead of the United Nation's agenda for the women's decade influencing Indian planning, it was the Indian agenda that got incorporated into the United Nation's mid decade Program of action through the mendicancy of the non–aligned Movement's special conference on women and development and India's membership of (i) the commission on the Status of Women (1978–80); and, (ii) the Preparatory Committee for the Mid-Decade Copenhagen Conference and Program of action.

The conceptual approach evolved through these few years identified women's developmental needs as incorporating multiple dimensions cutting across economic, social and political sectors requiring explicit examination of women's situation in various sectors industry, labour and employment, power, environment, energy, science and technology as well as the social and infrastructural sectors.

With twin emphasis on employment and productivity in the seventh plan, the approach paper highlighted the strategy of a direct attack on the problem of poverty, unemployment and regional imbalance with accelerated development of human recourse. There was greater emphasis on the provision of gainful employment to the unemployed, particularly women and youth.

The strategy of organising women around socio–economic activities was reiterated for the twin objective of making their projects economically viable and adding to their social strength for overall achievement of their status. During this period even Rural Development Department of the Govt. of India made extensive efforts to enhance the social status of Indian Women. The Department announced 30% quota for women in all anti–poverty programs for the rural areas. A special task force appointed by the department was recommended that such mandatory inclusions of the gender sensitisation were necessary for training of public servants of all categories. A parallel move was the appointment of the National Commission for Self–Employed women to help articulate the problems, needs and aspiration of working women in the poverty sector.

These year–long efforts of women movements and Govt. bodies resulted in the formation of the National Commission of Women to review the laws and government Policies. The National Commission of Women Act was passed in August 1990. Now The National Commission for Women is working in its full swing and hopes are there. In the year of 2001 National Policy for the Empowerment of Women was introduced. This policy identifies following factors as the effective tools of Women Empowerment among which most of them, as we see, are either social or need a positive social attitude for implementation:

(a) Education
(b) Health and Nutrition
(c) Housing and Shelter
(d) Science and Technology

(e) Drinking Water and sanitation
(f) Violence against Women
(g) Rights of the Girl Child
(h) Mass Media
(i) Environment

We shall bring only four of these under our notice as a vital tool to release women from their dependent and unequal status:

(a) Education
(b) Health and Nutrition
(c) Economic Measures
(d) Participation in political Bodies

(i) Education: In modern India history of women education takes its start from 1854 with Wood–Dispatch Commission. In 1882 The Indian Education Commission expressed its deep concern over the uneducated population of women. After independence in first Five Year Plan (1951–56) the need for education in women was emphasised. In second Five Year Plan (1956–61) these efforts were extended. During this period National Committee on Women Education, headed by Durga Bai Deshmukh, emphasised on formal education of Indian Women. This effort was resulted in National Council for Women Education. In Third Five Year Plan (19651–66) 'Condensed School Course' and Vocational Training Program for Women were started by the Govt. of India and continued even in the Fifth Five Year Plan (1969–74). In 1971 National Commission on Status of Indian Women, Organised by the Govt., realised that Special measures should be taken for girls to send them to school. Due to this realisation the Fifth Five Year Plan had a special provision to appoint maximum women as school teachers.

In the mean time the Women Development and Child care became core concern of International Community, hence, the year of 1975 was declared as International Women Year and later on a period of the years, *i.e.*, from 1975 to 1985 was declared as 'International Women's decade'. Though desired results were not achieved in those years, a focus on women's problem and their importance were well perceived due to these efforts.

In 1985 the Govt. of India started a special drive for women education under the head of 'National Perspective Plan for Women', which had an aim to achieve 100% literacy rate for Women in India till the end of the year 2000. Ironically this aim was failed to be achieved due to various reasons including slow process of enrollment of girls, particularly in rural areas. Not sending children to schools has something to do with families not getting need based wages. Due to our poor economic structure a large number of children have no option but to work. Indeed the problem of uneducated mass, especially in India, is a problem of education of girl child of weaker section since 80% of them are illiterate. A change in attitude toward girl child and growing economy can play positive role in this regard. However, effective majors are required there.

(ii) Health and Nutrition: In general women have high risk of malnutrition and diseases at the three stages: (i) infancy and childhood, (ii) adolescent and (iii) reproductive phase. This is also importance to in view the critical relationship between the health of a mother, where a result of her health is her childhood and adolescent, and the health of infant and child. The health of lactating mother is also much important for infants.

Though government bodies took serious note on the problem of health and nutrition in women, a large majority of girls and women is still deprived. From the third plan onwards the issue of population control acquired increasing priority. Family planning services were introduced within the health services. Family planning with maternity and child health (MCH) services could not be implemented properly. Program for supplementary nutrition to children and nursing expectant mothers from poverty groups were introduced by the Welfare Department, but could achieved less success.

In fact, marriage and motherhood should not become a disability in women's fulfilling their proper role in the task of national development. It is important that society, including women themselves must accept their responsibility in this field. It should be understood that the society and nation owes a special responsibility to women because of their child bearing role. Apart from their maternal responsibilities, the health of a woman is important ever for herself as 'health is wealth'. If she does not have her health facilities, and also a healthy physic, the goal of Empowerment will turn in vain.

In this regard traditional knowledge and attitude towards women's health and nutrition is also needed to be reviewed. Intra household discrimination in nutrition matters *vis-a-vis* girls and women should be sought to be ended through appropriate strategies like social awareness.

(iii) Economic Measures: Since women comprise the majority of the population below the poverty line, macro economic policies and poverty eradication programs are required to address, specifically, the need and problems of such women. Steps should be taken to mobilise poor women and convergence of services by offering them a range of economic and social options along with necessary support measure to enhance their capabilities. The contribution of a woman to socio–economic development as producer and worker should be recognised widely. Appropriate polices related to their employment and their working conditions should be drawn up. Since measures could include reinterpretation and redefinition of conventional concept of 'work' to reflect women's contribution as producer and worker. The contributions of an active house wife to run and to manage a family should be admitted as economically and socially productive and a contribution to national development. Her employment opportunity and earning power has to be given the highest priority.

In view of the critical role of women in agriculture and allied sectors concentrated efforts have been made (by NGOS and Government agencies) to train women in appropriate manner. National Policy of women empowerment (2001) has a goal to run training programs for women in soil conservation, social forestry, dairy development and other occupations allied to agriculture like horticulture, livestock including small animal husbandry, poultry, fisheries, sericulture *etc.*

Now a days women are playing an important role in non conventional sectors like industry and technology. For the optimum utilisation of national talent and working capacity this trend must be encouraged, hence, women should be given comprehensive support in terms of labour legislation, social security, transportation and other support services. To provide the support services for women, like child care facilities, including creches at work place and educational education should be expended and improved. Women friendly personnel policies should also be drawn up to encourage women to participate in economic functions.

(iv) Participation in political Bodies: Assessment of the role of Indian Women in Indian politics is a saga of the silent suffering of fair sex. It is quit disappointing that, despite of a number of pro women commitments of almost all the political parties and all the governments, the representation of women in parliament and state legislative assemblies is far behind the justified goal. A great majority of women have no access to ' political input' and hence are almost eliminated from political participation.

Reasons are there. As women have no control over economic resources and since they also lack in decision making power at the household level, they are naturally unable to contest the elections without the consent of a male sponsor. Hence, the fare sex is inevitably unable to enter the political battle field. Obviously, due to this reason the political empowerment of women is far from reality. Actions are needed to break the vicious circle.

The Gender Development Index (GDI) reveals the fact that among 130 countries India ranks 99 which shows that gender empowerment measures are urgently required to correct the balance. Though in Panchayati Raj Institution seats up to 33% are reserved for women (An incorporation of two paragraphs on the education for women's equality within the national policy of Education, for the first time, spread out the massage of women empowerment by changing the socio political construction of gender bias. During this period, for the very first time, the issue of effective representation of women in Panchayati Raj was raised but they are not in a decision making position due to male dominant patriarchal society.

Theoretically about 7 to 8 lakh women in the country are in a position to share the decision making power, but practically they are not in a position to avail the opportunity. This is a challenge for women activists and women organisations to find out effective majors. In this regard the policy prescription of The National Policy for Women Empowerment is notable "Women's equality in power sharing and active participation in decision making, including decision making in political process at all levels, will be ensured for the achievement of the goals of the empowerment. All measures will be taken to guarantee women equal access and full participation in decision making bodies at every level, including the legislative, executive, judicial, corporate, statutory bodies, the advisory Commission, Committees, Boards, and Trusts *etc.* Affirmative actions such as reservations/quotas: including in higher legislative bodies, will be considered whenever necessary on a time bound basis. Women Friendly Personnel policies will also be drawn up to encourage women to participate effectively in the development process".

NEW CHALLENGES OF WOMEN EMPOWERMENT AND GLOBALISATION

In this post modern era the Globalisation has presented and continuously presenting new challenge to the goals of Women Empowerment, especially in Indian society. The changing economic pattern and tremendous progress in science and technology bring a change in social and moral values and life style. The new values emerging out of the global pattern often run against the traditional ones.

In a country like India, which has a long cultural history and deep rooted traditions in its peoples psyche, these changing values are appeared to create a chaos like situation. On the other hand many of these changes, which are natural outcome of growing technology, are not bringing desired results in even manner, even in a geographical defined area. This inability to adjust the new values and lock of clear awareness about right social objectives are some of the main reasons for tension in both personal and professional lives.

Obviously the gender impact of Globalisation is a matter to be evaluated systematically. "From the micro level studies commissioned by the Department of Women and Child Development it is evident that there is a need for reframing policies for access to employment and quality of employment. Benefits of the growing global economy have been unevenly distributed.

This leads to wider economic disparities, the feminisation of poverty, increased gender inequality, deteriorating working conditions and unsafe working environment especially in the formal economy and rural areas. Strategies will be designed to enhance the capacity of women and empower them to meet the negative social and economic impacts, which may flow from the globalisation process."

SOME MORE CHALLENGES

A recent UN report notes that India has improved its score in education, employment and per capita income of women, but has not improved women's representation in Parliament, removed their unequal wages or lessens their debt burden. Budget allocation for women's welfare schemes is also reducing gradually. Women's health position is also not good in India.

It accounts for almost twenty five per cent of world's maternal death and the numbers of pregnancy related deaths in rural areas are still among the worlds highest. Women face a high risk of malnutrition, retardation in growth and development, diseases, disability and even death at three critical stages in their Lives viz. infancy and early childhood, adolescence and the reproductive phase. In the old age they face threats of breast and uterine cancer and menopause related problem.

They are largely denied their reproductive health rights in the conservative, traditional and religiously orthodox families. Women are not adequately represented in the legislative, executive and judiciary spheres of the government. Though in recent years due to reservation of seats, there have been increased participation of women at the grassroots democratic system but mostly are under the shadow of the husband, in–laws and parents.

Notwithstanding numerous welfare measures, the status of women has not been adequately hoisted and the women empowerment status varies from region to region, state to state, and even between rural and urban areas, Moreover, it also varies from one community to the other. The fruits of woman welfare measures are being largely enjoyed by the highly literate women and women belonging to socially, economically and politically advantaged upper strata of urban society. A colossal large percentage of women are engaged in the unpaid household activities and are largely employed in the informal and unorganised private sector.

Conclusion

Women are the vital human infrastructure and their empowerment economic, educational, social and political would hasten the pace of social development. Investing in women's "capabilities" and empowering them to achieve their "choices" and "opportunities" is the surest way to contribute to economic growth and overall development. Overlooking of empowerment of women means dispossession of half of human capital. It means an incomplete attempt for social development and a complete violation of Human Rights' for all.

4

Globalisation, Employment and Women's Empowerment

Introduction

The purpose of this chapter is to provide a an overall assessment of how globalisation, which is taken here to mean greater openness of economies to international trade and capital mobility, in diverse regional contexts since the early 1980s has impacted on the growth of real economies and their capacity to create employment. More specifically, the chapter attempts to trace how these policies have impacted on women's access to employment and their enjoyment of social rights. While there has been significant criticism of the way in which neo–liberal stabilisation and structural adjustment policies have impacted on poor women in much of the developing world, the debate on the impacts of trade liberalisation on female employment has been far more sanguine. In fact, one argument that is frequently made in favour of globalisation, and trade liberalisation in particular, is that it has brought about higher rates of employment in developing countries as the locus of manufacturing has shifted from the North to the South, and that within developing countries women have emerged unequivocally as the winners.

A related argument, often implicit in the literature on globalisation and female employment, which we scrutinise in this paper, is about the interlinkages between female employment and social policy. Given the fact that poor women in many developing countries enjoyed few social rights even prior to the neo–liberal era during the so called 'golden age' of capitalism critics argue that it is meaningless to condemn 'globalisation' for creating jobs for women that have few social rights attached to them. In other words, given that women were deprived of social rights even when developing country governments pursued various models of import substitution industrialisation (ISI) which essentially created jobs for a male 'labour aristocracy', and that the existing systems of social protection were frequently biased in favour of men who were assumed to be the 'breadwinners' while women were considered to be their 'dependents', there has been no regression or reversal of rights as far as women are concerned.

It is argued here that while it is crucial to recognise the shortcomings of Keynesian thinking that dominated development policy, and the ISI strategies that fell short of their objectives in several important respects (especially from a gender perspective), a constructive approach would have been to extend their achievements and to change their less successful interventions so as to make them perform better, rather than to reverse their gains.

Instead what we are witnessing today with the new direction of public policy is that poor women in many developing countries are being deprived 'of even the prospect of the progressive realisation of a non–discriminatory system of decent jobs and public services and broad based social security systems'. Today, employment objectives, the creation of decent jobs and broad based, redistributive social security systems are no longer the objectives of public policy in most countries. These concerns have now been relegated to the realm of 'safety nets', and small enterprise and informal sector specific programs, which very often lead to blanket exemptions from paying taxes and from observing environmental and labour regulations, thereby undermining the social policy agenda.

Explaining Globalisation

A great deal has been written about globalisation in recent years. The orthodox globalist position argues that there has been a sea change in the nature, magnitude and reach of cross border flows of products, people, capital and money in the last two decades of the twentieth century, forging a genuinely globalised economy in which territorial boundedness and geographical proximity have declining importance for economic accumulation. The tidal wave of free trade, open markets, capital flows and high technology, globalisation enthusiasts argue, will translate into higher rates of economic growth and improvements in people's standard of living. The orthodox position further posits the gradual demise of the state's domestic power over policy issues and a concomitant convergence in economic and social policies across diverse national entities. Given the overwhelming force of these globalising forces, the verdict is that sooner or later all national policies must, and will, succumb to the market based logic and converge towards the neo liberal American model of capitalism.

This position has been seriously questioned by a significant range of analytically nuanced and empirically based studies. While it is impossible for this chapter to summarise in any detail the many points of contention that have been raised by these critics, it will highlight some of the more fundamental qualifications they have made. To do so we first look at the broad facts of globalisation and note a number of reservations that have been entered in relation to the orthodox claims about the nature of the changes underway. The objections here are summarised in response to three key questions: Is the current period of globalisation historically unprecedented? Have world trade, production and investment flows become all encompassing in other words, genuinely global as the orthodox position claims?

To what extent and in what ways have national states become powerless over policy issues? Next we look at the more controversial question concerning the presumed impacts of globalisation on economic growth, poverty and human welfare. The key question we will be exploring can be stated thus: are free flows of capital and an ever more open trading system conducive to economic growth and equitable development? What impacts have these trends had on gender equality?

The Facts about Globalisation

First, from a historical point of view, as far as trade and capital flows are concerned, many of the studies concur that the present period of globalisation is by no means unprecedented. In fact, the process of international economic integration from the 1880 until 1913, most observers agree, surpassed many of the contemporary indices of globalisation, albeit perhaps not at the same pace. For example, OECD share of export trade to GDP in 1913 may have exceeded the level reached in 1973, and by 1991 the share did not enormously exceed that for 1913 (17.9 per cent in 1991 compared to 16 per cent in 1913, (cited in Weiss 1997)). Looking at the more contemporary era, while there is no doubt that both tariff and non tariff barriers to trade have been significantly lowered in recent years in East Asia and Latin America, for example, they were around twice as high in 1964–73 than they were in 1990, world exports were expanding far more rapidly between 1964 and 1973 than in the subsequent, trade liberal, era.

This should not, however, be taken to suggest that there is nothing new about contemporary globalisation: there are monumental changes taking place and the crucial role of technological change, particularly in communications, transport and information processing cannot be overemphasised. Today what happens in one part of the world carries far greater impact on other parts of humanity and does so much more quickly than was once the case; *the global financial market is arguably the most dramatic manifestation of this change.*

Second, while the orthodox globalist position predicts an all encompassing tendency in world trade, production and investment, in fact these flows have remained *highly concentrated*, largely within the rich OECD countries and only *some* developing countries, while *most* developing countries have not integrated into the so called 'global' economy.

In the case of FDI (foreign direct investment), for example, there are currently four FDI clusters (Köhler 2001): the European Union; North America (with US as lead FDI investor and host, and including Canada and Mexico); a group of countries in East and Southeast Asia comprised of China, Hong Kong, Republic of Korea, Singapore and Malaysia; and the Mercosur members Brazil and Argentina. Together these four clusters accounted for 90 per cent of all FDI inflows in 2000 (Kohler 2001).

It is in the finance sector that the reality of a *global* market seems indisputable. Since the removal of the gold standard in 1971 and the subsequent liberalisation of exchange controls, international capital flows have reached spectacular levels. However, just like FDI flows, financial flows have also been highly concentrated and uneven, with over three quarters of portfolio investment going to only ten or so developing countries the so called 'emerging markets'. Still, there have been important changes as far as a wider range of developing countries are concerned. Official financial flows, for example, which until the early 1980s accounted for the bulk of international capital flows to the developing world are now being overtaken by private flows (with the exception of sub–Saharan Africa and the Middle East where the former continue to predominate).

Financial liberalisation is also one of the most controversial components of external liberalisation (a point to which we shall return below). As persistent financial crises over the past two decades or so have shown, premature liberalisation in the context of weak financial regulation has turned out to be a recipe for macroeconomic and social disaster. There is a groundswell of opinion (among academics and policy analysts) urging the regulation of short term capital flows, for both economic and social reasons. However, international action to regulate short term capital flows and reduce their volatility is blocked by powerful financial interest groups that benefit from high capital mobility. In the absence of global regulation, most policymakers agree that domestic monetary policies and banking regulations ought to focus on the strengthening of prudential regulation and controlling destabilising short term capital flows.

Third, the extent to which national states have actually become powerless as a result of external liberalisation (especially financial liberalisation) since the 1980s an argument that is advanced by both advocates and critics of globalisation is a complex question because state capacity is so highly contingent. What is beyond doubt is that in the context of financial liberalisation, the choices in *macroeconomic* policymaking have been narrowed; deflationary and fiscally conservative policies have become the norm (*e.g.* high interest rates, tight monetary policies, and fiscal restraint).

Many observers rightly believe that it has become extremely difficult for governments to adopt expansionary policies and to determine macroeconomic policy through an open social dialogue in which different interest groups can meaningfully participate. This option has been effectively foreclosed by fear of pre–emptive exercise of the 'exit' option by financial institutions attributed to the openness of capital markets.

While this is an important area of concern and one to which we shall return further below, there are nevertheless a number of provisos that need to be taken into account. One important qualification is that for *many* developing countries the exigencies of globalisation are expressed not only through the spontaneous workings of the market, but also (and sometimes largely) through policies imposed on them by the Bretton Woods Institutions.

This does not mean that they have more room for policy maneuver than what the above mentioned scenario would seem to indicate. What it underlines is the *different sources* of constraint under which they operate, and the extent to which the international financial and trade institutions, though their 'policy conditionalities' (rather than the 'invisible hand' of the global market), constitute the most immediate force of globalisation.

A different argument, raised especially by scholars working on East Asia, is that 'there is much more to governing the economy than macroeconomic policy'. Industrial policy, they argue, continues to play a large role in the Asia region even though by its very nature '*the very capacity for industrial policy is one that requires the state to constantly adapt its tools and tasks*'. The point to emphasise is that 'because state capacities differ, the ability to exploit the opportunities of international economic change rather than simply succumb to its pressures will be much more marked in some countries than others'. In the aftermath of the Asian crisis, for example, the state in South Korea has once again taken charge of reorganising social and market institutions and is refocusing its goals (which may well include the liberalisation of the domestic economy) (Woo–Cumings forthcoming), while the real challenge for a country like Thailand is to 'overhaul it bureaucracy', which among other things, would mean increasing pay to improve its capacity to govern the economy.

Finally, the orthodox globalist claim of 'the powerless state' has also been applied to the social policy field. The argument is that the competition triggered by capital mobility the 'footloose' nature of multinational corporations tends to erode social norms and national regulations, by encouraging downward bidding among countries simultaneously aiming to attract FDI. This is presumed to reduce tax revenues, social insurance and other social expenditures, and to erode labour and environmental standards a scenario that is commonly referred to as 'social dumping' or 'race to the welfare bottom'. This is a controversial proposition and various objections have been raised in response to it.

First, regarding the role and significance of 'footloose' capital, while in some sectors of production where profits largely depend on the reduction of wage costs capital can simply take a 'random walk' in the global market and use the threat of exit, both the importance of cost reduction as the driving force behind capital mobility and the extent of global capital mobility may have been exaggerated. There are structural reasons why companies may wish to nurture a strong 'home' or regional base rather than 'go global'. Moreover, as was noted earlier, the great bulk of global FDI is located in the high wage (and in some cases, high tax) countries rather than in low wage developing countries. The world's largest recipient of multinational investment is not low wage India, Bangladesh or Tanzania, but high wage U.S. itself. and low wages and low labour standards are not an attraction, and can be a deterrent, to most FDI.

Interestingly, a country like China which is by far the single largest recipient of FDI inflows in the developing world, both in absolute terms and also in relation to national income, maintains a non–convertible currency, state control over its banking system and a broadly 'gradualist' strategy that violates some of the key elements of IMF/World Bank prescription for 'successful integration'. It is also important to underline the specificities of FDI flows into China: much of China's success in attracting FDI is probably owed to its linguistic, cultural and sentimental attraction for Hong Kong and Overseas Chinese businessmen. Still, the availability of 'cheap labour' with work discipline and a descent basic education and nutritional standard has no doubt been important in attracting such investment. But even here what is noteworthy about China's industrial trajectory, like that of Taiwan's (PoC) and Republic of Korea's a decade or two earlier, is the extent to which global industrial competitiveness has been underpinned by the highly redistributive agrarian transitions that were carried out prior to the industrial take off, which have effectively acted as a wage subsidy. The extent to which China can continue to capitalise on the benefits of earlier redistributions and investments in human capabilities, however, may be eroding very fast as the impacts of domestic liberalisation (of both land and welfare) lead to increasing inequality and the erosion of human capabilities.

Second, in opposition to the 'social dumping' thesis, others argue that external economic openness in fact requires the strengthening of mechanisms for social protection the 'social compensation' thesis. An important lesson from Europe, according to these analysts, is that more open economies (compared with the virtually self–sufficient continent of the USA) require greater social protection.

The historical record shows that some of the more successful open economies or trading nations including the Nordic countries and the Netherlands have had comprehensive social policies. Such policies have not only facilitated the creation of human capital through education (training) and better health, but have also made the costs of greater openness more politically acceptable. It is further argued that despite the initial fears that globalisation would lead to a reversal of some of the social gains that were made in the institutionalised welfare states, driving them down towards the 'lowest common welfare denominator', these have not been by and large substantiated (with the exception of New Zealand and United Kingdom where there have been some policy reversals). Instead, the evidence points towards the continued dominance of national institutional traditions of interest representation and political consensus building as important parameters that continue to shape growth, employment and welfare objectives.

Beyond the institutionalised welfare states, the 'compensation' thesis has also been advanced based on econometric analyses drawing on large data sets from a wide range of countries (including many developing and transition countries). One reliable study of this genre documents a positive and robust association between an economy's exposure to foreign trade and the size of its government. The most plausible explanation for this association is that government expenditures are used to provide social insurance against external risk. In other words, social protection may be the only alternative to trade protection, if social disintegration is to be avoided. *The implication is that a globalised world requires more social protection.* However, it is important to bear in mind that these quantitative analyses are highly sensitive to definitions of 'social spending'.

One concrete example from a comparative research project on social policy carried out by the ILO can help illustrate this point. Alber and Standing (2000) found that based on ILO statistics Chilean social expenditure ratio almost doubled between 1980 and 1992. Thus, according to the ILO statistics, Chile appears as an 'overproportionate welfare spender with expansionist social policies'. However, based on in depth information on institutional changes, and data on central government expenditures provided by the UN Economic Commission on Latin America and the Caribbean, Stephen Kay (2000), who was a member of the ILO research team, depicts Chile quite differently.

According to his analysis, which is cited in Alber and Standing's introduction, Chile is the country 'with the most radical liberal welfare reforms in Latin America, furthermore, his statistical data show Chile as curbing its social spending ratio between 1980 and 1996'. The point to underline is the sensitivity of quantitative outcomes to definitions of 'social spending', and hence the importance of cross–checking different data sources and 'triangulating' quantitative methods with qualitative or institutional analyses of social policy.

Which of these competing hypotheses 'social dumping' or 'social compensation' fits better with the facts as far as developing and transition countries are concerned? While a convincing answer to this question would require far more comprehensive comparative empirical research than what is currently available, what is clear even from the existing studies of social policy is the *absence* of a uniform response to the pressures of globalisation, which would conform to the idea of social dumping.

Southern European and most East Asian countries appear on a trail following the developmental path of the European welfare state pioneers; while Eastern European and Latin American countries are torn between institutionalist European and residualist American models to a degree which makes their future more uncertain. ... then, that there is marked heterogeneity in recent welfare policy developments with an astounding degree of country specific variations.

The findings of the ILO research project, summarised above, are broadly consistent with the fine grained country level research emerging from East Asia and Latin America. Ironically the region with a history of extensive social policies (with enterprise based entitlements to welfare under communism), Eastern Europe also appears to be the one where there have been more policy reversals, even though the authors find the notion of social dumping in response to globalisation inadequate when it comes to describing the social policy reforms undertaken in the region.

They argue that while there has been some privatisation (*e.g.* education, housing), the social expenditure ratio increased rather than declined in most countries, various taxes (payroll, corporate, and personal income) have been raised, and a good number of countries in the region appear to be moving towards different varieties of Western European welfare state model (rather than a residualist, liberal model), the outcomes having been largely dependent on political battles in which supranational and national actors were intertwined in various coalitions.

These findings, however, do not take into account how social policy reforms have impacted specifically on different strata of women in Eastern Europe. In the case of Poland, for example, which is considered by the ILO study to be moving towards an 'institutionalised welfare state model', women have seen numerous reversals of their social rights with detrimental consequences for their labour force participation and autonomy. A striking number of legal and policy changes that have been implemented since the transition to democracy have effectively stripped women of what in Poland are called their 'special privileges', such as paid leave to take care of sick children.

Furthermore, the restoration of democracy has coincided with a significant erosion of social rights that primarily benefited women. Severe cuts in the state budget have dealt a heavy blow to public infrastructure for infant care and childcare. Given these two sets of policy changes, it is not surprising that women's official labour force participation rate has fallen, while they constitute a disproportionate share of the unemployed. At the same time with the introduction of market principles many other social benefits (pensions, health insurance, and so on) that used to be universal rights associated with socialist versions of citizenship have been increasingly linked to formal labour force participation, which although not directly discriminating against women, indirectly places many women at a disadvantage by strengthening the so called 'male breadwinner bias' of social policy.

We will return to this theme further below when we re–visit social policies and consider how they are gendered. But what we need to retain from this short description is that the objectives pursued through social policy embody and reinforce diverse values and objectives, which may be politically contested, and which may become outdated as societies evolve and social norms and values undergo change.

The post war concept of full employment that underpinned European welfare states was often limited to the male breadwinner population. In these contexts social policy and industrial relations often worked in tandem. The family's dependence on the male wage and male entitlements, together with trade union struggles for a 'family wage', contributed in many contexts, especially in continental Europe, to keeping women confined to full time care work and dependent on the male wage and its concomitant entitlements.

As Elson and Cagatay remind us, the 'male breadwinner bias' constructs the ownership of rights to make claims on the state for social benefits (access to services, cash transfers, pensions) around a norm of full time, life long working age participation in the market based labour force. Those whose participation does not fit this norm typically have lesser rights, which they can frequently only exercise as dependents on those who do fit the norm. The result has been the exclusion of many women from entitlements, making them dependent upon men, especially during periods of their lives when they are intensively involved in taking care of children and elders, and when they themselves become old.

This should not come as a surprise because welfare systems construct and are constructed on notions of who is and who is not a full citizen. Hence, they exclude and stratify, by 'race', gender and social class. Welfare systems are thus the bearers of broader social relations of inequality. However, they are also a political stage for the constitution and contestation of notions of 'the public', and are thus important building blocks of legitimate democratic states. To end, we can conclude that while the current period of globalisation may not be without historical precedent, and while world trade, production and investment, have remained *geographically concentrated* rather than being genuinely global, there has nevertheless been a clearly discernible trend toward global economic liberalisation (compared to the previous three decades).

This has involved liberalisation of the international trade in goods and services on the one hand, and the flows of international capital (foreign direct investment, portfolio equity investment, borrowings, *etc.*) on the other. The extent to which external liberalisation has weakened the national state and led to 'social dumping' are complex questions given the *diversity* both in state capacity as well as in institutional and political forces that mediate the forces of globalisation. While there is increasing convergence in macro–economic policies, the same cannot be said about industrial and social policies which continue to be shaped by national institutional characteristics and histories, as well as political alliances and dynamics which are increasingly intertwined with clashes of interests and ideas among influential supranational actors (EU, IFIs, UN, and so on).

Globalisation and Economic Growth

Globalisation advocates premise their arguments for increasing external liberalisation on the beneficial outcomes in terms of economic growth, employment and human welfare expected to flow from greater openness. But globalisation enthusiasts have to confront a number of awkward questions.

A comparison of regional growth rates for the period 1960–1980, when developing countries were pursuing *dirigiste* policies (import substitution industrialisation, or ISI, for example), with those for the 1980–2000 period, when they were enticed to open up to world markets, raises a number of important questions. In Latin America, for example, GDP per capita grew by 75% from 1960–1980, whereas in the subsequent period (1980–2000) it has only risen by 6 per cent; the equivalent figures for sub–Saharan Africa are 36% and 15% respectively.

In fact, the only region that shows higher growth rates in the latter period is East Asia, which grew faster from 1980 to 1998 than in the previous two decades explained by China's quadrupling of GDP over the last 18 years. But as was noted earlier, China has taken a far more gradualist approach to liberalisation than is routinely advocated by the international financial and trade institutions. The lessons that may be legitimately drawn from the Chinese experience will not therefore provide categorical support for all out global integration along the lines advocated by these mainstream institutions.

This disappointing growth performance is enough to raise some serious questions about the policies that are advocated, and often imposed, on developing and transition countries where the 'social costs' are often justified in terms of higher growth rates. Clearly, the evidence cited above leaves a gaping hole in that argument. Having said this, how can the disappointing growth rocord of the past two decades be explained? The literature suggests two main causes: first, that the neo–liberal macro economic agenda has a strong '*deflationary bias*' which has, predictably, led to low rates of growth. And, second, that the disruptions caused by *financial liberalisation* have had a devastating impact on the growth of real economies. We will look at these two factors in turn.

As is now widely appreciated the debt crises of the early 1980s, in turn induced by US–led deflationary policies, provided a critical opportunity for Washington to try to impose a series of new policy regimes on indebted developing countries through the international financial institutions. This new macro–economic policy agenda included fiscal restraint, open trade and capital accounts, and privatisation, all of which reflect an acceptance of price stability as the primary concern of macroeconomic policy (described in some circles as the 'Washington Consensus'). In other words, the main targets of macro economic policy have been low inflation and balanced budgets, regardless of the implications for social development and indeed, as we have seen, for growth.

These items are seen by many observers as central to the policy agenda of finance capital a narrow but powerful interest group (distinct from industrial capital) that has moved to a position of dominance since the mid 1970s (Patnaik 1999). As one observer puts it: Financiers are creditors, and creditors wish above all to prevent inflation which erodes their returns; they wish to maintain high real interest rates, and they want complete freedom to move their finance in and out of countries in the search of the highest profits. *Deflationary economic policies combined with removal of all national barriers to the free movement of finance capital*, thus form the core of the policy agenda of finance capital.

Yet, macroeconomic policies that are 'sound', in terms of balancing the budget and keeping inflation low, can be quite detrimental if they destroy jobs, livelihoods and human capabilities. Many independent economists have raised serious questions about the cherished 'fundamentals' of orthodox macroeconomic policy that have been applied in countries as diverse as Russia, Brazil and Indonesia with pronounced contractionary consequences.

They urge a serious re–thinking of these 'fundamentals'. Orthodox economists, for example argue, on the basis of simple regressions, that low inflation is a significant contributor to growth, while high inflation is costly for the real economy. But critics contend that the relationship is spurious: governments whose economies are already in trouble tend to over expand their money supply which leads to inflation; but in these cases it is poor economic performance that leads to inflation, not the other way around.

What constitutes a 'sound' or 'prudent' macro economic policy then becomes an open question with no single optimal set of policies as the correct answer. What is a sustainable budgetary deficit? Above what rates does inflation become costly for an economy? Rather than a single unique answer to many of these questions, there is instead a range of alternative development paths, each deriving from different combinations of a large number of relevant factors. While this seems to be nothing more than a truism, the implications in term of development *policy* can be powerful. And yet changing the macro economic agenda will require more than clear analytical vision and strong empirical evidence. The economic agenda that devastates the livelihoods of large numbers of people is very beneficial to some groups; it serves 'the interests of financial institutions and those who own large amounts of money, preserving the value of their wealth and enabling them to augment it freely'.

A related factor that has contributed to the disappointing growth record over the past two decades is the much higher frequency of financial crises. The world economy has been experiencing a much higher frequency of financial instability in the 1980s and 1990s than in the post World War II period up to the early 1970s. These persistent 'booms in busts' have been in response to the much greater cross–border capital flows relative to GDP compared to previous decades, at least for the OECD countries and the developing countries known as 'emerging markets'.

It is for the latter group of countries that the strains caused by financial crises have been particularly high given the weakness of their financial systems. For example, in the case of the Mexican crisis of 1994, uncontrolled capital flight led to the devaluation of the currency and the collapse of the economy that could only be halted by a $50 billion rescue package from the US. While the financial crisis was short lived for investors, it had far reaching effects on the Mexican banking system, interest rates and prospects for longer term economic recovery; it has also meant increased vulnerability and slow (or negative) growth for other countries in the region that have become highly dependent on short term foreign investment.

There is now little serious disagreement that the East Asian economic crises since mid–1997 began as currency and liquidity crises. It is also increasingly clear that the crises were caused by the undermining of previous systems of international and national economic governance due to deregulation and other developments associated with financial liberalisation. In other words, the subversion of effective financial governance at both international and national levels created conditions contributing to the crises. As is now well known, the drastically tight monetary policies (interest rates as high as 80% in Indonesia) and fiscal austerity measures that were 'advised' by the IMF to Asian governments in response to the financial crisis led to massive job losses and surges in poverty. In other words, what was initially a 'relatively tractable liquidity problem was thus turned into a massive solvency crisis with enormous losses in employment and output'.

It has also been persuasively argued that financial crises in developing countries, and the fact that these crises are followed by long periods of negative or slightly positive growth, while the rich countries continue to grow even during their banking cum–currency crises (which are in any case less frequent) have contributed to the rising global inequality. And within countries (be it in East Asia, Eastern Europe or Latin America) it is arguable that financial crises have exacerbated gender inequalities as women have often born the brunt of managing household adjustment to these crises. According to regional studies from Asia, the most immediate and felt impact of the crisis was in the area of social reproduction (increases in prices and availability of basic food items), as well as medium–term impacts in terms of the intensification of women's labour force participation in low paying work in the services and informal sectors (including prostitution and domestic work) due to pressures of family survival and from limited opportunities provided by economic systems with marked sector based gender preference.

This section has considered some of the plausible explanations for the relatively slow rates of economic growth in the 1980s and 1990s. But we know that economic growth is not in itself sufficient to achieve social goals. What matters if the benefits are to be widely shared is the quality of growth: 'whether it entails a more equal distribution of income, more and better jobs, rising wages, more gender equality and inclusiveness'. In the following sections we will therefore be looking more specifically at some of the social issues, in particular the employment and poverty record. However one point that can be said with confidence is that with very low or negative rates of growth it will be extremely difficult (if not impossible) for countries to undertake policies that can significantly reduce poverty and inequality and enhance the standard of living the fiscal resources needed to set up comprehensive social programs, for example, will be much more difficult to muster when growth is sluggish. These difficulties are compounded by the fact that redistributive policies (such as agrarian reform, progressive income taxation, and redistributive and comprehensive social policies) have been marginalised in policy debates by the neo liberal ideological hegemony.

Poverty, Inequality and their Gender Dimensions

This section begins with the general picture of income poverty for different regions of the world over the past decade. The measure of income poverty used here is the standard measure employed by most international agencies: number of people (or proportion of the population) with a purchasing power equivalent to less than $1 per day. Arguably, this is a very low figure and seriously underestimates the extent of poverty. The picture is nevertheless far from encouraging: at least 1.2 billion people (or one–fifth of the world's population) were living in absolute poverty in 1998, roughly the same situation as a decade earlier.

Table: Poverty Trends: People living on less than $1 (PPP) per day (Millions)

	1987	1990	1993	1996	1998
East Asia and the Pacific	415.1	452.4	431.9	265.0	278.3
(Excluding China)	109.2	76.0	66.0	45.0	55.6
Eastern Europe and Central Asia	1.1	7.1	18.3	2.8	24.0
Latin America and the Caribbean	36.7	73.8	70.8	76.0	78.2
Middle East and North Africa	25.0	22.0	21.5	21.3	20.9
South Africa	474.4	495.1	505.1	504.7	522.0
Sub-Saharan Africa	217.2	242.3	273.3	289.0	290.9
Total	1,196.5	1,292.7	1,320.9	1,179.9	1,214.2
(Excluding China)	890.6	916.3	955	960.1	991.5

Source: World Bank. 1990a (cited in UNRISD 2000).

However as a recent UNRISD Report goes on to argue, 'the incidence of poverty has increased in the past few years not because the world as a whole is getting poorer, but because the benefits of growth have been unevenly spread.'. There has been a striking increase in inequality both between countries and within countries (even the rich industrialised countries), which raises pressing questions about the policies that have contributed to this worrying trend.

Ironically though, the issue of inequality has received little attention in policy circles (and some would say, in research too). The retreat from equality is evident across the literature on economic development, which has been far more concerned with issues of poverty than of inequality (and redistribution). It is also evident in the recent shift in social policy thinking away from ideas of universal welfare provision aimed at creating a more equal society, towards an emphasis on the provision of *basic* services targeted to the needy and the 'poorest of the poor'. The latter aims to reduce poverty and destitution, but is not concerned with the overall distribution of income and wealth within society.

Gendered Poverty

Poverty is increasingly seen as a multi dimensional phenomenon, which includes market–based consumption (or income), as well as the public provision of goods and services, access to common property resources and the intangible dimensions of a good life, such as low levels of disease and crime, clean air, dignity and autonomy. The proponents of the conventional approach argue that the income/consumption measure is still the best single proxy for poverty since it can incorporate non–market goods and services and a wide range of other utilities (clean air, democracy) and disutilities (noise, pollution), through 'shadow prices', into a monetary equivalent that is easy to compare over time and across context. But their critics argue that common property resources and state provided commodities have usually been ignored in practice, and the consumption of non traded goods has also been under–estimated. It is also questionable whether 'shadow prices' can meaningfully translate the different kinds of values that are embodied in non–market goods and services into monetary equivalents that are comparable.

In practice while most official studies of poverty, such as the World Bank's Poverty Assessments (PAs) begin by asserting the multi dimensionality of poverty, they end up giving priority to an income and/or consumption definition, a poverty line measure and a quantitative estimate of the percentage of people in poverty. At the same time, many of the potential insights about the nature of impoverishment, or poverty processes, which emerge from the qualitative and 'participatory' research are either marginalised or dropped from the analysis.

This is a fundamental methodological choice, since it locks these studies of poverty into reliance on expenditure data from household surveys, which tend to be unreliable and non–comparable. In most African and Latin American countries, household budget surveys are one off (non–repetitive) exercises, which make them unsuited as a device for monitoring poverty.

There is also little consistency in how the poverty line is established, even for the same country: in the case of the World Bank's PAs, some of them define the poverty line in absolute terms and others in relative terms; some deflate household expenditure by average household size while others use expenditure per adult equivalent. Such methodological inconsistency effectively defeats the purpose of collecting quantitative data, since one of the rationales for using quantitative data is precisely that they are comparable over time and across context.

The reliance on poverty lines and household expenditure data has profound implications for how gender issues are analysed. Measuring poverty on the basis of household expenditure data effectively ignores the long standing feminist concerns about intra household distribution. It is very rare to find standard surveys, such as those carried out in the context of the PAs, embarking on a quantitative exploration of intra household poverty. Per capita and adult equivalent measures make assumptions about *equal* intra household distribution of resources. Gillian Hart's (1995b) interrogation of the claims made by those using collective models of the household to be able to recover intra household distributional patterns from household surveys using sophisticated econometric techniques also reveals that they are for the most part exaggerated. In other words, if household surveys are to become useful tools for capturing and monitoring gender differentials in poverty, then intra household distribution issues need to be addressed at the very early stage and specifically built into questionnaire design.

The reliance on household expenditure data also means that one of the easier ways to make gender visible is by dividing the households into male headed and female headed ones, given that the characteristics of household heads (their gender, age, *etc.*) are invariably collected through these surveys and form a ready basis for sorting the data. The tendency to equate female headship with poverty has, however, been queried on both empirical and methodological grounds. The trajectories leading to female headship are clearly divergent, and the category of households labelled 'female headed' is a highly heterogeneous one. It includes lone female units, households of single women wage earners with young dependents, households in which women earners receive significant remittances from absent males, and so on. Some of these conditions may constitute what can be reasonably thought of as poverty risk factors, such as households with young children maintained by women alone. But by aggregating these distinct categories of households generated through different social processes (*e.g.* migration, widowhood, divorce), and constructing a simple dualism between male headed and female headed households, it becomes impossible to interpret the evidence in a meaningful way.

In short, there is a persisting reticence on the part of administrative and governmental structures responsible for data collection exercises to probe the intra household arena. This is surprising in view of the significant body of evidence and argument that has been brought to bear on this issue over the past two decades. This has effectively shaken the micro foundations of the conventional economic approach, and yet few national level surveys attempt to collect data at a more disaggregated level. In the absence of appropriate data it is very difficult to assess how processes of globalisation over the past two decades have impacted on intra household inequalities in income poverty. As a recent UNIFEM report concluded:

'Without a gender sensitive income poverty indicator there is no way of estimating the extent of feminisation of poverty leading to the use of global "guesstimates" such as the much repeated claim that 70 per cent of the world's poor are women. No one can identify the empirical evidence on which this claim is based, and demographic analysis has shown that it is not credible'.

Capabilities and their Gender Gaps

The capability framework, outlined in the writings of Amartya Sen (1985) within the economics discipline and elabourated in philosophical terms by Martha Nussbaum (2001), sets out an approach towards identifying 'the basic constitutional principles that should be respected and implemented by the governments of all nations, as a bare minimum of what respect for human dignity requires'. The idea of a basic social minimum is provided by focusing on human capabilities, that is, 'what people are actually able to do and to be in a way informed by an intuitive idea of a life that is worthy of the dignity of the human being'. Moreover, given that these 'beings' and 'doings' are directly measurable on the individual, gender inequalities can be made more readily visible. Not surprisingly, the framework has inspired a large body of feminist research on well being outcomes, documenting significant and sometimes alarming incidence of female disadvantage.

The indicators we will be looking at in this sub section very cursorily relate to female education (net primary and secondary enrolment or attendance ratios). The main concern, however, is female employment (including gender wage gaps, and social rights linked to employment).

As Elson (2001) rightly argues, there are many problems in assessing the impact of particular policy programmes on how women and men have fared (in terms of nutrition, life expectancy, and so on). One major source of problem continues to be the lack of timely, reliable, sex disaggregated data for many parts of the world. Moreover, as she goes on to argue, 'it is intrinsically difficult to examine causal links between policies and events that follow their introduction' since the policy may not have been fully implemented, or because of many significant events taking place at the same time (such as changes in the weather, or in social and political forces).

Let us take one capability for which data is more readily available and generally more reliable (compared to, for example, nutritional indicators), namely education. Enrolment ratios, it is widely agreed, provide an over–optimistic picture of the degree to which young people are educated. Enrolment ratios do not take into account drop out rates (which can be quite high, especially when economic conditions deteriorate); they do not take into account the content of education curricula (which can be gender biased); nor do they show how qualified people are when they complete their education.

Despite these weaknesses, given the fact that enrolment ratios are more widely available, they will be used here. Moreover, given the emphasis that has been placed on female education by diverse policy institutions over the past decade or so, it is also one of the few areas of social development where one can expect to see relatively more progress. However, as we will see below, there have been setbacks in some contexts, and many challenges remain.

During the period 1980–1994 the gap between girls enrolments and boys enrolment at primary level did indeed narrow in developing countries. But there are some important anomalies that stand out. In the case of sub Saharan Africa the closing of the gender gap in some countries is attributed to a decline in the enrolment of boys and only a marginal increase in the participation of girls. According to UNESCO data, the gross primary enrolment rate for girls in sub–Saharan Africa was 68 in 1980 and 66 in 1990, while that for boys was 87 and 79 respectively. In other words, the gender gap did indeed narrow, but not in a way that was consistent with the realisation of the right to education of either boys or girls. It is essential to look at absolute levels of enrolment of girls, as well as at the gender gap if we want to evaluate how far girls have enjoyed the right to education in the neo–liberal era.

If we examine girls' enrolment in secondary school, while the majority of countries have made progress, for about one quarter of countries there has been deterioration. Again the UNESCO data show that girls' net enrolment in secondary school declined between 1985 and 1997 in 10 out of 33 countries in sub–Saharan Africa; 7 out of 11 countries in Central and Western Asia; 2 out of 21 countries in Asia and the Pacific; 6 out of 26 in Latin America and the Caribbean; 6 out of 9 in Eastern Europe; and 1 out of 23 countries in Western Europe and other Developed Countries.

Again, the picture is mixed. But even enrolment ratios, which are widely believed to provide an over optimistic assessment, show that there have been regressions in some regional contexts and this despite the policy emphasis that has been placed on female education as the panacea for all development ills. One of the benefits of education for women should be to enhance their economic entitlements. Yet, despite the link between education and income, studies from diverse regional contexts indicate that equal years of education do not translate into equality of job opportunity for men and women.

Men everywhere tend to get better jobs than women with similar levels of education. A complex set of forces explain the persistence of gendered labour markets, from the more obvious factors such as continuing gender gaps in the fields of science and technology, to the more intractable differences in men's and women's relations/access to employment, the centrality of the 'care economy' in how women relate to labour markets, and gender discriminatory forces in how male and female labour are valued and remunerated regardless of human capital investments.

A far more comprehensive picture charting the relationship between gender inequalities in capabilities and neo–liberal policies over the past two decades is provided in Progress of the World's Women 2000 (UNIFEM 2000) and in Diane Elson's recent article on gender justice and neo–liberal economic policies (2001).

The picture that emerges from both the UNIFEM Report and Elson's comprehensive review is far from encouraging. It is worth citing Elson's conclusions, which contrast rather sharply with those voiced by a World Bank report Engendering Development (2001) that was recently released. Based on a limited and problematic data set, the World Bank Report concludes: While there is evidence to support both sides of the debate about the impact of structural adjustment, on balance the evidence suggests that females' absolute status and gender equality improved, not deteriorated over the adjustment period.

Elson's review ends with a far less sanguine conclusion: Overall, the picture with respect to women's enjoyment of specific rights in the neo–liberal era is not encouraging. The evidence reviewed above suggests that there has been regress rather than progress in the realisation of economic and social rights in many countries, even though in some countries progress has been made.

It is beyond the scope to assess these statements in any comprehensive manner. However, one issue that we will be looking at in some depth is the area of employment.

Globalisation and Employment

One argument that is frequently made in favour of globalisation, and trade liberalisation in particular, is that it has brought about higher rates of employment in developing countries as the hub of manufacturing has shifted from the North to the South. In turn, high rates of unemployment in the North are, according to this view, to be blamed on the same North–South migration of jobs. Is this argument supported by existing empirical evidence? Has trade liberalisation expanded employment opportunities in developing countries? These questions are explored below.

Women, in particular, are often seen as the winners of labour market changes unleashed by trade liberalisation. Are women the *net* beneficiaries in terms of employment generation and destruction consequent upon trade liberalisation? Which groups of women have gained and which groups have lost? What has women's increased presence in labour markets meant in terms of economic and social entitlements as well as in more qualitative terms as far as changes in gender relations are concerned?

Manufacturing Employment: North and South

There is a widespread perception among policy makers and some sections of the public in the North that processes of trade liberalisation over the past two decades have contributed to a significant shift in the structure of global manufacturing production, from the North to the South. A significant part of the academic literature on trade related employment (by economists) has been concerned with the impact of North–South trade on unemployment and wage inequality in the North. The effects of such global integration on workers in the South 'have generally been taken to be unambiguously positive', and have received surprisingly little empirical scrutiny. Only recently has more sustained attention been directed at the impact of global integration on workers in the South.

One of the main arguments emerging from the trade literature is that the expansion of North–South trade has brought about substantial employment gains in the South, while it has given rise to high rates of unemployment among the unskilled workers in the North. More recent studies raise serious questions about the extent to which high rates of unemployment (in Western Europe) and low wages among unskilled workers (in the United States) can be attributed to manufacturing trade with the South.

Looking at the share of different countries in world merchandise exports, one point emerges with clarity: the share of developing countries in world export of manufactures steadily increased from about 11 per cent in 1980 to about 25 per cent in 1999, while the share of industrialised countries over the same period steadily declined (from about 83 per cent to 72 per cent). These aggregate changes in world merchandise exports seem to support the view that jobs are being 'exported' from the North to the South. But such a proposition is weakened when a number of further considerations are brought into the picture. First we briefly look at the employment picture in the North and the extent to which North–South trade can be held accountable for the deteriorating conditions there. Next we turn to the employment picture in the South and scrutinise the proposition that is implicit in the very idea of 'exporting' jobs: if jobs are being 'exported' from the North, presumably they are being 'imported' into the South.

The evidence on trends in wages and employment of workers in the North over the past two decades clearly show a marked deterioration in labour market conditions: increasing unemployment in Europe; falling real wages and increasing casualisation of labour in the US; and the significant weakening of trade unions in both contexts. An important factor behind the rising rates of unemployment and increasing wage inequality in most industrialised countries over the past two decades has been job loss in the manufacturing sector, which has in turn been due to a displacement of unskilled labour on a significant scale in a number of industries in which developing countries have increased their market share (UNCTAD 2001).

Hence the public concerns about jobs and wages in the North are clearly well founded. Yet, the results of recent research indicate that there is very little basis for the popular perception that deteriorating conditions in the North are to be blamed on trade with the South. This conclusion is in turn based on a number of related arguments.

First, most manufacturing trade of the advanced countries takes place between these countries themselves and only a small part is with developing countries. It is rather difficult therefore to argue that the rise in income inequality and mass unemployment in the North are caused largely by the rather marginal trade with the South. Second, despite its increased manufacturing imports from the South, over the past three decades the North has generally maintained a surplus in manufacturing trade with the South.

Furthermore, neither mass unemployment nor de–industrialisation (*i.e.* the drop in manufacturing employment in the North) is associated with fluctuations in this trade surplus. It is further recognised that these unfavourable labour market conditions need to be explained by taking into account other important factors, such as trade imbalances between Northern countries themselves, cyclical movements in economic activity and its slow long–term growth, technical change, and changes in economic and social policy in these countries themselves.

Finally, while it is widely recognised that the main employment problem in the North is the insufficient demand for unskilled labour, even those economists who believe that there is a tendency for North–South trade to be detrimental to unskilled workers will recognise that this tendency can be overwhelmed by the 'lift all boats' effect of faster economic growth (as was the case in the 1950s and 1960s when there was a fast increase in imports from the then NICs, Japan and Italy, into the US but without any adverse impacts on employment and wages in the US). In other words, even if there were some adverse labour market outcomes in the 1980s and 1990s of trade with the South, these could have been overridden by faster economic growth.

The far more important question that needs to be looked at is whether North–South trade in manufactures has in fact led to significant employment expansion in the South, as is often claimed.

The first important point to note is that the much cited changes in the trade relations between the industrialised and the developing economies, or between the North and the South, actually reflect shifts in the position of a small number of developing economies in the global market for manufactures referred to as the 'Group of 13'. It is the export performance of this small group of countries that explains almost all the significant increase in developing country manufacturing exports over the past two decades and therefore accounts for what is often regarded as a major shift in trade relations between the North and the South. Thus the share of these countries in total merchandise export from the South increased from 33 per cent in 1980 to 72 per cent in 1996, while their share of manufactured exports of the South went up from the already high figure of 73 per cent to 88 per cent over the same period.

Inevitably, the nature of economic relations between the North and the rest of the South (*i.e.* excluding the 'Group of 13') remains largely unaltered, and they have been for the most part unable to shift their export base from primary commodities to manufactures. It is fair to conclude therefore that the international division of labour between the developing countries *excluding the 'Group of 13'* and the North 'underwent no major qualitative change'. Consequently, it would be meaningless to argue that the developing countries as a group have gained (in terms of structural change, export earnings, employment, and so on) from North–South trade in manufactures given that no such shift in trade has actually taken place.

The next important question to consider is the extent to which shifts in North–South trade, and the export orientation of manufactures among this small group of countries has led to significant employment gains. As one author puts it, 'Obviously, if manufacturing jobs have been going anywhere, then it must have been to these locations, since they account for the lion's share of manufacturing exports of all developing countries' .

Using the UNIDO database for the period 1980–96, Ghose (2000) compares the labour intensity of export oriented industries in some of these dynamic developing countries to their import competing industries, as well as the employment elasticity of manufacturing over the period when growth of manufactured exports accelerated. He reaches the conclusion that in a number of countries (China, Indonesia and Malaysia) trade liberalisation did increase the employment elasticity of manufacturing. He also explicitly rejects the argument that trade liberalisation in developing countries has reduced employment in the import competing industries. Some possible explanations are offered for this counter intuitive finding: first, trade might have eased the foreign exchange constraints which would in turn have stimulated the growth of manufacturing; second, trade could have stimulated the inflow of FDI into both export oriented and import competing industries.

His overall conclusion about the gains to be made from trade liberalisation as far as developing countries are concerned is therefore positive: with greater openness and more trade the employment intensity of manufacturing production will rise in developing countries; and within the Asian developing countries (but not Latin America) the export oriented industries show higher employment elasticities of manufacturing production than the import competing industries. His findings therefore seem to confirm the predictions from neo classical trade theories.

These conclusions are put in question by another recent study which uses both UNIDO and ILO datasets, and examines patterns of manufacturing employment expansion as a whole rather than relying on the factor content approach which is used by Ghose. First, it is clear from the datasets used by Ghosh that with a few notable exceptions, China, Malaysia and Chile many of the even supposedly dynamic developing countries experienced only a low to moderate employment growth in manufacturing, and that for several countries (*e.g.* Brazil, Argentina, Mexico) such employment actually declined in absolute numbers over the said period.

Female Employment in the 1980s and 1990s

Women are certainly more likely to be working outside the home than ever before. Between the 1950s and the end of the 1990s, the proportion of women aged 20–59 who were in the labour force increased from around one third to one half. The current participation rates by region range from 14 per cent in North Africa to 76 per cent in East and Central Europe. In many cases, women's participation has increased at the expense of men's. In half the developing countries for which data were available, over the period 1975–95 the female participation rate rose while the male rate fell. The global labour force has become more female rising from 36 per cent in 1960 to 40 per cent by 1997.

But it is also important to underline an important counter trend taking place in the 'transition' economies of East and Central Europe, where women's formal employment has fallen since the on set of economic reforms. The female labour force participation rate was lower in 1997 than in 1985 in all transition countries, and the drop in female employment was as drastic as 40% in Hungary, although this may hide the increasing informalisation of female labour not only in Hungary but also elsewhere in the region.

To some extent the increase in participation (in all regions except Eastern and Central Europe) is a statistical artefact it reflects better ways of recording seasonal, unpaid family and casual wage labour. But it does also reflect a number of real changes. First, more women must now work to ensure family survival in the face of declining real wages and the increased monetary cost of subsistence resulting from cutbacks in both public services and subsidies for staple foods. In an increasing proportion of two adult households, both partners now work.

A second factor is the increase in the number of women headed households in which women are required to meet the monetary cost of household survival from their own labour. A third reason is that there has been a greater demand for women workers in particular sectors of the economy that have experienced long term growth. Many industries employing a high proportion of women have expanded rapidly in response to globalisation. Much of this is low skilled manufacturing notably in garments, footwear and electronic products and 'non–traditional' agricultural products such as cut flowers, seasonal fruits and vegetables. At the same time, with the increasing emphasis on cost–cutting competitiveness, firms have been searching for ways to reduce their labour costs.

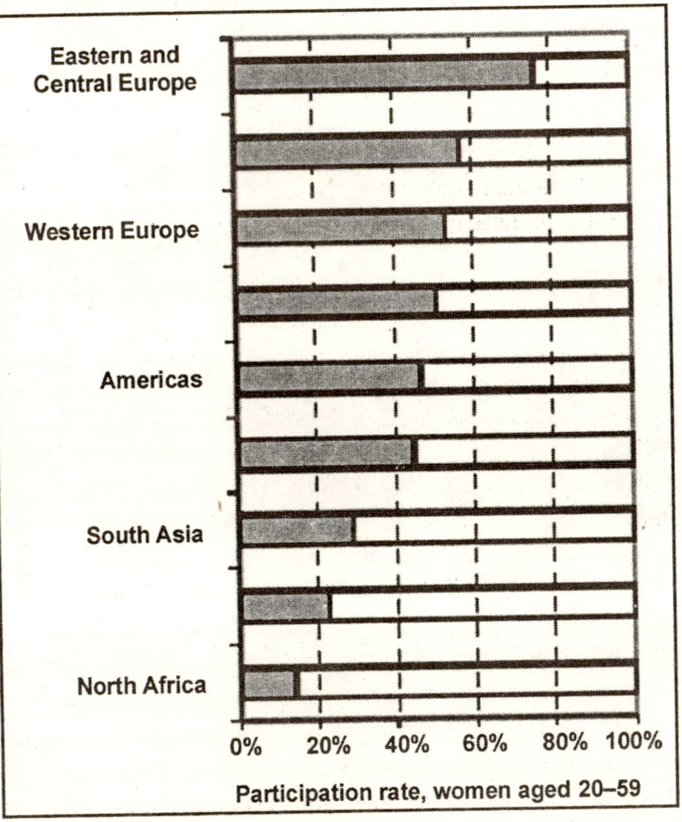

Fig. *Women's labour force participation, 1980s and 1990s*

This has often meant changes in the structure of the labour market away from formal, full time employment with entitlements, such as unemployment and sickness insurance, pensions and maternity benefits. Instead, people must work in more 'flexible' ways whether part time, temporary or casual. And this is more likely to involve women. In most industrialised countries, women make up 70 to 80 per cent of part time employees. Women also make up the majority of home workers. Other important factors behind the increase in women's labour force participation are: changing social norms, increasing levels of education among women and declines in fertility.

While many see women's entry into the labour force as empowering (economic independence, wider social contacts, and so on), there are several important questions that are also raised. What is the quality of employment? Is labour force participation translated into economic and social rights? Have gender relations been transformed and are women experiencing more autonomy or does it mean a 'double load' with little change in the division of domestic labour? Some of these questions are explored in greater depth below.

Female Employment in the Manufacturing Sector

It is widely argued that industrialisation in the context of globalisation is as much female led as it is export led. By the mid 1990s a clear consensus had emerged which considered the growth in international trade to be, on the whole, favourable to women's participation in the paid labour force. The increased absorption of women workers into the manufacturing sector in developing countries, it was argued, has clearly been driven by changes in trade performance in two senses. 'On the one hand, women have been the actively preferred labour force in exporting industries, and on the other, the change in trade orientation has entailed the relative decline of privileged male employment in autarkic industry'.

While some important elements of this assessment still hold true, a number of trends since the mid 1990s in the employment patterns of developing countries, raise noteworthy questions. First, what was perhaps not sufficiently highlighted by some of the early assessments of the benefits of trade for women is the simultaneous destruction of jobs as cheap imports replace domestically manufactured goods a point that was raised above. So the net impact of trade liberalisation may not be as positive as the gross employment figures for the export oriented sector suggest.

The second important factor is the slow down in the capacity of the export oriented sector to create employment in more recent years even in the more dynamic Asian and Latin American developing countries. The third important factor to take into account is the apparent de–feminisation of employment in some sub–sectors of export oriented manufacturing, apparently as export production becomes more skill and capital intensive. In elabourating these points, particular attention will be paid to developments in Asian labour markets, since the impacts of globalisation on female employment have been particularly marked in this region.

To begin it is important to reiterate the obvious point that among the newly industrialising countries of Asia (and others like Mexico, Morocco and Mauritius) where manufacturing production has been successfully oriented towards exports, the share of women in these industries has increased significantly. The available employment data, disaggregated across industrial sub–sectors, suggest that female labour shares have been highest in the relatively low skill, labour intensive and often export oriented sub sectors.

To give some idea of the magnitude of change, in South Korea, which is considered to be one of the pioneer 'first tier' newly industrialised economies (NIEs), the female share of manufacturing workers rose from 26.6 per cent in 1960 to 32.9 per cent in 1970, 39.0 per cent in 1980, and a high point of 42.6 per cent in 1990 before declining to 35.3 per cent in 1999. In the second tier Southeast Asian NIEs like Malaysia, where the strategy of export oriented industrialisation was adopted later in time, the female share of manufacturing workers rose from 38.2 per cent in 1980 to a peak of 47.6 per cent in 1990, before declining to 40.3 per cent in 1999. Similarly in Thailand the female share of manufacturing workers rose from 37.6 per cent in 1960 to a peak of 50.4 per cent in 1991 before declining slightly to 49.3 per cent in 1999.

Perhaps the single most striking piece of evidence for the feminisation of the labour force engaged in export oriented manufacturing production is the very high share of women in EPZ industries. Women also occupy a significant place in the less visible part of the so called 'global assembly line' through sub contracted piece rate work that takes place outside factory premises, in very small units as well as through home based work. Dispersed across the urban and rural hinterland, it has been very difficult to reach any quantitative estimates of the numbers of workers thus engaged, but there are indications that this type of work may be on the rise in many parts of the world, and that the workforces involved are heavily feminised. Indeed, some estimate that the percentage of home workers in garments ranges from 30 to 60 per cent in different Asian and Latin American countries.

The first qualification that needs to be raised in response to the optimistic scenario noted above, is that the growth of export oriented production processes (and employment therein) can take place simultaneously with the destruction of jobs in other parts of the manufacturing sector because of import penetration following trade liberalisation. Unfortunately, there is little empirical evidence documenting the magnitude of jobs destroyed through trade liberalisation for different regions of the South, even though there are important country studies providing a clear picture of this phenomenon.

But two important trends at the aggregate level seem to suggest that such processes of job destruction are indeed taking place. First, as we have already noted, over the past decade the South on the whole has had a negative trade balance with the North, even in the case of manufactured goods, suggesting that Northern imports may be displacing Southern domestic production (note, however, that displacement of domestic production can also take place as a result of South–South trade, as Hart shows for South Africa where imports of cheaper knitwear produced in China through Taiwanese investments is destroying jobs in South African factories producing similar products).

Second, and as we have already seen, the overall net employment outcome for the Southern manufacturing sector has not been as positive as one would have expected from the increase in the Southern share of manufactured goods exports. At the same time, adding to the downward pressures on employment from import liberalisation, many state owned and state protected industries have come under pressure as government subsidies and protections have been withdrawn. While it is sometimes claimed that these industries provided jobs for a male 'labour aristocracy', the validity of such statements becomes questionable when we look more closely at variations across countries.

Looking more specifically at the gender composition of employment, one would need to compare those groups of women who have been able to find employment in the expanding export oriented sectors of manufacturing with the 'losers' in other parts of the manufacturing sector. The comparison is not simply about numbers of 'losers' versus 'winners' (although that is an important consideration).

It is also important to bear in mind that the profile of women workers in the different sub sectors may be very different (in terms of age, life cycle, levels of education, and so on). To continue with the case of China, while it is clear that export processing industries depend more heavily than the older state owned industrial sector on female workers (many of them young rural migrants), this does not mean that the latter were/are insignificant employers of women. While the new export processing enterprises employ a highly feminised work force female workforces of the order of 80% according to many studies at the same time the Chinese State Statistical Bureau figures for 1994 show that 39.3% of the workforce of state–owned enterprises and 50% of the urban collectives' workforces were women.

The numbers of women having lost their jobs already, and those now facing the risk of job loss in the near future as China further liberalises its economy are thus significant.

Another example worth citing is Bangladesh. This is an important case to consider given the fact that the heavy presence of young women in the readymade garments industry that has mushroomed in and around the capital city, Dhaka, in the 1980s and 1990s has often been held up as evidence of how women, even in a highly restricted cultural context, can be liberated from the confines of home based work through trade liberalisation. While some crucial elements of that argument remain valid, it has tended to gloss over some of the complexities and counter trends. It is clear, for example, from more recent studies that policies of import liberalisation since the early 1980s have adversely affected the output growth and employment performance of several large and medium scale industries that compete with imports (the so called import competing industries), such as paper, cotton textile and sugar, which have all experienced regression over the same period.

The other more worrying trend is that the overall employment in the industrial sector has fallen sharply, from 7 million in 1989 to 4.1 million in 1995–6, and much of this sharp reduction in employment in the manufacturing sector has evidently occurred in the small and cottage industry sector. A large part of the job destruction, therefore, is likely to have taken place in the informal sector industries that are located in both the urban and rural areas of the country, employing large numbers of men and women and very often catering to demand from the poorer strata of the population; interestingly, it is the decline in agricultural wages and incomes due to import liberalisation substantial imports of cheap foodgrains which have depressed domestic foodgrain prices that is behind the fall in demand for the products produced by these rural industries. While we do not have gender disaggregated data to ascertain the gender composition of job losses in these informal sector industries (or in the import competing industries noted above), a significant proportion has been for the category of 'unpaid family workers' which must include significant numbers of women.

The second qualification that needs to be made is that employment expansion in several regions have already slowed down and are likely to decline even further as the global economy further decelerates. We have already elabourated this issue, and so it will not be pursued any further here. Suffice it to say that with a few notable exceptions China, Malaysia and Chile many of the even supposedly dynamic developing countries experienced only a low to moderate employment growth in manufacturing, and that for many other countries such employment actually declined in absolute numbers from 1985 to 1998. Another important trend is that those countries that have accelerated their manufactured exports, like Malaysia and Indonesia, have been facing diminishing terms of trade between 1985 and 1995, despite significant increases in the ratio of exports to GDP and the ratio of manufactures to total exports.

There thus appears to have been a relative decline in the prices of manufactured exports from the South compared to manufactured imports into the South, especially from the North. These trends have been so worrying that observers warn that the 'enhanced productivity and competitiveness in East Asia may well have contributed to a variant of "immiserising growth", *i.e.*, of productivity gains that are less than proportionately reflected in rising real incomes or living standards'.

One of the explanations offered for this apparent paradox is the technology content of the manufactures in which these countries have specialised: most developing countries have concentrated on labour intensive and low technology products, and the emergence of low wage countries like China as major producers and exporters has exerted further downward pressure on the terms of trade of developing countries' manufactured exports since the mid–1980s. In other words, labour intensive manufactured exports from developing countries are behaving more and more like traditional commodities, facing terms of trade losses. Yet, despite these adverse trends, stabilisation and adjustment policies continue to promote manufactured exports, thereby contributing further to world surpluses and intensifying the fallacy of composition.

There is also a plausible gender dimension to this argument. As is well known by now, one of the main features of countries that have embarked on the labour intensive export strategy, through the so called 'low road to industrialisation', is the availability of an abundant supply of 'cheap' and 'docile' female labour.

However, low wages and low value added in exports can keep export prices low and weaken the terms of trade, resulting in a form of immiserising growth along the lines noted above. 'Thus to the extent that gender inequalities and gender biases are allowed to keep wages perennially low', Gita Sen asserts, 'these can reinforce structural inequalities in global trade between South and North'. The policy implication of Sen's argument is that the challenge for industrial policy is to forge a transition from the so called 'low road' (based on cheap labour) to the 'high road' (based on increasing worker productivity), (and one would add) combined with better policy coordination at the global level to avoid the 'fallacy of composition' likely to result when a large number of countries pursue a similar strategy.

This, however, takes us to the third qualification we wish to raise in this section. What happens to the gender composition of the labour force when such a transition takes place? The employment trends in East Asia, especially among the first tier NIEs that have successfully restructured and up graded their labour intensive exports by shifting towards skill intensive products, are highly informative in this respect.

In the latest issue of the United Nations Report, The 1999 World Survey on the Role of Women in Developmen, it is argued that since the late 1980s 'in many middle income countries the demand for women's labour in manufacturing has been weakening, as export production became more skill and capital intensive'. As examples of this trend, the report cites Singapore, Taiwan, South Korea and the *maquiladoras* in Mexico. In South Korea specifically, it notes that 'the composition of the workforce in the electronics industry has changed in favour of male workers, as production in this sector shifted to more sophisticated communication and computer products'.

In a recent paper prepared for UNRISD, Jomo (2001) traces the trends in female employment as the manufacturing sector in different East Asian countries has gone through various structural changes over the past two decades. First, what is clear is that while the manufacturing share of total employment has begun to decline in the three first tier East Asian newly industrialised economies (NIE) of Hong Kong, Singapore and South Korea from 1971, 1981 and 1989 respectively, the same cannot be said of the three second tier Southeast Asian countries of Malaysia, Thailand and Indonesia, with the possible exception of Malaysia, which began absorbing more labour into manufacturing much earlier than the other two.

Importantly, the female proportion of manufacturing workers peaked at different times in the different economies (and declined thereafter): around 1982–84 in Hong Kong, 1989 in Singapore, 1990 in South Korea and Malaysia, 1991 in Thailand and thrice (1976, 1982 and 1993) in Indonesia. The recent declines in the female share of manufacturing labour in Thailand and Indonesia have been modest, compared to the sharper fall in Malaysia. While the sequence of de–feminisation seems to follow that for the peaks in manufacturing's share of total employment, there is no clear pattern in relation to the timing.

However, while the facts of de–feminisation are more or less conclusive, the mechanisms leading to it are far from clear. A number of different explanations have been offered for the observed de-feminisation of manufacturing employment. Ghosh, for example, argues that the observed de–feminisation of the manufacturing labour force in East Asia may be attributed to the narrowing of the gender wage gap in the region. The figures she cites show a gradual (and, one could say, rather marginal) rise in women's wages compared to male wages. For example, in South Korea, the ratio of average female wages to male wages increased from 50 per cent in 1990 to 56 per cent in 1997, while in Malaysia it moved from 49 per cent to 57 per cent between 1990 and 1995.

According to Ghosh, what this narrowing of the gender wage gap has meant is that 'women became less cheap as labour in exporting industry' a tendency that was reinforced by several legislative moves in the region towards protecting women workers' rights and interests (such as more generous maternity benefits). In other words, as women workers have become less 'cheap' and less 'docile' thanks to their struggles and to public policy responses to their demands they may have lost their 'comparative advantage' vis–a–vis male labour. But this hypothesis sits uneasily with the fact that Singapore one of the countries where there has been a clear de–feminisation of employment is also exceptional among the East Asian economies in being the only economy studied where the gender gap in manufacturing wages has actually widened in recent years.

Joekes (1995) argues that the swing back from female intensity in Singapore's manufacturing as it has pursued its goal of product up grading, may be attributed, as a proximate cause, to the fact that women workers with the needed technical qualifications were not available in sufficient numbers for recruitment to new technical and other skilled grades. However, Jomo (2001) notes in response, that it is not clear that this was necessarily a region wide phenomenon since the facilities for pre–employment industrial vocational training in the rest of the region have been less well developed (though they are likely to be as gender biased).

Given the fact that the precise mechanisms and relations are still poorly understood, it would be very difficult to reach any definitive conclusions about the causes and mechanisms behind de–feminisation. What can be concluded with some certainty is that there appears to have been a general regional pattern of increased female employment in manufacturing during the early period of rapid labour intensive industrialisation, probably accelerated by the availability of export markets. However, with full employment, more sophisticated or skill intensive manufacturing and other related developments, both manufacturing growth and industrial employment growth appear to have tapered off, and the female share of such employment also appears to have declined, reflecting the gender preferences (or biases) of the new industrial employers, though the existing evidence does not allow a more careful and detailed examination of the processes at work. This is, however, clearly an area that requires far more empirical and analytical scrutiny.

Female Employment, Wages and Wage Gaps

The discussion so far has raised some questions about the *quality* of female employment in the export oriented industries where women have made significant *quantitative* inroads in recent decades (recent setbacks notwithstanding). Needless to say, many of the same concerns about working conditions would apply forcefully, almost by definition, to the 'informal' sectors (of agriculture, manufacturing and services) where increasing numbers of women and men are concentrated (often as part of household survival strategies). However, what we would like to suggest in this section is that even if the distinction between 'formal' and 'informal' sectors was useful or relevant in the 1960s and 1970s (many argued then that the distinction was dubious), it has become even less useful as a descriptive and analytical device in the present era.

As it is widely known, since the early 1980s labour markets around the world have undergone profound transformations. There has been a massive trend towards casualisation of the labour force: trade unions have been sidelined and coerced in many contexts, and labour forces have been deliberately casualised through sub contracting arrangements and the like.

At the same time there has been a continuing process of 'feminisation' of the labour force, where the concept of feminisation is understood to mean both an increase in women's labour force participation, as well as a recognition of the fact that labour market conditions in general for men as well as women have deteriorated and become more like the precarious labour market conditions that have typically characterised many 'women's jobs'. There has been a decline in the proportion of jobs that have security of employment, rights against unfair dismissal, pension rights, health insurance rights, maternity rights and the like, while there has been rapid growth in 'informal employment' which lacks social protection. In India, for example, during the decade of the economic reforms (the 1990s) it is the informal sector that has grown fastest and absorbed most labour: in agriculture, manufacturing, construction, petty trade and services.

Similarly in Africa there has been rapid growth in 'informal employment'. It is estimated that well over half of the urban jobs in Africa and Asia are informal, while the figures for Latin America and the Caribbean could be around one quarter; it is also argued that the share of informal employment is higher for new jobs, with as many as 83 per cent of new jobs in Latin America and 93 per cent in Africa being informal. Women's share of informal employment is typically higher than their share of formal employment.

Women in many economic sectors today therefore rarely enjoy the wide spectrum of social rights specified in national and international legislation, such as the right to favourable conditions of work, the right to equal pay for equal work, the right to social protection or the right to form and join trade unions and increasingly the same description could apply to many male workers. The absence of many of these rights in export oriented factories across the world is well documente and does not require repetition here. What such evidence points to, however, is the questionable distinction between the 'formal' and 'informal' sectors when working conditions in much of the socalled formal sector barely differ from those found in the informal sector. The distinction between the two sectors is also ambiguous given the linkages between production processes in the two sectors (through sub contracting and the like).

Given these labour market trends, have gender wage gaps narrowed? The availability, reliability and inter pretability of the data on pay relativities by gender pose major problems. A recent UNIFEM report (2000) made a heroic effort to tackle this question, but was constrained by the limited range of countries for which internationally comparable datasets were available (especially to assess change over time), as well as the incomplete coverage of different economic sectors, with a bias towards urban 'formal' sectors. The report argued that in industry and services, women on average earned about 78 per cent of what men earned in the late 1990s. As was noted above, in East Asia for which more reliable datasets are available, there is some evidence that the gender wage gaps have narrowed in a number of countries during the 1980s and 1990s, but it must be underlined that even after some convergence the gender wage gaps in this region remain large by international standards. For many other developing countries the UNIFEM report cautions that data on the gender wage gaps is likely to reflect mainly the earnings of those in full time 'formal' employment, given the biases of statistical surveys in many countries.

One piece of research that is frequently cited is by Tzannatos (1995). It asserts a positive correlation between trade liberalisation and reduced gender wage gap, based on wage data for Cote d'Ivoire, Brazil, Colombia, Philippines, Thailand and Indonesia. The implicit assumption seems to be that with export growth (which is supposed to be facilitated by trade liberalisation) the demand for female labour increases faster than for male labour, so that female wages also rise faster than male wages, and eventually converge. Leaving aside issues of statistical coverage and reliability, it is difficult to attribute the apparent closing of the gap in wages in these six countries to trade liberalisation *per se*; the analysis, for example, does not take into account the rise in women's educational attainment relative to men's over the same period. Evidence presented by Joekes for a number of other countries reveals no systematic divergence or convergence over time.

The other major problem with some of the evidence on wage convergence (including the study by Tzannatos) is that it does not make a distinction between convergence of male and female wages through a process of 'harmonising up' and 'harmonising down'. In other words, is the gender gap in wages narrowing because women's wages are catching up with men's, or is it rather because men's wages are being levelled down? In some contexts, such as in Singapore during the late 1970s, successful export oriented industrialisation did create a tight labour market for both men and women, and women's wages in particular did rise somewhat faster than men's. But as Phongpaichit (1988) rightly argues, Singapore's population is small and hence its experience somewhat different from that of many Asian countries which rely on migrant labour from a much wider rural hinterland.

In Bangladesh, for example, the availability of a generally elastic supply of unskilled female labour has meant that wage increases in the highly feminised garments manufacturing have been more or less the same as wage increases across a wide range of other sectors, despite a substantial rise in garments manufacturing profit margins and real value added over the same period so that there is little evidence of male and female wages converging.

Finally, it needs to be born in mind that the kinds of mechanisms that determine the value of labour in labour markets include important social and gender norms. This happens, for example, in how 'skills' are defined and labour is categorised processes which very often carry implicit gender biases. As evidence from different contexts has shown, the lower wages that women often command in labour markets cannot be adequately accounted for simply in terms of workers' experiences, skills and levels of education. There are both implicit and explicit exclusionary and discriminatory processes at work. The policy implication is that the norms and social mechanisms that shape and structure labour markets cannot be tackled through female education alone. There is clearly a need for gender aware trade unions and women's NGOs to contest the seemingly 'objective' mechanisms through which women's labour is devalued in labour markets.

The issue of gender wage gaps is clearly an important area of concern and a powerful indicator of gender inequality. However, monitoring and evaluating the broader conditions of employment is equally (if not more) crucial, especially from the point of view of *women* workers. The significance of this area stems from women's centrality to the 'care economy', *i.e.* their socially ascribed responsibilities for child care and elderly care, and how those prior obligations shape the kinds of work they are able to take up during different phases of their life cycle.

Women's groups have repeatedly emphasised the need to recognise that women stand at the cross roads between 'productive' activities and the care of human beings (the care economy). Subsidised childcare and elderly care facilities, public healthcare programmes, public transport and piped water/electricity help women meet their dual responsibilities.

As the literature on the gender impacts of structural adjustment has convincingly shown, when state resources are not channelled to such services, women must work more to compensate for the shortfall. In theory, women's work in the care economy is central to economic activity and should therefore carry economic rights or entitlements. But attracting resources when there are many competing claims on budgets has been a major challenge for women's movements worldwide.

Thus, while young unmarried and childless women have been able to benefit from labour–intensive industrial strategies (albeit under working conditions that are far from ideal), *in countries where those strategies have been successful* (important qualification), these labour market opportunities have been far less open to older women with dependants. They have found it far more difficult to enter these industries in the absence of adequate social provision of childcare and other services. We will therefore consider the area of social policy which is inextricably tied up with issues of employment. However, before we do so we would like to consider one more issue that has been somewhat controversial, namely women workers' own assessments of these jobs.

Female Employment and Women's Empowerment: Subjective Assessments

So far we have looked at employment trends, wages and working conditions. But we have not said much about how women workers themselves assess their jobs. Has their position as workers in export oriented factories, earning a monetary wage, given them more autonomy and voice in terms of their intra household relations? Has the ability to leave the confines of home based production been empowering in some respects? What weight should these 'subjective' assessments carry, and more controversially, how should they be read?

One of the contentious issues dividing feminists who are writing on this subject concerns the interpretation of women workers' voices. According to Gita Sen (1999a) the fact that young women sometimes voice a preference for this type of work to going back to the confines of rural patriarchal households only emphasises how harsh the conditions of rural poverty and rural patriarchal dominance are for these women, rather than being a positive indicator of the conditions of work in the factories. Providing a somewhat different reading of women's voices, Kabeer (1995) has argued that work in export industries (in Dhaka, Bangladesh) has helped households meet basic survival needs, improved their security, and begun a process by which women are being transformed from representing economic burdens on their families into economic assets a process that can in some ways be seen as empowering.

One of the analytical insights that emerged from the 1980s gender and development literature, and which can be seen as an area of cross fertilisation (or overlap) between feminism and critical institutionalism, was the gender critique of markets, captured in Ann Whitehead's (1979) distinction between gender relations that are 'intrinsically gendered' (conjugal relations) and those that become the 'bearers of gender'. The labour contract was seen as a poignant illustration of the latter, and was elabourated by Elson and Pearson (1981) in their path–breaking work on women's incorporation into export oriented manufacturing in world market factories.

In many ways this early analysis was nuanced and insightful enough to stand the test of time. Rather than providing a deterministic framework, what they did was to distinguish 'three tendencies' in the relation between factory work and the subordination of women which suggested that factory work could either *intensify* the existing forms of gender subordination, *decompose* them, or *recompose* new forms of gender subordination. However, as Pearson (1998) herself has recently argued, their analysis left uncontested the idea that women workers' interactions with capital and patriarchy were somehow structurally determined rather than open to negotiation and reconstitution by women workers themselves. Structuralist accounts, critics argued, rendered women workers 'faceless and voiceless' and attributed much more personality and animation to capital than to the women it exploits. At a more general level, the oversight highlighted some of the difficulties of integrating an actor–orientation in structuralist analyses.

Some of the feminist research that was recording women's own understandings of their work, and their experiences of engagement with factory management, provided somewhat diverse answers to some of the key questions that Elson and Pearson (1981) had posed. The Javanese factory daughters who figured prominently in Wolf's (1992) account of industrialisation in rural Java, did not seem to submit their needs to the betterment of the family economy in the way that Taiwanese daughters did. Wolf in fact argued that factory work in Java was giving young women the tools with which to 'hack and whittle away at parental and patriarchal controls over their lives, at least for a certain period, with longer term implications such as deciding when and whom to marry'. A similar conclusion was emerging from some of the situated analyses of garments factory workers in Dhaka, Bangladesh.

In the case of Bangladesh, the phenomenon of factory women was in many ways remarkable for a country where women's entry into the public domain in search of employment had been generally associated with dire economic need. Factory work, it was argued, had not altered some of the striking features of gender subordination in this context, such as women's dependence on male *protection* (even though it may have reduced their dependence on male *provision*). Nevertheless the ability to earn a wage (whether their wages disappeared into a common pool, was retained under their own management or handed over to or appropriated by household heads or other senior members), had made a difference in how women were perceived and treated, as well as their feelings of self worth. The increased sense of power became even more visible in moments of crisis when the expanded possibilities offered by the strengthening of women's 'fall back position' allowed them to walk out of, or not enter into, relationships that undermined their agency in unacceptable ways.

While Kabeer (1995) did not explore the gendered patterns of shop floor politics, Wolf (1992) argued that the increased field of manoeuvring that factory work had offered the Javanese daughters at home was matched by different patriarchal controls in the factory setting that kept these factory women 'relatively acquiescent, poorly paid and vastly unprotected in industrial jobs that are often dangerous'. Moreover, the increased voice and agency in the familial sphere did not seem to carry over into the factory, despite the attempts of some women to 'rock the boat'; the managers and the work discipline seemed to be much less flexible and much more overwhelming than were parents in their rules and discipline.

Ching Kwan Lee's (1995) comparative analysis of two gendered regimes of production in Shenzhen (southern China) and Hong Kong, however, showed how two factories owned by the same enterprise, managed by the same team of managers, producing the same products, and using the same technical labour processes, developed distinct patterns of shop floor politics. These gendered regimes were in turn explained in terms of local and communal institutions like localistic networks, kin, and families which underpinned the social organisation of the labour markets. The comparative analysis also highlights the negotiated (rather than imposed) aspects of a factory regime where the workers themselves actively engage in the construction of cultural notions of workers' gender. In the Shenzhen factory where the labour regime was highly hierarchical and 'despotic', Lee tries to explain why young women subscribed to the notion of 'maiden workers' and came to terms with localistic, despotic control.

Many of these young women had fled home to evade arranged marriages. Many also had personal goals like gaining experience, saving for dowries, or financing their educations. Because they intended to marry at some point, factory employment was preferred to other service jobs because of the popular association between factory work and endurance for hardship and disciplined labour, traits deemed desirable for future wives. Thus, entering the factory meant preserving the appropriate femininity of maidens while earning a cash income and enjoying the freedom to explore romantic relationships.

The export oriented production processes had in some ways reproduced gender hierarchies, providing employment that was in many ways exploitative under working conditions that were far from ideal Lee's account of labour control in the Shenzhen plant, in particular, provides a vivid illustration of this point. But these 'despotic' labour regimes were at the same time social constructions that were both contested, and invested with different meanings and purposes by different parties. In the Hong Kong plant, Lee shows how the women workers used familial discourses as a pretext for circumventing certain managerial demands; women cited gender based inconvenience and their mothering burdens at home to reject management demands for assignments which required cross border commuting and overnight stays.

These fine grained feminist accounts which provide a contextual analysis of labour force formation (workers' histories, familial and kinship relations and localistic networks) and take workers' subjectivities seriously, can also provide better insight into issues relating to collective action why traditional trade union strategies have proven so problematic in some contexts. In South Africa, for example, where Taiwanese industrialists have invested in garment factories employing women, Hart (1995a) argues that the fact that trade unions have experienced extreme difficulties in organising clothing workers to press for higher wages and better working conditions reflects not only the adamant opposition of the foreign industrialists, but also broader processes of labour force formation and the desperate search by huge numbers of dispossessed people for a modicum of economic and social security.

This is not to suggest that working conditions in export oriented factories are by any means satisfactory or 'humane' in many cases they are clearly not. But at the same time the analysis of working conditions in the export oriented sectors needs to be fully attentive to the fact that in the more populous developing countries in particular there invariably exist large reserve armies of unskilled, low productivity labour that has to make ends meet by any means, and is in search of work at any price. The challenge therefore must be to forge coalescing strategies and policies that can help 'lift all boats'.

Clearly, despite being problematic very few women would like to see their jobs in export oriented factories disappear, and as far as I know, none of the advocates of women's rights argue that these jobs should be taken away from the women concerned! Rather the point is that the labour intensive strategy relying on 'cheap' labour needs to be up graded: this is Gita Sen's argument about making a transition from the 'low road' to the 'high road' of industrialisation. At the same time, it is important to widen the agenda to include the conditions for social reproduction more broadly through gender sensitive social policies. It is to social policies that we now turn.

Social Policy through a Gender Lens

There has been a global shift in the consensus over the role of the state in welfare provision, which carries many serious and adverse implications for women. Selectivity in social policy has thus gone hand in hand with a trend towards 'multi tierism' in modes of provision of social protection in several important areas of social policy pensions in particular, but also health care and education. While selectivity means narrowing the targets for support, multi teirism means reducing the state component and partially privatising social protection. There is thus increasing reliance on private provision and community support, or indeed an increased need for these sources to fill the gaps left open by diminishing public provision.

As feminist economists argue, market economies assume that new workers appear costlessly at the factory gates already healthy, nourished, educated and socialised; all the employer must do is pay for that day's labour. In fact the public funding and delivery of a wide range of goods and services such as health care, education, welfare services such as day care, care for the aged, care for the retired and disabled is vital to women who are ultimately the ones who have to balance their time and energies between income earning activities and the care of human beings.

This in fact has been the great advantage of the so called 'service heavy' Swedish welfare state, for example, compared to the more 'transfer heavy' welfare states of the continental European variety. The public funding and delivery of social services, has been the cornerstone for gender equality in advanced welfare states and significantly, some of these states have held up those important funding priorities, and expanded them, despite all the expectations to the contrary. While in many industrialised countries the welfare state takes some of the responsibility for social reproduction, in developing countries the task remains primarily one for the household, and within the household for women and increasingly so.

The global shift in the consensus over the role of the state in welfare provision has in many contexts entailed the down sizing of public services and the re allocation of service delivery to commercial interests, charitable groups, NGOs and *families*. This devolution of responsibility to 'civil society' for managing welfare and development raises serious questions, especially as far as women are concerned. In the case of Chile, for example, one of the novel features in the new (post Pinochet) system of social provisioning, has been the role that NGOs are playing in the delivery of welfare.

However, while there clearly are some positive aspects to this involvement, Veronica Schild (2001) argues that it depends upon an unpaid or poorly paid and unregulated workforce of female 'extension workers'. Ultimately what this means is that claims for more 'efficient' social spending, through a 'partnership' of state and civil society, rely on what Elson (2001) refers to as the 'unspoken and invisible safety net of women's unpaid work', whether in their capacity as mothers and wives or as NGO and community workers.

Furthermore, it is not clear whether both the coverage and the quality of service that this patchwork of NGOs with their poorly paid staff and army of volunteers delivers is in any way adequate.

As the state devolves responsibility for welfare delivery to non state actors there is therefore a danger of even further reliance on women to perform low paid or unpaid care work as NGO workers, and as members of families and communities. Implicit in the claims for more efficient social spending, through a 'partnership' of state and civil society organisations, is the notion that communities and households can take up the slack for what the state no longer invests in. Ultimately this means that *women*, who have traditionally been responsible not only for the well being of family members but also of their communities, have to pick up where the state leaves off.

Privatisation of pensions and healthcare: The term social security is generally applied to social insurance programs that protect the target population against the risk of loss of income due to sickness, maternity, occupational accidents, disability, old age and unemployment. Social security programs also provide services, most prominently health services. Enrolment in these programs is very often employment based and affiliation to the programs is mandatory for all employees in the occupational categories covered. In the case of developing countries, coverage has tended to be limited due to two factors: first, the large size of the informal sector, and second, the high rate of evasion of contributions, even by employers and employees in the formal sector.

For these reasons social security schemes may not be the most effective vehicle for extending coverage to the majority of the population in developing countries. Instead, universalistic programs that are financed through taxation not employment based contributions and with entitlements to basic benefits based on citizenship or residency criteria may have a much greater potential to contribute to human welfare and to developmental objectives. This is particularly the case as far as women are concerned, given their shorter, more informal and more intermittent employment trajectories. Politically, however, it is much easier to mobilise resources via contributions to specific programs. And for this reason, many countries may opt for social security schemes. If this route is taken, then coverage cannot be employment based; contributions for members of the informal sector have to be heavily subsidised in order for them to be included and to facilitate universal coverage. Costa Rica, for example, has managed to extend health insurance to the members of the informal sector.

One of the most controversial and significant areas of social policy reform, both in fiscal terms and as far as the life chances and welfare of citizens are concerned, is pension reform. In Latin America alone nearly ten countries have enacted structural reform of pensions during the past decade, in many instances as an integral part of their on going structural adjustment programs.

The neo liberal reformers in many of these countries opted for privatisation of pensions even though many other options were available. Political forces and institutional characteristics that vary across countries have shaped and influenced the final policy outcomes. Half of the ten countries undergoing reform, Chile, Bolivia, Mexico, El Salvador and Nicaragua have gone for the full privatisation of pensions, while others have adopted *parallel* (public and private) or *mixed* (basic public and supplementary private) systems.

Those promoting privatisation, IFIs and domestic neoliberal reformers argued that privatisation would be superior to all other options on several accounts: expansion of coverage; competition; administrative cost of the system; and its impact on capital markets, national savings and investment. Yet, contrary to the claims and predictions of those promoting privatisation, the reforms appear to have been implemented based on assumptions that data show, have not in fact materialised. The evidence on pension reform in Latin America provides a poignant account of the discrepancies between neoliberal nostrums and realities an astounding case of misguided perceptions shaping major policy decisions.

The first claim was that of increased *population coverage*. In reality, coverage in many countries has actually declined and a significant proportion of affiliates do not contribute. A second unfulfilled claim is that of *competition* within the private sector. One of the key objectives of the structural reform was to break the state monopoly and establish freedom of choice for the insured to select the system and change/choose administrators. In practice the private sector has become highly concentrated.

In some countries (*e.g.* Mexico and Bolivia) the insured have no freedom because everyone must join the 'private' system. In small countries with a limited insured market, there are only two or three administrators; but even in countries with a more extensive insured market and a fair number of administrators, there is a high degree of concentration of the insured.

The third claim was that the *administrative costs* of private accounts would be less burdensome than those of collective ones. But contrary to such expectations the administrative costs have tended to be very high and they have not declined over time. In countries like Peru and Bolivia where attempts have been made to reduce costs, it has been by sacrificing some of the benefits of the insured (by not granting minimum pensions, for example).

The fourth assumption was that of *capital accumulation* and increase in national savings. The reality is that even where there has been significant capital accumulation as high as 40 per cent of GDP at the end of 1998 in the much touted Chilean case it needs to be interpreted with two important caveats in mind. First, the figures for capital accumulation are gross figures; fiscal costs must be deducted so as to show the net balance. To continue with the Chilean example, the net return has been estimated to be negative (annual rate of –2.6 per cent). Second, in all cases, except Chile, the pension programs began to operate in the 1990s when international markets were producing very high returns. The financial crises in the mid and late 1990s reduced the yields considerably. What this means is that the welfare of the insured is hostage to the oscillations of capital markets.

As research in other contexts has shown, the best way of reducing poverty among the entire aged population is to provide a universalistic citizenship or residency based basic pension, which can then be supplemented by earnings or contribution related pensions. *One of the other major drawbacks of the private system is its in built gender bias.* Due to gender discriminatory forces within the labour market and women's care responsibilities, women tend to earn lower wages and work fewer years than men. Thus, in private systems where benefits are calculated strictly based on contributions, women tend to be at a disadvantage.

The system of individualised contributions removes the cross subsidy that women are able to receive under the public system. This is in fact indicative of a much broader problem: the private system is antithetical to redistribution and equity. Those advocating privatisation of social security schemes simply skirt these issues. Social values like redistribution, equity and solidarity have no place in a private fully funded individual account pension system.

Yet redistributive action has been central to the project of nation building in both developed and developing countries. Highly redistributive healthcare systems, for example, embed the inequalities of society within those systems (*e.g.* through socially inclusive insurance mechanisms) while also using those systems as a platform for redistribution. The lesson from both European and non European contexts is that effective redistribution involves compromises with the middle class: social equity, with high levels of social welfare provision accessible to all, has been secured and retained when those services have been available to, paid for and used by, the professional and middle classes. At present the opposite approach is dominant in the development mindset, which according to Mackintosh (2000) endorses three main thrusts: privatisation; safety nets; and community provision.

Privatisation: The liberalisation of private provision, with its implicit legitimation of inequality, is undermining government commitment to redistribution in many developing countries. Marketisation tends to drive out cross subsidy, generating an institutional split between provision through exchange and redistribution via government. Historical evidence shows that highly inclusive systems of health care have been built from patchworks of public, mutual, charitable, employment based and private. In general, systems that are not highly socially segmented, and not dominated by private care, are easier to universalise. Conversely, systems dominated by private fee for service provision are extremely hard to universalise. This is another reason why the current trends towards privatisation are so worrying.

Community provision: There has been an enormous emphasis over the past ten years in the economics literature on 'social capital', 'personalised networks' and 'trust'. As Mackintosh (2000) puts it, by and large this literature highlights the greater ease of sustaining cooperation and reciprocal trust in small communities than in large scale impersonal interactions. These analyses facilitate the policy shifts towards decentralisation and community involvement in health care provision. The emphasis on cooperation within small communities, however, obscures the sharp divisions within small communities, and the difficulties of achieving redistributive outcomes within small communities.

Indeed there is often a theory driven confusion between *collabouration* and *equity* which are not the same. One of the outcomes of the emphasis on collabouration and trust has been to marginalise issues of redistribution. What is needed are more systematic explorations of the conditions for effective *redistributive* behaviour by governments, service providers, funding institutions and communities. That problem seems practically absent from the policy debate.

Targeting: The current social policy and development mindset is also enamoured with 'safety nets' and 'targeting'. Targeted schemes, however, are very difficult to implement, demanding well established and legitimate administrative structures. Ironically, these were the very arguments on the basis of which neoliberals dismissed strategic industrial policies, alleging that governments do not have the information and the capacity to implement selective industrial policies. But in their enthusiastic embrace of targeted welfare schemes these advocates seem to have forgotten their own reasoning (which would be even more relevant to targeting of poor *individuals*). Moreover, there is no evidence for the underlying assumption that targeted public provision is the way to achieve greater inclusion. Targeting and means testing are likely to produce on the contrary increasing inequality.

Critics allege that the models of import substitution industrialisation (ISI) that shaped labour market conditions in many developing countries prior to the neo liberal reforms of the 1980s did not in fact guarantee the universal coverage of social rights. Not only was the entire *working* population not covered by its legal and social provisions in particular those engaged in voluntary work, care work or community work, who were largely excluded but a significant part of labour in the developing world never gained the wide spectrum of rights that became institutionalised under the European welfare states. This was particularly the case as far as women are concerned. In India, for example, only a small proportion of the workforce was in the organised sector on regular wages or salaries, in registered firms and with access to state social security system and covered by its statutory framework of labour laws. It is argued therefore that even though liberalisation has been highly regressive, significant numbers of people were left out and deprived of social rights even when developing country governments pursued various models of ISI.

In response we would argue that while it is imperative to recognise the shortcomings of the Keynesian development model that dominated development thinking in the so called 'golden age' of capitalism, and although the ISI strategies fell short of their objectives in several crucial respects (especially from a gender perspective), a constructive approach would have been to extend their achievements and to change and fine tune their less successful interventions so as to make them perform better, rather than to reverse their gains. By the 1970s, however, the criticisms directed at ISI were extended to the social polices associated with them. They were accused of 'urban bias' and, in the urban areas of favouring a male 'labour aristocracy' in the formal sector. According to the neo–classical critique of ISI, the social policies were fiscally not sustainable and a source of high deficits. They were also accused of distorting the labour market, and thereby contributing to the high capital intensity of production and the uncompetitiveness of domestic industry. Associated with putatively flawed industrialisation, the social policies were jettisoned, though of course with considerable resistance.

As Elson and Cagatay (2000) argue macro–economic policy approaches that rely solely or principally on full employment to achieve socially desirable outcomes are severely limited because they fail to recognise unpaid forms of work that are just as much at the heart of provisioning human needs as paid work. It is not just labourers whose rights need to be upheld, but different kinds of workers who make different kinds of contributions to society.

However, as they go on to suggest, with the massive and pernicious process of privatisation and commodification of social policy and care that is underway, the 'male breadwinner' model that was pervasive in the post–WWII era is being superseded *not* by a gender egalitarian reform of state based entitlements which accords equal rights and entitlements to men and women for different kinds of work (be it employment, training, care or voluntary work), but by a drastic reduction of state based entitlements and their replacement by a market based, individualised system of social services for those few who can afford them, and elusive safety nets, poverty and overwork for the great many who cannot.

Conclusion

This chapter began by looking at some of the broad facts of 'globalisation' which is taken here to mean greater openness of economies to international trade and capital mobility. While questioning some of the claims of global enthusiasts, it argued that there has nevertheless been a clearly discernible shift toward global economic liberalisation which has involved liberalisation of the international trade in goods and services on the one hand, and the flows of international capital, on the other. The impacts of these major policy shifts on regional growth rates seem far from encouraging not to mention the social disruptions caused by financial liberalisation.

The extent to which external liberalisation has weakened the national state and led to 'social dumping', we argued, are complex questions given the *diversity* both in state capacity as well as in institutional and political factors that mediate the forces of globalisation. While there has been increasing convergence in macro economic policies towards neo liberal deflationary policies, the same cannot be said about industrial and social policies that continue to be shaped by national institutional characteristics and histories, as well as political alliances and dynamics which are increasingly intertwined with clashes of interests and ideas among influential supranational actors. The resistance to neo liberal models of social policy seems to be most marked among the institutionalised welfare states of Europe, while the trends in East Asia also appear to be encouraging. Hence while the room for maneuver has clearly narrowed, there are still policy *choices* to be made, and contestation and struggle at both the national and global levels can have an impact on the liberalising juggernaut.

Looking more specifically at the impact of trade liberalisation (one important component of 'globalisation') on employment patterns, a number of findings emerged from our review of the literature. First, while labour market conditions especially in the manufacturing sector in the North have clearly deteriorated since the mid–1970s, it would be very difficult to attribute these negative trends to the rising, but still rather marginal, North/South trade in manufactures. Moreover, even if there were some adverse labour market outcomes in the 1980s and 1990s of trade with the South, these could have been overridden by faster economic growth. Second, as far as the South's much cited employment gains from trade liberalisation in manufactures are concerned, the picture looked far less optimistic on closer scrutiny.

For a start, the gains in manufacturing employment appear to be confined to a small group of developing countries (the so called 'Group of 13'). Moreover, even within this group there are clear indications that employment expansion through export oriented industries has coincided with the destruction of jobs in other sectors of manufacturing due to competition from imports, so that the net employment expansion has been far less impressive in most cases than is often assumed (although we suggested that this is an area that requires far more rigorous data and analysis).

The same holds true as far as women are concerned: while some groups of women (young, rural migrants) are over represented in the export oriented industries, other groups of women (in state owned enterprises and in import competing industries) have suffered job destruction consequent upon trade liberalisation an issue that has tended to be neglected. Finally, for the handful of countries that have succeeded in expanding their manufactured exports and employment in recent years (*e.g.* Malaysia, Indonesia and Chile), there are worrying signs of deteriorating terms of trade and of so called 'immiserising growth', *i.e.* of productivity gains that are less than proportionately reflected in rising real incomes or living standards.

This, we argued, raises questions about both global policy coordination (or more accurately, lack thereof), as well as national industrial strategies (the limits of labour intensive growth which has been predicated upon women's 'cheap' and 'docile' labour).

The third important area of concern that we have tried to probe is the interface between female employment and social policy provisions. Given the fact that poor women in many developing countries enjoyed few social rights even prior to the neo–liberal era, some critics argue that it is almost meaningless to criticise 'globalisation' for creating jobs for women that have few social rights attached to them. Models of import substitution industrialisation (ISI) essentially created jobs for a male 'labour aristocracy', and their associated systems of social protection were biased in favour of men who were assumed to be the 'breadwinners' while women were considered to be their 'dependents'. There has thus been no regression or reversal of rights as far as women are concerned.

What we have tried to argue is that while it is crucial to recognise the shortcomings of Keynesian thinking and the ISI strategies that fell short of their objectives in several important respects, especially as far as women are concerned, a constructive approach would have been to extend their achievements and to change their less successful interventions so as to make them perform better, rather than to reverse their gains. A gender sensitive approach to social policy and to macro economic policy more broadly must start from the premise that women have a different relation to employment than men; approaches that premise social rights and entitlements on labour market contributions will remain gender biased given that for the majority of women their labour market contribution has to be interwoven with their care obligations (they thus work part time, and withdraw from the labour market during some periods of their lives when they are intensively involved in care activities). Thus social entitlements based on citizenship or residence can reach women far more effectively. These are the lines along which the Keynesian development model should have been re-structured and reformed.

Instead what we are witnessing today with the new direction of public policy is that poor women in many developing countries are being deprived 'of even the prospect of the progressive realisation of a non–discriminatory system of decent jobs and public services and broad based social security systems'. Employment objectives, the creation of decent jobs and broad based, redistributive social security systems are no longer even the objectives of public policy in most countries. What we are witnessing instead in many contexts is the drastic reduction of state based entitlements and their replacement by a market based, individualised system of social services which inevitably only responds to the needs of a few privileged men and women who can afford them, while the great many who cannot are left with elusive safety nets, overwork and increasing vulnerability.

5

Women and ICT

Information and Communication Technology (ICT) is a key enabler of globalisation. It allows for an efficient and cost effective flow of information, products, people and capital across national and regional boundaries. ICT is not a panacea for rural development problems but it has the potential to help the rural poor leapfrog some of the traditional barriers to development, by improving access to information, expanding their market base, enhancing employment opportunities and making government services work better.

Imports of ICT affect the local modes of production and employment. Internet technologies facilitate the way companies can locate and manage production away from the main site to geographically distributed centers. This expands employment possibilities of women who live away from metropolises, in suburbia, in rural areas both in the manufacturing and services sector. Such technologies allow women to have possibilities of flexible location and flexible hours, through tele–working or with the use of neighbourhood centers. It also allows women to have new forms of business: such as selling telephone services and Internet services through Internet and telephone kiosks or cellular phones. There are examples of such initiatives in India and Bangladesh.

These potentials, however, become reality only when the policy makers can create the necessary enabling environment. Effective ICT strategies must provide the basic infrastructure for connectivity and access, develop human capacity, offer affordable demand driven ICT services and involve local stakeholders and beneficiaries in project design and implementation. Special attention should also be given to disadvantaged women, youth and the persons with disabilities during project development and implementation.

This chapter looks at the general situation of women *vis-a-vis* their technological and information contexts. What are some of the main barriers to women's full use of ICTs, and strategies for overcoming those barriers. This chapter is based on examples of women's experiences and activities. The final section contains guidelines and recommendations for to facilitate women's participation in the information society.

ICT AND THE GLOBAL CONTEXT

The world is in the midst of a rapidly expanding information and communication technology (ICT). ICT comprises a diverse set of technological tools and resources to create, disseminate, store and manage information. Traditional ICT tools such as television, radio and the telephone have proved their use in effecting development in marginalised areas. The emergence of computers, the Internet and wireless communication technology, along with powerful software for processing and integrating text, sound and video into electronic media, have formed the modern ICT.

The spread of the global electronic network of computers, also called the Internet, and wireless telephony has generated an unprecedented global flow of information, products, people, capital and ideas. The Internet needed only four years to reach 50 million users. It took 38 years for radio to capture 50 million listeners. TV took 13 years to reach that figure.

Technological advancements have also slashed the costs of information and communication. Email is becoming a free service. Internet telephony is offering a much cheaper long distance communication than the traditional telephone. Costs of transmission of digital information anywhere in the world has also fallen dramatically. This cost reduction has enabled developing countries to partly benefit from modern ICT.

The number of people with access to the Internet grew exponentially from less than 20 million in 1995 to more than 400 million in 2000. This number is expected to reach 1 billion by 2005.

The number of web sites also grew rapidly from fewer than 200 in mid 1993 to about 20 million in late 2000. Since the early 1990s, the web has been the mainstream environment for creating and disseminating digital information.

At present, access to the Internet is almost exclusively from personal computers. This could change in the near future with the emergence of data enabled wireless phones and web enabled PDA (Personal Digital Assistants). Internet access through wireless devices is expected to outstrip personal computers access by 2005. This development could bring the web to remote areas without basic ICT infrastructure. Also coming soon is a whole new range of the so called Internet appliances for use in the home, at work or in the car

Today, ICT is the fastest growing industry in the world and is poised to become the largest global industry. Global spending on ICT is projected to grow from US$ 2.2 trillion in 1999 to US$ 3 trillion by 2003 providing many niche opportunities for service providers in developing countries. Establishment of national ICT infrastructure and policy framework are prerequisites for them to participate in the emerging global ICT business.

6

Feminist Movements from Global to Local, Women Empowerment Process, Patriarchy and Status of Nepali Women

In the global perspective, ever since feminist movements heightened since 1970s there are many discussions and counter discussion on women's liberty on sexuality and gender equality undergoing till the date. Mass immigration and globalisation process have not only sought financial freedom of women but also emancipation of knowledge and resistance against male domination in each social domain. The ongoing discourses have demanded more studies in gender and gender equalities both in West and the third world. Besides these, women's active participation in economy and enlightenment through media and technology in reproduction, the underdeveloped country such like Nepal stands for social transformation through gender equality practice in culture and legislations. Compare to last a few decades, it can be experienced that women have been much more empowered not only in West but also in underdeveloped countries. Homosexuality, lesbianism, transgendered sexuality have taken wider public discourses which were socially stigmatised in past. As soon as women are empowered through education and economy, new gender roles and sexuality are accepted through legislation, that have helped to create new social reconstructions on feminism.

This chapter deals with interpretation of patriarchy in relation to women's oppressed position and how they are lagged behind due to the deprivation of mobility and economic freedom. Finally it deals with world feminist movements and its impact on local level gender equality practice.

Understanding Feminist Movement

The struggles for the women's emancipation have three major waves in the mid twentieth century; those movements carried the discourses of women's situation as subordinate, oppressed and discriminated on the basis of sex category. In the advancement of feminism discourse, further deconstruction of feminism through intersectionality such as class, race, and sexuality added new gender studies encounters.

Meanwhile, post colonial perspective of feminism added a new contour in feminist discourse. Feminism became a part of world politics where new power relation was defined by French feminism theorist after western female scholars identified their status of oppression or male domination. New sexuality, gender roles and hetero normativity became new social encounter especially after Michel Foucault introduced the history of sexuality. On the other hand, women's reproductive characteristic became a discourse in power politics. Davis mentions, 'women are not just the biological reproducers of the nation but also its cultural reproduces ... transmitting it to the children and constructing the home in a specific cultural style'.

In context to divided feminist world by class, race, and social structures, a continue search for transversal politics is underway to reunite world women together. In the regime of power in global to local institutions, feminism has become a search of power equation. Through the world summits such as CEDAW and BEIJING Conference feminist have successfully tried shed lights on power discourse for gender equality. Addressing the situation of women as subordinate to men, much has been discussed on different forms of dominating factors excluding masculinity, most criticised factor is the patriarchy system.

There after a wide discussion took on social construction of sex and work division under the sex category. To fight against the discrimination, oppression it has been proposed of an idea as gender equality. This idea was the first effort to dismantle the configuration of patriarchal structure which was supposed to be a significant hazard. While discussion, this section will also throw the light on those attempts to examine interrelation of feminist movement in the form of global politics and its impact on local. A Nepali case is an example to bring more understanding the context.

Patriarchy, Oppression and Subordination

Connell (2002) in her introductory book 'Gender' mentions that gender is a key dimension of personal life, social relations and culture. She further emphasises the factors that influence our everyday life because there are amasing amount of prejudice, ideology, myth, misinformation and outright falsehood. Gender is the term coined as social construction of notion where differences are made and practiced on the ground of biological differences.

These different practices have been categorised under the division of work based on gender relations. Escobar (1995) portraits women's role was unproductive before the wave of 1970s feminist movement. In the power politics through economic contests, the feminist movement was able to visualise women as productive force. Until this idea was debated or, essentialised women's equal part in the gender equality struggle, they were viewed as mothers engaged in feeding babies, pregnant or lactating, procuring water for cooking and cleaning, dealing with children's diseases, or in the best of cases growing some food in the home garden to supplement the family diet.

This view has been based on historically constructed idea that advocated men's superiority under patriarchy. In fact, women being oppressed can be defined when the world order is defined under the patriarchy. In the patriarchal society, these practices are well defined in everyday life that what men should do and what women shouldn't do and they are culturally legitimated. These gender practices which obviously reflect women as subordinate to men exist where the patriarchal structure and culture are. Acker (2006) well anchors gender in patriarchy by mentioning that a basic structural relation between women and men roots in male dominance which is found primarily in family.

Broadening to male domination out of family geography, Lloyd (2005) deferred from other radical feminists points that in order to understand feminism from local, national and global scale, it is essential to capture the structural institution of patriarchy in which all pervasiveness of women's oppression at the hands of men. She quotes Kate Millett 'The fact is evident at once if one recalls that the military, industry, technology, universities, science, political office, and finance in short every avenue of power within the society, including the coercive force of the police is entirely in male hands'.

She concludes that patriarchy is a system of male power that permeates all aspects of life at all times and in all places. Although, dismantling the patriarchy could be the uniting agenda for all women, there are still problems of identification of various forms of domination and subordination. Lloyd (2005) contrasts within feminist movement on men's power as liberal feminists keen to acquire equality with men sharing power where as radical feminists argue male power is domination that require repudiation and overthrow. However feminists agree that different sectionalities such as class, ethnicity and sexuality vary from geographical locations and cultural constructions.

Beside the idea of being subordination and subjugation of men, new feminists brought new theories in gender where race and colonial power have made women as subject to regulate organic crisis. Gail (2000) well mentions, 'at a time of organic crisis...arena of local state is identified as a key institution in the mediation of this contestation'. In this respect, NGOs and INGOs are similar form of regulating institutions to mediate women empowerment. Besides other ideas on feminism it would be better to discuss Mohanty's post colonial feminism. Mohanty (1984:5) highlights the post colonial perspective of feminism and its theoretical framework from new sociological, anthropological cultural and economical perspective. She indicates that all the feminist scholars from West demarcated employing theories of feminism in terms of racism, immigration, Euro–centrism, critical white studies, heterosexism and imperialism.

These feminist studies mostly see the new developments of feminist movement from Eurocentric perspective and advocate liberalisation, women's right on body and sexuality and normativity of heterosexuality. Loomba (1998, 2005) argues, 'when we discuss feminism in the light of colonial discourses, the cultural/racial differences form a different ideological standpoint, we are fingering, these are tricky questions and we will approach them by examining various discourses about racial differences and how they work in relation to class, gender, sexuality and other social hierarchies.

Although these in differences in feminism coexisted, there were perpetual searches for common ground to reunite the women from all over the world. Transversal politics in feminism provoked the idea of identity as women through the collective narratives of women as oppressed group in capitalist world order. Now in present, the biology of women is the positivist discourse to achieve gender equality. Not only other study of feminist geography, globalisation has also contributed new empiricism in feminist movement from global to local. In the globalisation process, the state lost the grip on locals because northern NGOs directly approached the local NGOs which are the actors for empowerment of women. World summit on women agendas is appropriate to discuss here shortly.

World Conference on Women's Right

Moghadham (2005) argues that self identified feminists have various priority concerns, but the wider goals are women's empowerment, as well as legal changes and societal transformation. In this respect, it is required to see how global institutions including states effort to highlight women's rights through world summit and conferences. In 1979 UN general assembly drafted women's right (CEDAW) to set up international norms to avoid all types of dominations against women.

This bill constituted 30 points descriptions of various forms of discriminations in view of male domination in the background of patriarchy. After UN convention the responsibility came to the state however there were fewer achievements. In September 1995 the fourth world conference held in Beijing China ratifying 38 strategic points to bring gender equality practice. In fact Beijing Conference further enhanced the guideline and generated a space for the wider discourse. Following world summits on peace and environment, children and millennium development goals: all the conferences equally gave much importance to women's indispensable participation in the arena of all social development fields. 'Women's right is human right' agenda played essentialising power politics through feminism. Ever since, feminism strongly appeared in the global, national and local power politics, various measures were sought for women's emancipation such as legislative, reproductive, resource access, power sharing and responsibility.

Empowerment as Goal

In search of gender equality, it has been much debated and sought instrument is women empowerment. Within the frame of women's oppression, subordination and domination, there are several aspects in everyday life to experience inequalities. Many feminists advocate about sharing power equality whereas some of the feminists look male domination is power which has to be overthrown. Though there are many states and development actors working on mainstreaming gender, the outcome is not satisfactory. According to SIDA's report no 3 it says 'In June 2000, a follow–up of the Beijing conference was held in New York. Five thousand delegates from one hundred and eighty eight countries participated. The outcome document established that, although recognition of the gender dimension of poverty is increasing, the economic gap between women and men is widening. At the same time as globalisation is bringing opportunities and autonomy to some women, it has marginalised others'.

In this context, gender awareness is preceding factors until the knowledge is produced and disseminated. Developing countries are suffering both economic opportunity and knowledge gain. Those, who have access to bigger network with power, knowledge and economy, (a very fewer) in another words, a type of so called women elites are much benefitting from globalisation and gender knowledge. Davis (1997) interestingly mentions the third world women want their men free from western oppression to come up equality with their counterpart. Meanwhile, talking about impact of globalisation, Perrons (2004:320) argues that there are big gap within superstar cities where some good skilled and with acknowledged women are incredibly paid high where as informal female workers receive nominal pay. This phenomenon indicates that a perpetual dialogue between economic class and race required sharing the experience of male dominance and create a platform to voice jointly.

Globalisation, Women's Right and Nepali Context

There are several NGOs and INGOs working in Nepal for women's empowerment however I would like to pickup and discuss a few good examples. Among many, one of the leading NGO Sancharika Samuha is a strongest feminist NGO which is working in the field of knowledge distribution through the media. This NGO has published a book 'Mother, Sister Daughter: Nepal's Press on Women' consisting several collective memories of women's situation in Nepal. Rana, B. and Navin Singh in the preface of the book accept that the Nepali society largely influenced by patriarchal norms and values. These patriarchal norms and values have extensively limited Nepali women for the mobility and economic participation to make self identity in their periphery.

After all, the first way out to make women self confident is to expand the knowledge and experience of outer world. Let them know their situation and compare to all other aspects. Let them know their fundamental right to search an identity through financial independence. For it, the state and policy have to be favourable. But it needs cooperative social networks. Especially in Nepal the family and social networks are very fluctuating when one is very poor. The basic fact is that economically strong women can tackle several other problems. In connection with economic stands, Ramila Thapa in the book *Mother, Sister Daughter* shares her experience as: People are only close when you have money. If a person is self sufficient and has good income, people automatically come closer.

This excerpt is one of the aspects of Nepali women which show their weak position in patriarchy. This also advocates that working in foreign land and collecting money and experience is individual right whatever the individual's sex identity is. Compared to past, Nepali Society is greatly influenced by Globalisation which has at least encouraged many migrant workers especially women in terms of making efforts to economic sustainability. Perrons (2004) mentions the impact of globalisation as 'space has been compressed by fast modes of communication making it possible for money, ideas, goods and people to flow around the world ever more quickly with significant implications for the organisation of economic activities and the security and stability of employment'.

It is true that empowerment could be achieved by expanding women's mobility and participation in the economic activities. In context to Nepal, the larger part of economy depends on remittance however; women are discouraged to go to foreign land to earn money for their livelihood. Beside this the government policy is discriminating to the women on their participation for foreign employment. If sufficient legal procedures, training, orientations and security are provided to women, they can easily handle the problems working in foreign lands however, instead of enhancing capacity to women, Nepal government is hiding its weaknesses.

This is the one fact of women being discriminated in practice within the country. General Federation of Nepalese Trade Unions (GFONT) reports that according to nation population Census 2001 has reflected that 95% of the female workforce is in informal employment. Similarly, the report mentions that in the wage employment, their participation as permanent workers is in a very small proportion having daily wage worker to be 61% of the total female workforce. The report further mentions that the gender discrimination in general starts from the birth in the socio economic structure of the Nepali society. According to report major features to the status of Nepali women are very pity as low paid wage, long working hours, no fringe benefits, no incentives and fast increasing home based character. Theoretically Perrons' (2004) analysis of globalisation and its impact has largely implicated to Nepali women. Perrons appropriately make a big question.

Why is it that all the statistics...widening inequalities between rich and poor countries, between rich and poor people within countries and between men and women, even though there are so many conferences, policies, strategies, resolutions and accords for tackling development, challenging inequality, empowering the poor, mainstreaming gender issues and empowering women?.

Mass immigration and globalisation process have added more theories in gender. New encounters on inclusion of marginalised and ethnic minorities such as black, Asian, Caribbean women in the racialised subjects are debated in the British Parliament. Normalisation of life in the inner cities has become objective of the centre government and local governments are instrumentals. Despite these efforts to encounter new challenges, a question still persists how these process are controlled in the power hierarchies where men invisibly dominant figure in modern world. In general, women's active participation in economy and enlightenment through media and technology in reproduction largely enhanced the status of women. In Nepal, women have become very active group compared to last few decades. Obviously, girl trafficking for sex market has incredibly declined and domestic violence is a matter of public debate as criminalisation.

Additionally the feminist movement has brought awareness of reproductive rights and legal rights but the question still rises for whom? Is that only for women in the urban? Or is that for few women elites acknowledged of women's right? It has been observed that within feminist institutions, there is fierce contestation among women and keep knowledge gap. The situation questions whether men are oppressive or women themselves are hazards to unity. Has feminist movement lost its way in gender equality struggle? In fact, there is still a big gap between women from different geographical regions in terms of women empowerment.

According to Nepal Human Development Report 2001, the ratio of gender related development compared to national average (0.466) is dispersed within different geographical and development regions. Despite this fact, Nepali socio economic structure is transforming significantly. Recently women occupies one third of total seats in Constitution Assembly however, those who are in the policy making level themselves are weak because they are selected by party high command where gender inequality exists. Women empowerment through knowledge is upmost requisite however, in this respect, we can thankful to NGOs and INGOs and civil society which are working hard and well trying to influence the state's power hierarchies. In consequence, in new economy order, new gender roles and sexuality are accepted through legislation, however insufficient in practice. The Nepal Human Development report 2001 well recommends that Nepal needs to stress the education and training of women at higher levels. The government should also consider taking appropriate measures to increase women's participation in the political process and the recruitment of more women into professional and administration.

Conclusion

I have largely discussed about power, contestations of gender and patriarchy in terms of challenges to feminist movement. The world has no geographical boundaries due to rapid globalisation process. And this process has influenced the feminist's movement through world conferences however, when there are social norms and values obstacle to women's empowerment, there is no way except to find a common ground to challenge the power politics especially male domination in sex category. Although there are differences within feminism, Davis meticulously suggests the transversal politics and empowerment process of 'shifting' and 'rooting' which according to her can help to distinguish between differences of context and terminology and differences of values and goals to find a common ground to unite and revive stronger feminist movement. All the way, third world like Nepal needs massive empowerment process through knowledge production of gender and strict implementation of gender mainstreaming projects in the field level. Alternatively, feminist institutions need strong and open coordination to identify the forms of oppression and effort to eliminate them.

7

Measuring the Global Gender Gap

This study is a first attempt by the World Economic Forum to assess the current size of the gender gap by measuring the extent to which women in 58 countries have achieved equality with men in five critical areas: economic participation, economic opportunity, political empowerment, educational attainment, and health and well-being. Countries that do not capitalise on the full potential of one half of their societies are misallocating their human resources and undermining their competitive potential. Consolidating publicly available data from international organisations, national statistics and unique survey data from the World Economic Forum's Executive Opinion Survey, the study assesses the status accorded to women in a broad range of countries.

Even in light of heightened international awareness of gender issues, it is a disturbing reality that no country has yet managed to eliminate the gender gap. Those that have succeeded best in narrowing the gap are the Nordic countries, with Sweden standing out as the most advanced in the world. These are followed by New Zealand (6), Canada (7), United Kingdom (8), Germany (9) and Australia (10), countries that have made considerable progress in recent decades in removing obstacles to the full participation of women in their respective societies. France (13) ranked ahead of the United States (17) among the 58 nations. Seven East European nations hold places among the top 25, with Latvia (11), Lithuania (12) and Estonia (15) the highest ranking in that group. Switzerland (34), Italy (45) and Greece (50) perform poorly, lower in rank than many of the East European group, and below Latin American nations such as Costa

Rica (18), Colombia (30) and Uruguay (32). Brazil (51), Mexico (52), India (53), Korea (54), Jordan (55), Pakistan (56), Turkey (57) and Egypt (58) occupy the lowest ranks.

These country comparisons are meant to serve a dual purpose: as a benchmark to identify existing strengths and weaknesses, and as a useful guide for policy, based on learning from the experiences of those countries that have had greater success in promoting the equality of women and men. The study provides concrete measures of the gender gap within the five categories identified above, providing an unambiguous framework for future policy making in each of the countries. By quantifying the size of the gap in each of five key categories, the study highlights the priority areas for reform.

The Status of Women: Current Reality

The past three decades have witnessed a steadily increasing awareness of the need to empower women through measures to increase social, economic and political equity, and broader access to fundamental human rights, improvements in nutrition, basic health and education. Along with awareness of the subordinate status of women has come the concept of gender as an overarching socio cultural variable, seen in relation to other factors, such as race, class, age and ethnicity. Gender is not synonymous with women, nor is it a zero sum game implying loss for men; rather, it refers to both women and men, and to their status, relative to each other. Gender equality refers to that stage of human social development at which "the rights, responsibilities and opportunities of individuals will not be determined by the fact of being born male or female," in other words, a stage when both men and women realise their full potential.

In recognition of the importance of establishing gender equality around the world, the United Nations Development Fund for Women (UNIFEM) was established as a separate fund within the United Nations Development Program (UNDP) in 1984. At that time, the General Assembly instructed it to "ensure women's involvement with mainstream activities." The Platform of Action resulting from the 1995 Beijing World Conference on Women expanded this concept, calling it "gender mainstreaming" *i.e.* the application of gender perspectives to all legal and social norms and standards, to all policy development, research, planning, advocacy, development, implementation and monitoring as a mandate for all member states. In this way, the gender factor is no longer to be only a supplement to development but central to the practice of development.

As a result of the Beijing conference and the many years of work leading up to it more than 100 countries announced new initiatives to improve the status of women. In 2000, the follow up Beijing conference further strengthened the application of the mainstreaming concept, and used it to highlight the need for more progress in reaching equality worldwide.

Achieving gender equality, however, is a grindingly slow process, since it challenges one of the most deeply entrenched of all human attitudes. Despite the intense efforts of many agencies and organisations, and numerous inspiring successes, the picture is still disheartening, as it takes far more than changes in law or stated policy to change practices in the home, community and in the decision making environment. In many parts of the world rape is not considered a crime, goes unpunished and continues to be used as a tool of war. Even in highly developed countries, violence against women of all kinds is routine, and often condoned. Female sexual slavery and forced prostitution are still terrible "facts of life" for poor, often very young, women. Genetic testing for defects of the unborn is used in some parts of the world to determine the sex of the foetus, so that females can be aborted, while in some countries, female infants are buried alive.

Forced marriage and bride burning are still prevalent in the Asian sub–continent. A pregnant woman in Africa is 180 times more likely to die of pregnancy complications than in western Europe. Women, mostly in rural areas, represent more than two–thirds of the world's illiterate adults. In the United States, 90% of AIDS cases under 20 years of age are girls. In many developed countries, where basic gender equality appears to have been achieved, the battlefront has shifted to removing the more intangible discrimination against working women. Women still hold only 15.6% of elected parliamentary seats globally. It is clear that the world has a long way to go to achieve equality and that this work will require concentrated efforts on many fronts. The work of the United Nations and many other agencies in advancing gender equality has converged in three closely interconnected areas: strengthening women's economic capacity, with a focus on new technologies and the new trade agenda; promoting women's leadership and political participation; eliminating violence against women and supporting the implementation of the Convention on the Elimination of Discrimination Against Women (CEDAW).

The Contribution of the World Economic Forum

In recent years, the Women Leaders Programme of the World Economic Forum has been focused on supporting the advancement of women to positions of leadership in society, and on promoting consideration of other issues affecting women's lives. Furthermore, for the past four years, the Forum's Global Competitiveness Reports have provided data on the qualitative aspects of women's participation in the workforce. The Forum has begun to explicitly incorporate in its measures of competitiveness aspects of gender equality, recognising that, far from being a matter of mere political correctness, the advancement of women is an important strategic issue. Countries which do not capitalise on the full potential of one half of their societies are misallocating their human resources and compromising their competitive potential.

Despite worldwide evidence of the low levels of female participation in social, educational, economic and political spheres, there is still a tendency to see it as a real problem only in a limited number of countries. Yet, as noted above, the reality is that no country in the world, no matter how advanced, has achieved true gender equality, as measured by comparable decision-making power, equal opportunity for education and advancement, and equal participation and status in all walks of human endeavour. Gender disparities exist, even in countries without glaring male domination, and measuring these disparities is a necessary step towards implementing corrective policies. Yet measurement is challenging and country performance difficult to assess using disaggregated and diverse data for each nation.

Our study is an attempt to consolidate these data in a manner that allows us to take a closer and more structured look at relative country strengths and weaknesses. The year 2005 marks the tenth anniversary of the Beijing World Conference on Women, bringing renewed focus and energy to the efforts to empower women. Thus, it is timely for the Forum to undertake the present study, in order to facilitate the work of aid agencies, governments and policy makers by providing a benchmarking tool to assess the size of the gender gap in 58 countries, ranking these nations according to the level of advancement of their female population and identifying successes and failures, based on economic, political, educational and health based criteria.

Criteria for Measurement

Five important dimensions of female empowerment and opportunity have been chosen for examination, based mainly on the findings of UNIFEM, concerning global patterns of inequality between men and women:

1. Economic participation
2. Economic opportunity
3. Political empowerment
4. Educational attainment
5. Health and well–being

The gender gap in each dimension is then quantified using two types of recent available data:

(a) Published national statistics and data from international organisations, and

(b) Survey data of a qualitative nature from the annual Executive Opinion Survey of the World Economic Forum.

The economic participation of women their presence in the workforce in quantitative terms is important not only for lowering the disproportionate levels of poverty among women, but also as an important step towards raising household income and encouraging economic development in countries as a whole. Amartya Sen makes a compelling case for the notion that societies need to see women less as passive recipients of help, and more as dynamic promoters of social transformation, a view strongly buttressed by a body of evidence suggesting that the education, employment and ownership rights of women have a powerful influence on their ability to control their environment and contribute to economic development. Economic participation concerns not only the actual numbers of women participating in the labour force, but also their remuneration on an equal basis. Worldwide, outside of the agricultural sector, in both developed and developing countries, women are still averaging slightly less than 78% of the wages given to men for the same work, a gap which refuses to close in even the most developed countries.

While globalisation has generated opportunities for local producers and entrepreneurs to reach international markets, it has at times intensified existing inequalities and insecurities for many poor women, who already represent two thirds of the world's poorest people. Since the gains of globalisation are often concentrated in the hands of those with higher education those who own resources and have access to capital poor women are usually the least able to seize the longer term opportunities offered. Instead, as demonstrated in East Asia in the 1990s, it is all too often the case that women are only able to secure employment during rapid expansions, employment that is usually transitory and insecure, and performed under harsh conditions.

Globalisation has dramatically changed the conditions under which the struggle for gender equality must be carried out, especially in developing countries. One of the important tools of gender mainstreaming, aimed principally at poverty reduction, has been the concept of "gender budgeting," *i.e.* focusing attention in the process of budget formulation within a given country in order to assess whether a particular fiscal measure will increase or decrease gender equality, or leave it unchanged.

Gender budget initiatives (GBIs) not only identify targeted expenditures, or allocate more money to women, but also aim to "break down and identify the differentiated impact and incidence of general public revenue and expenditure on women and men...and significantly contribute to overall objectives like equity, equality, efficiency, transparency, the realisation of social, economic and cultural rights, and good governance," thus offering a practical way of evaluating government action (or inaction). Close monitoring and analysis of gender effects has become a mechanism for holding policy makers increasingly accountable for the impact of policies on the lives of both women and men, so that the large percentage of women who participate economically in the informal sector, and who in some parts of the world provide upwards of 70% of agricultural labour, and produce over 90% of the food yet are nowhere represented in budget deliberations can be taken into account in the economic adjustment measures which might directly affect their welfare.

The present study attempts to capture the gap between men and women in terms of economic participation by comparing unemployment levels, the levels of economic activity and remuneration for equal work.

Economic opportunity concerns the *quality* of women's economic involvement, beyond their mere presence as workers. This is a particularly serious problem in developed countries, where women may gain employment with relative ease, but where their employment is either concentrated in poorly paid or unskilled job "ghettos," characterised by the absence of upward mobility and opportunity. This is most commonly the result of negative or obstructive attitudes, and of legal and social systems which use maternity laws and benefits to penalize women economically for childbirth and child care responsibilities, and discourage or actively prevent men from sharing family responsibilities.

The ghettoisation of female labour is a phenomenon which crosses all cultural boundaries, and professions, affecting women in virtually all countries. Internationally, women are most often concentrated in "feminised" professions, such as nursing and teaching, office work, care of the elderly and disabled termed "horizontal occupational segregation" where they tend to remain in lower job categories than men. Typically, because these functions are carried out by women, they are the lowest paid, in addition to offering limited or no opportunity for advancement. The term "feminisation of poverty" is often used to illustrate the fact that the majority cf the 1.5 billion people living on US$1 a day or less are women and that the gap between women and men caught in the cycle of poverty has not lessened, but may well have widened in the past decade.

At the other end of the spectrum, advancement within professions, such as law, medicine and engineering, in which women are increasingly well represented in developed countries, is of great concern. One survey of graduates carried out by Yale Law Women points to the growing numbers of women attorneys (25–35%), only a small number of whom are partners in firms (5–15%), and to the importance of what they call "family friendly" and "female friendly" practices in the profession.

United Nations Economic and Social Council (ECOSOC) figures indicate that the vast majority of the world's countries offer paid maternity leave, often with a guaranteed wage of 50–100% of salary. Interestingly, the United States offers women 12 weeks, but with no pay whatsoever, putting it in league with Lesotho, Swaziland and Papua New Guinea.

Although, as of 2000, women are wage employed in roughly equal numbers with men worldwide, the number of women represented in managerial positions is much smaller. Women have made slow and uneven progress in obtaining a share of managerial positions, which, according to 2002 statistics of the ILO, ranged between 20–40% in 48 out of 63 countries. In addition, women who are in managerial positions often need to make a painful choice between a successful career and family. A study in the United States has found 49% of high achieving women to be childless, as compared with only 19% of their male colleagues.

In this study, we use data on the duration of maternity leave, the percentage of wages paid during the covered period and the number of women in managerial positions to capture the variation between the economic opportunities available to women in different countries. In addition, we have included a unique dataset on qualitative elements such as the availability of government provided childcare, the impact of maternity laws on the hiring of women, and wage inequalities between men and women for private sector employment. These data, obtained from the World Economic Forum's Executive Opinion Survey, are particularly useful in quantifying "ground level" realities. Very often there are discrepancies between the *de jure* environment and the *de facto* situation. By quantifying the perceptions of business leaders in the 58 countries these anomalies can be identified.

Political empowerment refers to the equitable representation of women in decision making structures, both formal and informal, and their voice in the formulation of policies affecting their societies. The Inter Parliamentary Union reports a world average of only 15.6% in combined houses of parliament. The statistics by region offer few surprises, ranging from 6.8% in the Arab States to 18.6% in the Americas, and 39.7% in the Nordic states. While women are poorly represented in the lower levels of government, they are rarer still in the upper echelons of decision making.

The absence of women from structures of governance inevitably means that national, regional and local priorities *i.e.* how resources are allocated are typically defined without meaningful input from women, whose life experience gives them a different awareness of the community's needs, concerns and interests from that of men. For example, a study in three widely differing countries showed that, were women to have a greater say in spending priorities, they would be far more likely to spend family and community resources for improving health, education, community infrastructure and the eradication of poverty, as opposed to the military, alcohol or gambling.

Indeed, the demand for changed priorities is heard from virtually all women's organisations, from the most advanced and politically savvy in developed countries, to fledgling women's NGOs in the developing world. However, in order for spending and development priorities to change, there must be at least a critical mass of women represented, who are learning the rules, using the rules and changing the rules of the decision making "game," and thus having an impact on discourse and decisions at all levels, from the family, to the nation, to the international community.

Here, we have measured the dimension of political empowerment by using data on the number of female ministers, seats in parliament held by women, women holding senior, legislative and managerial positions and the number of years a female has been head of state (president or prime minister) in each of the 58 countries.

Educational attainment is, without doubt, the most fundamental prerequisite for empowering women in all spheres of society, for without education of comparable quality and content to that given to boys and men, and relevant to existing knowledge and real needs, women are unable to access well paid, formal sector jobs, advance within them, participate in, and be represented in government and gain political influence. Moreover, the risk increases for society as a whole that the next generation of children will be similarly ill prepared.

If, as a broad body of empirical work has shown, education and literacy reduce mortality rates of children including the bias toward female child mortality and help reduce fertility rates, the importance of literacy for women is all the greater, considering that women still constitute two thirds of the world's illiterate population. Although the ECOSOC statistics show that girls actually outnumber boys in tertiary level education in a very few countries most notably in some of the Middle East and former Soviet bloc countries an obvious gender gap in education tends to appear early in most countries, and, on average, grows more severe with each year of education. In addition, the number of women represented among tertiary level educators is lower than among primary level educators.

However, if the content of the educational curriculum and the attitudes of teachers serve merely to reinforce prevalent stereotypes and injustices, then the mere fact of literacy and education does not, in and of itself, close the gender gap; schooling as a catalyst for change in gender relations will be more effective only if appropriate attention is also given to curriculum content and the retraining of those who deliver it.

Information and communication technologies, which have become a potent driving force of the development process, represent yet another dimension in which a knowledge gap has emerged between women and men: a gender based digital divide. A study by the USAID has found that countless women in the developing world are further removed from the information age because of their lower levels of education and deeply ingrained negative attitudes towards other forms of achievement. "Without access to information technology, an understanding of its significance and the ability to use it for social and economic gain, women in the developing world will be further marginalised from the mainstream of their communities, their countries and the world."

In the present study, gender disparities in educational attainment are captured using data on literacy rates, enrolment rates for primary, secondary and tertiary education and average years of schooling across the population. In this way, we are able to illustrate not only the current levels of women's empowerment through education, but also the potential of future generations of women in a particular nation.

Health and well being is a concept related to the substantial differences between women and men in their access to sufficient nutrition, healthcare and reproductive facilities, and to issues of fundamental safety and integrity of person. According to the World Health Organisation, 585,000 women die every year, over 1,600 every day, from causes related to pregnancy and childbirth. The Planned Parenthood Federation America quotes estimates that of the annual 46 million abortions worldwide, some 20 million are performed unsafely, resulting in the deaths of 80,000 women from complications, accounting for at least 13% of global maternal mortality, and causing a wide range of long-term health problems.

Women's particular vulnerability to violence is perhaps the most obvious aspect of reduced physical security and integrity of person, but one which is perhaps the least amenable to accurate statistics. Even Sweden, long recognised as a leader in the area of gender equality was recently called to task by Amnesty International, which stated that "the prevalence of gender biased violence shatters many people's image of Sweden as being the most gender equal country in the world". A recent front page article in the International Herald Tribune also noted that the implementation of violence related laws in Sweden was marred by "spotty prosecutions, vague statistics, old fashioned judges and unresponsive governments".

The complexity of the social and cultural issues, combined with the stigma and fear of disclosure lead a situation where only a small proportion of the crimes of sexual assault, child abuse, wife battering and gun-related violence are ever reported, making accurate data extremely difficult to obtain. Indeed, it is difficult to measure the true extent of violence against women as *most* incidences of domestic violence and sexual assault go unreported. It is typical for women themselves to be blamed for "provoking" the violence perpetrated against them by men often those closest to them.

The victims of such violence are then frequently stigmatised and isolated in society, even forced into marriage with their violators, with little or no control over their own persons. Each year an estimated two million girls, usually aged 4 to 8, are forcibly subjected to female genital mutilation (FGM), which routinely leads to death, chronic infection and bleeding, nerve tumours, obstructed childbirth, painful scarring, *etc.* Although most prevalent in Africa and the Middle East, the practice of some form of FGM has been reported among immigrant communities in parts of Asia and the Pacific, North and South America and Europe. While we lack reliable data on violence against women, we have incorporated several other variables related to the dimension of health and well being. Since women are often the majority of the victims of poverty, we have included data from the Executive Opinion Survey on the effectiveness of governments' efforts to reduce poverty and inequality. In addition, we include the adolescent fertility rate as an indicator of health risks among women aged 15 to 19 years, and as an indicator of the lack of other choices available to young women.

Finally, we include reproductive health data, such as the percentage of births attended by skilled health staff, and maternal and infant mortality ratios. Since these variables are particularly affected by the level of poverty in a given nation, *i.e.* poor health facilities in general as opposed to poor *reproductive* health facilities, we have adjusted these data by the number of physicians available per 1,000 people, as an indicator of the quality of the country's health system in general. In this way, we do not penalise developing countries in particular, but all those nations that provide poor reproductive health facilities to women, given the existing health infrastructure.

Calculating the Scores

The goal of our methodology is to provide cross-country comparisons, a broadly comprehensive assessment of the extent to which countries are capitalising on the full potential of their societies.

This is obtained by combining raw figures on the national economy, politics and education with the perceptions of the business community on the employment of women in their respective countries. We have attempted to consolidate in one index several dimensions of gender equality, including those that form part of the prominent indexes currently present in the literature, most notably the political factors that enter the UNDP Gender Empowerment Measure, and the literacy and health-related factors that form part of the Gender Related Development Index. In addition, we provide a measurement of the participation *per se* of women in economic activity, as contrasted with the opportunities available to them once they become participants in the labour force.

The ranking of the 58 countries in our study is by no means inclusive of all the issues that affect women. There are other approaches to prioritising global gender inequality in the current literature, such as that of the United Nations Millennium Project's Task Force on Gender Equality, where it is defined in terms of capabilities (education, health and nutrition), access to resources and opportunities (income, employment, property) and security (vulnerability to violence). However, since our work is exclusively quantitative, data availability has imposed limitations on our choice of variables. For example, insufficient global data on violence against women prevented us from including this variable in the "health and well being" dimension, but does not negate the importance of this factor in capturing gender equality. Nevertheless, the index provides valuable comparisons across countries in economic, political, health and educational realms.

The set of 58 countries covered in the current study includes all 30 OECD countries and 28 others from the "emerging market" world. Overall, the set of countries covers much of Europe and North America, in addition to providing relevant examples from Asia, Latin America, Africa and the Middle East. The existence of reliable data has been the main consideration in our choice of countries, and lack of such data has necessitated omitting many countries from the developing world.

The data used in this study come from publicly available sources, including the *World Development Indicators* of the World

Bank, and the *Human Development Report* of UNDP, as well as the annual *Executive Opinion Survey* of the World Economic Forum. In 2004, the *Executive Opinion Survey* recorded the opinions of nearly 9,000 business leaders in 104 countries. Respondents were asked to record their views on the importance of a broad range of factors central to creating a sound business environment, including the quality of fiscal management, labour practices, the quality of the country's infrastructure and its educational institutions. For example, one of the variables included in the Economic Opportunity category, the "impact of maternity laws on the hiring of women", was derived directly from the following Survey question:

In your country, maternity laws:

1 = impede the hiring of women

7 = are not a hindrance for hiring women

As described earlier, the questions from the Executive Opinion Survey included in this study have a similar format and use a 1 to 7 scale. The mean response of all respondents in a particular country is the final score reported for that country on the relevant variable. Clearly, the "hard" data taken from other international organisations is reported on different scales or units. To make all data comparable, hard data was normalised to a 1 to 7 scale, with the best value in each category being allotted a 7, and the worst value a 1. For example, out of the 58 countries covered by the study, Egypt had the shortest maternity leave allowed (approximately 7 weeks) and therefore Egypt was allotted a 1, while Sweden had the longest leave (52 weeks) and was therefore allotted a 7. All other countries were assigned a value between 1 and 7. Similar methods for normalising hard data have been used in several previous reports of the Forum's Global Competitiveness Programme. Once both survey and hard data are on the same scale, the scores for each country are calculated by taking the unweighted mean of all the variables within a particular category. Finally, the overall scores for each country are calculated as an unweighted average of the scores obtained in each of the five categories.

Since all five of these dimensions are inextricably linked, it is essential, ultimately, that gender equality be achieved in all of them.

For example, equal educational opportunities cannot be effective, if women are barred entry into the workforce. Entering the workforce, in and of itself, does not mean that women will not be ghettoised or encounter a "glass ceiling;" having work of whatever kind may be immaterial, if the conditions under which it must be endured are intolerable or life threatening, or if it must be sustained in the face of overwhelming additional burdens beyond the hours of paid labour. The disproportionate representation of elderly women among the poor means that economic participation may mean little, if the tax regime does not take into account income disparities and the differing capacities of women and men to contribute to an old age safety net. For these reasons, we have assigned equal weights to all five dimensions when calculating the final scores as well as within each dimension when adding the scores obtained on each variable.

Thus, however difficult comparisons may be, measuring the gender gap as well as possible, in each of these dimensions, both within and between countries, provides guidance to policy makers as to where efforts must be made in each country.

TABLE: THE GENDER GAP RANKING

Country	Overall rank	Overall score	Economic particip-ate	Economic opportu-nity	Political empowe-ment	Educational attainment	Health and well-being
Sweden	1	5.53	5	12	8	1	1
Norway	2	5.39	13	2	3	6	9
Iceland	3	5.32	17	7	2	7	6
Denmark	4	5.27	6	1	20	5	2
Finland	5	5.19	12	17	4	10	4
New Zealand	6	4.89	16	47	1	11	26
Canada	7	4.87	7	27	11	12	14
United Kingdom	8	4.75	21	41	5	4	28
Germany	9	4.61	20	28	6	34	10
Australia	10	4.61	15	25	22	17	18
Latvia	11	4.60	4	6	10	24	48
Lithuania	12	4.58	10	11	13	19	44
France	13	4.49	31	9	14	31	17
Netherlands	14	4.48	32	16	7	42	8
Estonia	15	4.47	8	5	30	28	46
Ireland	16	4.40	37	51	12	9	12

United States	17	4.40	19	46	19	8	42
Costa Rica	18	4.36	49	30	9	14	30
Poland	19	4.36	25	19	18	20	38
Belgium	20	4.30	35	37	25	15	16
Slovak Republic	21	4.28	14	33	29	23	35
Slovenia	22	4.25	26	15	39	22	19
Portugal	23	4.21	27	18	31	36	20
Hungary	24	4.19	30	3	28	39	40
Czech Republic	25	4.19	24	4	43	25	23
Luxembourg	26	4.15	48	8	33	21	25
Spain	27	4.13	45	34	27	35	5
Austria	28.	1.13	42	22	21	38	13
Bulgaria	29	4.06	11	14	23	50	55
Colombia	30	4.06	41	38	15	13	52
Russian Federation	31	4.03	3	10	47	29	57
Uruguay	32	4.01	36	26	36	2	56
China	33	4.01	9	23	40	46	36
Switzerland	34	3.97	43	42	17	39	7
Argentina	35	3.97	55	29	26	3	54
South Africa	36	3.95	39	56	16	30	21
Israel	37	3.94	28	40	32	28	39
Japan	38	3.75	33	52	54	26	3
Bangladesh	39	3.75	18	53	42	37	37
Malaysia	40	3.70	40	36	51	32	15
Romania	41	3.70	43	31	35	51	47
Zimbabwe	42	3.66	2	56	34	52	41
Malta	43	3.65	56	43	45	16	24
Thailand	44	3.61	1	39	49	54	32
Italy	45	3.50	51	39	48	41	11
Indonesia	46	3.50	29	24	46	53	29
Peru	47	3.47	50	34	38	47	31
Chile	48	3.46	52	20	44	14	45
Venezuela	49	3.42	38	13	52	33	58
Greece	50	3.41	34	48	50	45	22
Brazil	51	3.29	36	21	57	27	53
Mexico	52	3.28	37	35	41	44	51
India	53	3.27	54	35	24	57	34
Korea	54	3.18	34	55	57	48	27
Jordan	55	2.96	58	32	58	43	33
Pakistan	56	2.90	53	54	37	58	33
Turkey	57	2.67	22	58	53	55	50
Egypt	58	2.38	57	50	55	56	49

The preceding table illustrates the overall rankings, as well as the scores obtained in the five dimensions surveyed. Scores for the developing and middle income countries clearly demonstrate that even the most basic criteria for gender equality are unmet, especially those concerning maternal health and primary education. Moreover, while high income countries, such as those in the OECD, have made great progress over the past half century in removing some fundamental gender biases, they continue to display significant disparities in the opportunities presented to men and women in the workplace and in the political realm.

Not surprisingly, the top five places are occupied by Nordic countries, characterised by strongly liberal societies, protection of minority rights and comprehensive welfare systems. While women in these countries clearly have access to a wider spectrum of educational, political and work opportunities and enjoy a higher standard of living than women in other parts of the world, it is interesting to note that the rates of economic *participation* in some of these countries are not necessarily the highest in the world.

For example, although Norway and Iceland occupy the second and third places in the overall ranking, they hold ranks of 13 and 17 in terms of economic participation. This is not necessarily the result of barriers to women's entry to the workforce, since it is certainly the case that women in some developed countries are in the fortunate position of being able to choose *not* to work outside their homes. It is a potential caveat of the economic participation methodology that it does not take into account those who may voluntarily choose not to participate. However, it should be noted that while some women may indeed have chosen to "opt out," that choice is usually made in a structure where work family issues are seen as problems primarily facing women, while decision making structures are dominated by men.

These are followed by a number of "woman friendly" nations such as New Zealand, Canada, the UK, Germany and Australia. Several Eastern European and transition economies place well, appearing among the top 25. This is not too surprising, considering that these countries subscribed for long periods of time in recent history to a socialist ideology, which, however nominally, encouraged a "worker woman" notion of equality, albeit one in which women had to do everything: all the work inside the home, while at the same time participating in industry and all the professions. The most notable of these are Latvia (11), Lithuania (12) and Estonia (15), the first two coming ahead of France (13) and all three appearing ahead of the United States (17). It should be noted, however, that while these nations perform well in terms of economic opportunity, economic participation and educational attainment, they lag far behind in terms of health and well being, ranking 48, 44 and 46 respectively. The poor reproductive health statistics, despite the profusion of health professionals, indicate an inefficient use of health facilities in providing reproductive healthcare to women.

The United States (17) performs particularly well on educational attainment and only slightly less so on economic participation and political empowerment. However, the United States ranks poorly on the specific dimensions of economic opportunity and health and well being, compromised by the meagre maternity leave, lack of maternity leave benefits and limited government provided childcare. Moreover, the health and well being rank of the United States is brought down, in comparison with other developed nations, by the large number of adolescents bearing children and by the high maternal mortality ratio especially given the relatively high number of physicians available.

The four European nations Switzerland (34), Malta (43), Italy (45) and Greece (50) rank low overall, falling below Latin American nations such as Costa Rica (18), Colombia (30) and Uruguay (32), and (in the case of the latter three) below Asian countries such as Bangladesh (39) and Malaysia (40), a clear reflection of the shortcomings of these so called "advanced" nations in implementing gender equality. Although Switzerland performs well on the health and well being dimension (7), and relatively high on political empowerment (17) a notable achievement for a country which gave women the right to vote and stand for national election only in 1971 the country lags behind not only in economic participation and economic opportunity, but also in educational attainment, being one of the very few developed nations where female enrolment rates are consistently lower than male rates. As is to be expected of countries notorious for their patriarchal cultures, Italy and Greece each perform particularly poorly on the economic participation and economic opportunity dimensions. While the rankings speak for themselves, they both confirm many commonly held beliefs, on the one hand, and dispel some prevailing myths, on the other. In the United States, for example, the low rank of 46 for economic opportunity appears to corroborate the much discussed "glass ceiling."

And while American women have generally high levels of economic participation, they also appear to be subject to a lack of opportunity for advancement in their careers. Given China's labour policies, it will probably not surprise many that China ranks high in economic participation (9), but falls close to the bottom of the rankings in education (46) and political empowerment (40). With an overall rank of 33, the Chinese government's muchtouted gender equality objective still falls far short of expectations. Nonetheless, China remains the highest ranking nation in Asia, followed by Japan (38). The Russia Federation (31) shows similar results to those of China, boosted in the rankings by a high economic participation (3), but compromised by low political empowerment (47) and health and well being (57).

Costa Rica (18) occupies first place in Latin America by a large margin, followed by Colombia (30), Uruguay (32) and Argentina (35). Peru (47), Chile (48), Venezuela (49), Brazil (51) and Mexico (52) all fare badly, due to poor performances on all five areas of this index, with the exception of the economic opportunity ranks of Venezuela (13), Chile (20) and Brazil (21). The problem here appears to be not in the lack of opportunity, once women have entered the workforce, but rather in giving them access to the educational training and basic rights, such as healthcare and political empowerment, that will enable them to join the workforce. Out of the seven predominantly Muslim nations covered by the study, Bangladesh (39) and Malaysia (40) outperform Indonesia (46), while Jordan (55), Pakistan (56), Turkey (57) and Egypt (58) occupy the bottom four ranks.

There is little doubt that traditional, deeply conservative attitudes regarding the role of women have made their integration into the world of public decision making extremely difficult. As the newly independent Arab governments of Egypt and Jordan focused on modernisation more than half a century ago, they neglected the needs of women, one of their most important assets.

In recent times however, some progress has evidently been made. Bangladesh performs relatively well on economic participation (18), Malaysia on health and well being (15), Indonesia on economic opportunity (24) and Turkey on economic participation (22), no doubt reflecting the economic freedoms that are increasingly available to women in Islamic countries. While it is encouraging that the countries of the Middle East and North Africa region have invested impressively in women's education in recent years, increasing their productive potential and earning capacity, it is clear from the low ranks of these countries on labour force participation among the lowest in the world that the region is not benefiting from the potential returns on this investment. Despite having ratified the Beijing Convention for the Elimination of All Forms of Discrimination Against Women, most of these nations lack a coherent strategy for empowering women. Such a strategy will be necessary for building on the achievements thus far, learning from past mistakes, and improving the future of women in these economies.

Regional and Country Performance

Finally, we provide two correlation plots: one showing the correlation between the Gender Gap Index ranks and the Growth Competitiveness Index ranks for 2004–2005 and the other showing the correlation between the Gender Gap Index ranks and the log of the GDP per capita. While correlation does not necessarily entail causation, these comparisons provide a preliminary indication of the link between women's empowerment and a nation's long term growth potential.

True models of gender equality do not exist. Given the lamentable international picture, no one who studies the gender gap can doubt that no country in the world has yet managed to achieve it. True, the Nordic countries are getting closer, leading the way in providing women with a quality of life almost equal to that of men, with almost comparable levels of political participation, and with relatively equal educational and economic opportunity and participation. Yet, as this study indicates, other countries show wide variation, lagging far behind in particular areas, some across all five dimensions. Aside from this general conclusion, and broad country comparisons, the data we have presented here shed light on the disparities within countries, in some cases either confirming information gathered in other ways, or, in others, countering prevailing assumptions. By identifying and quantifying the gender gap, we hope to provide policy makers with a tool offering direction and focus for the work of significantly improving the economic, political and social potential of all their citizens. In addition, we hope that this work provides the impetus for policy makers to strengthen their commitment to the idea of women's empowerment, and to concentrate the political will, energy and resources, in concert with aid agencies and civil society organisations, to make gender equality a reality.

8

Globalisation: Empowering Women through Information

Globalisation can be a major force for prosperity only if it is backed by adequate national policies and conducive social and economic environment. This paper will give an overview of what the forces of globalisation have in store for the women of India. A large group of working women of India are in the rural and unorganised sectors.

Socially the majority of Indian women are still tradition bound and are in a disadvantageous position. Since globalisation is opening up the Indian economy suddenly at a very high speed, without the required economic and social policies to provide the much required safety net, women who have been involved with production in the traditional ways, have to cope with numerous problems and yet try to avail of the opportunities which an open economy promises. The changing scenario will diversify the information needs of women at different levels.

Globalisation is a fact of life, which has come to stay. It is expected to be a major for prosperity. The essentials of the new economic policy are:

- Privatisation
- Globalisation
- Modernisation
- Improving productivity and grow the rate.

The Structural Adjustment Programmes (SAP) undertaken to implement these objectives will require:

- Decontrol and deregulate
- Freedom of entry of foreign goods and investment
- Adoption of market friendly fiscal exchange, trade and policies
- Cut back in public expenditure
- Adoption of new technologies
- Concentration of government investment in infrastructure building education, health *etc.*
- Exit policy
- Withdrawal of subsidies.

This chapter tries to give an overview of what is in store for women in India in this process of globalisation and what type of information needs are likely to evolve due to this major change in the new socio economic scenario. The new Structural Adjustment Programmes to usher in globalisation in traditional economies like India will reach the expected goal only IF the process of globalisation well backed by properly planned national policies in a conducive social and economic environment.

Globalisation is a double edged process as far as women are concerned. On one hand, majority of women in India and other developing countries find themselves stripped off the benefit of social security, government subsidy protection of labour and than safety nets. On the other hand there are possibilities of better education facilities and opportunities at the transnational sense which are very attractive to the privileged few. It is however necessary to understand that effective development requires integration of women in the development process as agents of change as well beneficiaries because Indian women can be utilised as development resources in ways.

Problems encountered by Indian-women over the ages:–

- Patriarchy and social pressures.
- Caste based discrimination and social restrictions
- Inadequate access to productive resources
- Poverty
- Insufficient advancement facilities
- Powerlessness

These basic problems have plagued the lives of Indian women with little respite. But in the new circumstances created by SAP for globalisation are diverse and encompass all aspects of women's lives in India. It has affected both the quantity and the quality of work available to the majority of women in India.

- The traditional role of women in agriculture, livestock and animal husbandry, Khadi and village industries including handicrafts, handlooms fisheries, etc, is being undermined because mechanisation and automation is becoming prevalent in the market based economy which will adversely affect the village based traditional economy.
- Privatisation and reduction of public services will reduce regular employment opportunities for women.
- Globalisation has increased the number of low paid, part time and exploitative jobs.
- Occupational sex segregation will be a stark reality in the open economy. This will tend to result in worse working condition, lower pay and inferior career opportunities.
- Curtailment of state provisions in child care, community care and social security, will increase the dual burden of employment and family responsibilities for women in general.
- With male migration on the increase from the rural to urban sectors, the women have to bear the triple burden of caring, farming and paid employment in the rural sector.
- In the neo liberal work practices, contract work, unsocial hours of work, cooperative practices, payment by result make it very difficult for women to cope with their multiple responsibilities.
- With the disappearing social and financial safety nets and government subsidy, the poverty alleviation programmes, universal education, and woman oriented health programmes will be adversely affected.
- Trade liberalisation will allow MNCS to enter into food processing and other feminised industries which will lead to reduction in low skilled women labour.
- Privatisation of education and training will increase the cost of getting educated. When family budgets are readjusted, the

female children will be the main casualty because most of the resources will be spent to educate the male children.

- Migration of women specially for economic reasons often give rise to exploitation and trafficking in women at the local, regional and global levels.
- Open market economy leads to price rise in food and other basic necessities. Women who have to directly deal with family subsistence have to cope with such changes.

Basically liberalisation and globalisation of the economy will marginalise majority of women in India due to reduction of employment opportunities, reduction of wages, casualisation of jobs and women workers, exclusion from the modernised production process due to lack of education and training.

Possibilities and Opportunities

On the positive side globalisation has contributed to bring about welcome changes in the lives of women who have been able to avail of the opportunities, which have opened up in the various sectors of development. These are:

- Prospects of higher and quality education have become feasible for those women who can afford them, economically and socially.
- Employment in technological and other advanced sectors, which have global bearing, has opened up for suitably qualified women.
- With changing attitude towards women, especially in the urban areas, women enjoy more egalitarian set of gender relationship.
- Augmentation of women's movements through exposures at the international level will help bring about major changes in the economic, social and political lives of women.
- Reduction in gender inequalities will have positive effect on women's empowerment in the socio–economic context.
- Attitudinal changes towards women's role in the family due to good education, benefits of family planning and health care, child care, good job opportunities *etc.* will surely help in the development of more confident and healthy women.

- Positive approach to economic and cultural migration will facilitate women to be exposed to better prospects at the international level.

Steps to cope with the changing scenario: It is seen that the situation facing the majority if Indian women is far from positive. However efforts are underway to circumvent many of these problems through governmental and the non governmental programmes. Both the government and NGO's seem to be aware of the fact that the globalisation process require proper focus on rural development, education, health and child care and proper gainful employment for the underprivileged at the initial stages. Since poverty alleviation programmes are the main responsibilities of the Government, there are direct and sector wise schemes. Some of the important schemes are:

- Public Distribution system for food security
- Work security through various schemes
- Health schemes and services
- Child care schemes
- Credit schemes
- Insurance schemes

There are also sector wise schemes through Small Farmers Development Agency and other schemes .of the Department of Agriculture, schemes of the Dairy Development Boards in the dairy sector, schemes of Forest Corporation in the forestry sector *etc.* The main goal of the Department of Women and Child Development is to empower women and to bring them within the purview of the mainstream development process.

Also the capacities and capabilities of women addressing their own development have been the main focus of important NGOs and women's organisations. Innovative approaches for poverty alleviation such as savings, credit, and asset creation for poor women have evolved in India as well as in other developing countries. These experiments have been able to organize poor women to—

- Strengthen their capacity to survive
- Meet there social needs

- Enter into income generating activities
- Increase their savings
- Utilise the savings along with available credit
- Improve their socio–economic conditions and that of their families
- Sustain the process

NGOs such as Self Employed Women's Association (SEWA) in Ahmedabad, Working Women's Forum (WWF) in Madras, Centre for Women's Development Studies (CWDS), New Delhi etc have done commendable work in these directions. The Government departments have also given such experiments the necessary boost through the support for expansion in many ways.

The Role of Information in Rural Development Process

It is believed that the modern day phenomenon of Information and Communication Technology is the key to information flow for development. Especially in the Globalisation and liberalisation scenario, ICT can surely act as the major component in the developmental process.

In the World Development Report 2000–2001 it is observed that the spread of relevant information through technology will help in bridging the gaps between the information haves and the have nots. This will be a major step towards poverty reduction. India has seen a number of experiments to wire the rural sector to provide the right information to the right person at the right time and place. In Rajasthan, the village named Neyla has the Information kiosk 'Rajnidhi' which is a project to use ICT especially the Internet to replace traditional form of governance with more open and responsive service delivery system.

Gyandoot a prominent information facilitation programme in Madhya Pradesh has connected many villages through an intranet and has kiosks called Soochanalayas. The M. S. Swaminathan Research Foundation have set up Knowledge Centres which give access to information on Government programmes well as information relevant to fishing. There is farmer bazaar. com in Punjab for marketing the rural produce. The Warna Wired Village Project of the

Kolhapur and Sangli districts of Maharashtra is a joint venture of the Government organisation NIC and the Maharashtra State. Most of these projects disseminate information meant for the disadvantaged groups which includes:

- Government circulars/notifications regarding programmes of assistance
- Leaflets released by NGOs about their programmes to spread awareness among the rural poor
- Public health bulletins especially for family planning, health and childcare *etc.*

Some of these ICT based information system deal with wide ranging topics such as:

- Agriculture produce market rates
- Copies of land records
- On line registration of applications
- On line public grievance filing
- Rural e–mail
- Village auction sites
- On line matrimonial sites
- Information pertaining to government programmes
- Career counselling service
- Technical expertise programmes regarding agriculture, animal husbandry, health, *etc.*
- Online application forms
- Weather information for the fishing community.

Some of these programs also use digital media clubbed with audio and video capabilities to give access to information to those who cannot read.

Information Needs of Women

The programmes mentioned above are efforts to make available relevant information to the rural sector and specially to the disadvantaged groups. Women being the lowest in the socio–economic rung should be given the privilege of being one of the most important recipients of information meant to reduce the socioeconomic gap.

What Happens at the Ground Level

- All these commendable projects act as information supply agents which do not deal with information demands of special groups such as women.
- The information disseminated through most of these programs still caters to the English educated middle class. However there are efforts to give Hindi and regional language facilities in many programs. But the slant is still on the educated and literate few.
- The information, thus disseminated and often not need based. Such information is also not professionally organised for proper access and dissemination in the ICT environment.

Information Needs of Women

Information needs of women in the new globalised environment are as diverse as the socio– economic scenario. Treating women, as a monolithic group will over simplify their information needs. Within women's group itself, globalisation has created the haves and the have nots i.e those who are in an advantageous position due to globalisation and those relegated further into disadvantaged position under the new economic policy. The information needs will also differ accordingly.

The urban educated women need information mainly pertaining to:

- Research
- Educational opportunities including prospects abroad
- Career advancement facilities
- Job/ employment prospects in India and abroad
- Matrimonials
- Fashion and market values
- Health and child care facilities which includes sexual and reproductory information
- Art and entertainment

- Social support system for working women
- Legal rights and provisions

Urban lower middle class women however will specially need information on:

- Inexpensive educational facilities
- Career advancement and job opportunities in the city itself
- Matrimonial within the restrictions of caste and class
- Inexpensive health and childcare
- Inexpensive social support systems for working women
- Legal rights and provisions against social injustice, domestic violence, dowry system *etc.*

A large chunk of women who have been adversely affected by the globalisation process are the poor urban slum dwellers and women. To say the least they are the most marginalised people in the urban sector. Their information needs are only for subsistence.

They need to know about:

- Health services and child care facilities which are available free of cost.
- Job opportunities in the low paid informal sector including domestic services
- Housing availability specially in slums
- Free educational facilities for their children specially for boys
- Information regarding Govt. programmes for the poor and how to deal with the procedure
- Legal provisions against sexual harassment, domestic violence and social injustice.

Information Needs of Women in the Rural Sector

Once again women have to be divided on the basis of economic and social positions in the rural society to understand their information needs. Elite women in the rural sector are mainly from the landed gentry class or from the highly sophisticated politically important families. They are also usually from the upper castes. Their information needs are akin to that of the urban elite women excepting for the fact that they often are passive viewers in the changing socio–economic scenario because they are bound by the upper caste traditions where patriarchy rules supreme. The rural educated middle class women are more prone to change. They are in the process of gradually breaking the caste and class barriers and are working towards better education and economic independence. They are in urgent need of information regarding their new entitlements—

- Educational opportunities outside the village
- Job opportunities in both formal and informal sectors
- Govt. assistance programs for career advancement within the restriction of traditions
- Health services including sexual reproductive health
- Modern child care facilities
- Legal provisions to counter sexual harassment, domestic violence and social injustice.

The largest group, which has been marginalised from getting any need based information is the rural poor. Though this is the most active group of women in the rural sector, they have never been specially considered for information dissemination. Information system specially designed for the rural poor has to be need based because this group has been worst affected by the process of globalisation. Their information needs will encompass their economic, social and familial roles. Therefore the system must include:

- Agricultural assistance programmes
- Sector specific assistance programmes
- Technical training facilities *i.e.* hands on training
- Traditional and new job opportunities
- Health programs specially family planning and reproduction
- Children's development programmes
- Prices and market information
- Environment and its implications
- Water and soil management
- Adult education and literacy programs
- Educational opportunities for children
- Migration facilities/ possibilities

Who Gives Information to Women?

There has been no research conducted in India on the information needs of women, though this is a very vital aspect and a prerequisite for any developmental process. Women get information through various sources that are often not geared to their specific requirements.

- NGOs and the Govt. departments. generate information about women and prepare leaflets, indigenous newspapers, and small booklets *etc.* for distribution.
- The ICT based information systems give pertinent information concerning the rural sector activities but these are still general in nature. They however help women as well to a certain extent.
- Public libraries are a total failure at the rural sector because they are still traditional libraries dependent mainly on the print medium.
- Family members and friends are often the main source of information.
- The male members of the family who have better access to information source often share relevant information.

What is the Way Out?

Just as NGOs and the Government have come together to make poverty alleviation programmes successful through women centric initiatives in which poor women have been organised to circumvent the problems of liberal development processes, similarly women have to be made aware of their information needs as well. Once women make their decisions based on information relevant to them, their requirements will also be fulfilled as per their own terms. Presently someone else thinks for them and gauges their needs *e.g.* libraries and other information centres, media, educational/ Research institutions in the urban sector and the NGOs, government departments and recently the ICT managers in the rural sector prepare information capsules and disseminate for use.

There is a strong case for bringing together the expertise of library/information professionals, Government department officials who deal with women's problems, health workers, child care workers, NGOs and the ICT managers to envision communication centres in both urban and rural sectors to deal with the information requirements of urban and rural poor marginalised women, to give them the rightful opportunities for empowerment.

Relevant information have to be prepared in need based comprehensible formats in the regional languages to reach the unreached. ICT managers have to utilise audio and video, facilities to reach the illiterate women who are otherwise competent and worthy in their own fields of activities. Libraries in the rural sector have to act as communication centres and shed the traditional bias towards the print medium. Mass media and interpersonal communication should be used extensively to improve information dissemination.

Conclusion

It is only through full understanding of the plight of women in the Globalisation process can the government, NGOs, decision makers and information managers prepare proper strategies to empower women and bring them into the mainstream developmental process. This is the greatest challenge, which confronts India and its women because globalisation will stay but with half the population suffering under its yoke will only make it draconian and not a facilitator of progress.

9

National Policy for the Empowerment of Women

1.1. The principle of gender equality is enshrined in the Indian Constitution in its Preamble, Fundamental Rights, Fundamental Duties and Directive Principles. The Constitution not only grants equality to women, but also empowers the State to adopt measures of positive discrimination in favour of women.

1.2. Within the framework of a democratic polity, our laws, development policies, Plans and programmes have aimed at women's advancement in different spheres. From the Fifth Five Year Plan (1974–78) onwards has been a marked shift in the approach to women's issues from welfare to development. In recent years, the empowerment of women has been recognised as the central issue in determining the status of women. The National Commission for Women was set up by an Act of Parliament in 1990 to safeguard the rights and legal entitlements of women. The 73rd and 74th Amendments (1993) to the Constitution of India have provided for reservation of seats in the local bodies of Panchayats and Municipalities for women, laying a strong foundation for their participation in decision making at the local levels.

1.3. India has also ratified various international conventions and human rights instruments committing to secure equal rights of women. Key among them is the ratification of the Convention on Elimination of All Forms of Discrimination Against Women (CEDAW) in 1993.

1.4. The Mexico Plan of Action (1975), the Nairobi Forward Looking Strategies (1985), the Beijing Declaration as well as the

Platform for Action (1995) and the Outcome Document adopted by the UNGA Session on Gender Equality and Development and Peace for the 21st century, titled "Further actions and initiatives to implement the Beijing Declaration and the Platform for Action" have been unreservedly endorsed by India for appropriate follow up.

1.5. The Policy also takes note of the commitments of the Ninth Five Year Plan and the other Sectoral Policies relating to empowerment of Women.

1.6. The women's movement and a wide–spread network of non–Government Organisations which have strong grass–roots presence and deep insight into women's concerns have contributed in inspiring initiatives for the empowerment of women.

1.7. However, there still exists a wide gap between the goals enunciated in the Constitution, legislation, policies, plans, programmes, and related mechanisms on the one hand and the situational reality of the status of women in India, on the other. This has been analysed extensively in the Report of the Committee on the Status of Women in India, "Towards Equality", 1974 and highlighted in the National Perspective Plan for Women, 1988–2000, the Shramshakti Report, 1988 and the Platform for Action, Five Years After An assessment"

1.8. Gender disparity manifests itself in various forms, the most obvious being the trend of continuously declining female ratio in the population in the last few decades. Social stereotyping and violence at the domestic and societal levels are some of the other manifestations. Discrimination against girl children, adolescent girls and women persists in parts of the country.

1.9. The underlying causes of gender inequality are related to social and economic structure, which is based on informal and formal norms, and practices.

1.10. Consequently, the access of women particularly those belonging to weaker sections including Scheduled Castes/Scheduled Tribes/ Other backward Classes and minorities, majority of whom are in the rural areas and in the informal, unorganised sector to education, health and productive resources, among others, is inadequate. Therefore, they remain largely marginalised, poor and socially excluded.

Goal and Objectives

1.11. The goal of this Policy is to bring about the advancement, development and empowerment of women. The Policy will be widely disseminated so as to encourage active participation of all stakeholders for achieving its goals. Specifically, the objectives of this Policy include:

(a) Creating an environment through positive economic and social policies for full development of women to enable them to realise their full potential

(b) The *de–jure* and *de facto* enjoyment of all human rights and fundamental freedom by women on equal basis with men in all spheres political, economic, social, cultural and civil

(c) Equal access to participation and decision making of women in social, political and economic life of the nation

(d) Equal access to women to health care, quality education at all levels, career and vocational guidance, employment, equal remuneration, occupational health and safety, social security and public office *etc.*

(e) Strengthening legal systems aimed at elimination of all forms of discrimination against women

(f) Changing societal attitudes and community practices by active participation and involvement of both men and women.

(g) Mainstreaming a gender perspective in the development process.

(h) Elimination of discrimination and all forms of violence against women and the girl child; and

(i) Building and strengthening partnerships with civil society, particularly women's organisations.

Policy Prescriptions

Judicial Legal Systems

2.1. Legal–judicial system will be made more responsive and gender sensitive to women's needs, especially in cases of domestic violence and personal assault. New laws will be enacted and existing laws reviewed to ensure that justice is quick and the punishment meted out to the culprits is commensurate with the severity of the offence.

2.2. At the initiative of and with the full participation of all stakeholders including community and religious leaders, the Policy would aim to encourage changes in personal laws such as those related to marriage, divorce, maintenance and guardianship so as to eliminate discrimination against women.

2.3. The evolution of property rights in a patriarchal system has contributed to the subordinate status of women. The Policy would aim to encourage changes in laws relating to ownership of property and inheritance by evolving consensus in order to make them gender just.

Decision Making

3.1. Women's equality in power sharing and active participation in decision making, including decision making in political process at all levels will be ensured for the achievement of the goals of empowerment. All measures will be taken to guarantee women equal access to and full participation in decision making bodies at every level, including the legislative, executive, judicial, corporate, statutory bodies, as also the advisory Commissions, Committees, Boards, Trusts *etc.* Affirmative action such as reservations/quotas, including in higher legislative bodies, will be considered whenever necessary on a time bound basis. Women–friendly personnel policies will also be drawn up to encourage women to participate effectively in the developmental process.

Mainstreaming a Gender Perspective in the Development Process

4.1. Policies, programmes and systems will be established to ensure mainstreaming of women's perspectives in all developmental processes, as catalysts, participants and recipients. Wherever there are gaps in policies and programmes, women specific interventions would be undertaken to bridge these. Coordinating and monitoring mechanisms will also be devised to assess from time to time the progress of such mainstreaming mechanisms. Women's issues and concerns as a result will specially be addressed and reflected in all concerned laws, sectoral policies, plans and programmes of action.

Economic Empowerment of women

Poverty Eradication

5.1. Since women comprise the majority of the population below the poverty line and are very often in situations of extreme poverty, given the harsh realities of intra–household and social discrimination, macro economic policies and poverty eradication programmes will specifically address the needs and problems of such women. There will be improved implementation of programmes which are already women oriented with special targets for women. Steps will be taken for mobilisation of poor women and convergence of services, by offering them a range of economic and social options, along with necessary support measures to enhance their capabilities

Micro Credit

5.2. In order to enhance women's access to credit for consumption and production, the establishment of new, and strengthening of existing micro–credit mechanisms and micro–finance institution will be undertaken so that the outreach of credit is enhanced. Other supportive measures would be taken to ensure adequate flow of credit through extant financial institutions and banks, so that all women below poverty line have easy access to credit.

Women and Economy

5.3. Women's perspectives will be included in designing and implementing macro–economic and social policies by institutionalising their participation in such processes. Their contribution to socio–economic development as producers and workers will be recognised in the formal and informal sectors (including home based workers) and appropriate policies relating to employment and to her working conditions will be drawn up. Such measures could include: Reinterpretation and redefinition of conventional concepts of work wherever necessary *e.g.* in the Census records, to reflect women's contribution as producers and workers. Preparation of satellite and national accounts.Development of appropriate methodologies for undertaking (i) and (ii) above.

Globalisation

5.4. Globalisation has presented new challenges for the realisation of the goal of women's equality, the gender impact of which has not been systematically evaluated fully. However, from the micro–level studies that were commissioned by the Department of Women and Child Development, it is evident that there is a need for re–framing policies for access to employment and quality of employment. Benefits of the growing global economy have been unevenly distributed leading to wider economic disparities, the feminisation of poverty, increased gender inequality through often deteriorating working conditions and unsafe working environment especially in the informal economy and rural areas. Strategies will be designed to enhance the capacity of women and empower them to meet the negative social and economic impacts, which may flow from the globalisation process.

Women and Agriculture

5.5. In view of the critical role of women in the agriculture and allied sectors, as producers, concentrated efforts will be made to ensure that benefits of training, extension and various programmes will reach them in proportion to their numbers. The programmes for training women in soil conservation, social forestry, dairy development and other occupations allied to agriculture like horticulture, livestock including small animal husbandry, poultry, fisheries *etc.* will be expanded to benefit women workers in the agriculture sector.

Women and Industry

5.6. The important role played by women in electronics, information technology and food processing and agro industry and textiles has been crucial to the development of these sectors. They would be given comprehensive support in terms of labour legislation, social security and other support services to participate in various industrial sectors.

5.7. Women at present cannot work in night shift in factories even if they wish to. Suitable measures will be taken to enable women to work on the night shift in factories. This will be accompanied with support services for security, transportation *etc.*

Support Services

5.8. The provision of support services for women, like child care facilities, including crèches at work places and educational institutions, homes for the aged and the disabled will be expanded and improved to create an enabling environment and to ensure their full cooperation in social, political and economic life. Women friendly personnel policies will also be drawn up to encourage women to participate effectively in the developmental process.

Social Empowerment of Women

Education

6.1. Equal access to education for women and girls will be ensured. Special measures will be taken to eliminate discrimination, universalise education, eradicate illiteracy, create a gender–sensitive educational system, increase enrolment and retention rates of girls and improve the quality of education to facilitate life long learning as well as development of occupation/vocation/technical skills by women. Reducing the gender gap in secondary and higher education would be a focus area. Sectoral time targets in existing policies will be achieved, with a special focus on girls and women, particularly those belonging to weaker sections including the Scheduled Castes/ Scheduled Tribes/Other Backward Classes/Minorities. Gender sensitive curricula would be developed at all levels of educational system in order to address sex stereotyping as one of the causes of gender discrimination.

Health

6.2. A holistic approach to women's health which includes both nutrition and health services will be adopted and special attention will be given to the needs of women and the girl at all stages of the life cycle. The reduction of infant mortality and maternal mortality, which are sensitive indicators of human development, is a priority concern. This policy reiterates the national demographic goals for

Infant Mortality Rate (IMR), Maternal Mortality Rate (MMR) set out in the National Population Policy 2000. Women should have access to comprehensive, affordable and quality health care. Measures will be adopted that take into account the reproductive rights of women to enable them to exercise informed choices, their vulnerability to sexual and health problems together with endemic, infectious and communicable diseases such as malaria, TB, and water borne diseases as well as hypertension and cardio pulmonary diseases. The social, developmental and health consequences of HIV/AIDS and other sexually transmitted diseases will be tackled from a gender perspective.

6.3. To effectively meet problems of infant and maternal mortality, and early marriage the availability of good and accurate data at micro level on deaths, birth and marriages is required. Strict implementation of registration of births and deaths would be ensured and registration of marriages would be made compulsory.

6.4. In accordance with the commitment of the National Population Policy (2000) to population stabilisation, this Policy recognises the critical need of men and women to have access to safe, effective and affordable methods of family planning of their choice and the need to suitably address the issues of early marriages and spacing of children. Interventions such as spread of education, compulsory registration of marriage and special programmes like BSY should impact on delaying the age of marriage so that by 2010 child marriages are eliminated.

6.5. Women's traditional knowledge about health care and nutrition will be recognised through proper documentation and its use will be encouraged. The use of Indian and alternative systems of medicine will be enhanced within the framework of overall health infrastructure available for women.

Nutrition

6.6. In view of the high risk of malnutrition and disease that women face at all the three critical stages viz., infancy and childhood, adolescent and reproductive phase, focussed attention would be paid to meeting the nutritional needs of women at all stages of the life cycle. This is also important in view of the critical link between the health of adolescent girls, pregnant and lactating women with the health of infant and young children. Special efforts will be made to tackle the problem of macro and micro nutrient deficiencies especially amongst pregnant and lactating women as it leads to various diseases and disabilities.

6.7. Intra household discrimination in nutritional matters *vis-a-vis* girls and women will be sought to be ended through appropriate strategies. Widespread use of nutrition education would be made to address the issues of intra household imbalances in nutrition and the special needs of pregnant and lactating women. Women's participation will also be ensured in the planning, superintendence and delivery of the system.

Drinking Water and Sanitation

6.8. Special attention will be given to the needs of women in the provision of safe drinking water, sewage disposal, toilet facilities and sanitation within accessible reach of households, especially in rural areas and urban slums. Women's participation will be ensured in the planning, delivery and maintenance of such services.

Housing and Shelter

6.9. Women's perspectives will be included in housing policies, planning of housing colonies and provision of shelter both in rural and urban areas. Special attention will be given for providing adequate and safe housing and accommodation for women including single women, heads of households, working women, students, apprentices and trainees.

Environment

6.10. Women will be involved and their perspectives reflected in the policies and programmes for environment, conservation and restoration. Considering the impact of environmental factors on their livelihoods, women's participation will be ensured in the conservation of the environment and control of environmental degradation. The vast majority of rural women still depend on the locally available non–

commercial sources of energy such as animal dung, crop waste and fuel wood. In order to ensure the efficient use of these energy resources in an environmental friendly manner, the Policy will aim at promoting the programmes of non conventional energy resources. Women will be involved in spreading the use of solar energy, biogas, smokeless chulahs and other rural application so as to have a visible impact of these measures in influencing eco system and in changing the life styles of rural women.

Science and Technology

6.11. Programmes will be strengthened to bring about a greater involvement of women in science and technology. These will include measures to motivate girls to take up science and technology for higher education and also ensure that development projects with scientific and technical inputs involve women fully. Efforts to develop a scientific temper and awareness will also be stepped up. Special measures would be taken for their training in areas where they have special skills like communication and information technology. Efforts to develop appropriate technologies suited to women's needs as well as to reduce their drudgery will be given a special focus too.

Women in Difficult Circumstances

6.12. In recognition of the diversity of women's situations and in acknowledgement of the needs of specially disadvantaged groups, measures and programmes will be undertaken to provide them with special assistance. These groups include women in extreme poverty, destitute women, women in conflict situations, women affected by natural calamities, women in less developed regions, the disabled widows, elderly women, single women in difficult circumstances, women heading households, those displaced from employment, migrants, women who are victims of marital violence, deserted women and prostitutes *etc.*

Violence against Women

7.1. All forms of violence against women, physical and mental, whether at domestic or societal levels, including those arising from customs, traditions or accepted practices shall be dealt with effectively with a view to eliminate its incidence.

Institutions and mechanisms/schemes for assistance will be created and strengthened for prevention of such violence, including sexual harassment at work place and customs like dowry; for the rehabilitation of the victims of violence and for taking effective action against the perpetrators of such violence. A special emphasis will also be laid on programmes and measures to deal with trafficking in women and girls.

Rights of the Girl Child

8.1. All forms of discrimination against the girl child and violation of her rights shall be eliminated by undertaking strong measures both preventive and punitive within and outside the family. These would relate specifically to strict enforcement of laws against prenatal sex selection and the practices of female foeticide, female infanticide, child marriage, child abuse and child prostitution *etc.* Removal of discrimination in the treatment of the girl child within the family and outside and projection of a positive image of the girl child will be actively fostered. There will be special emphasis on the needs of the girl child and earmarking of substantial investments in the areas relating to food and nutrition, health and education, and in vocational education. In implementing programmes for eliminating child labour, there will be a special focus on girl children.

Mass Media

9.1. Media will be used to portray images consistent with human dignity of girls and women. The Policy will specifically strive to remove demeaning, degrading and negative conventional stereotypical images of women and violence against women. Private sector partners and media networks will be involved at all levels to ensure equal access for women particularly in the area of information and communication technologies. The media would be encouraged to develop codes of conduct, professional guidelines and other self regulatory mechanisms to remove gender stereotypes and promote balanced portrayals of women and men.

Operational Strategies

Action Plans

10.1. All Central and State Ministries will draw up time bound Action Plans for translating the Policy into a set of concrete actions, through a participatory process of consultation with Centre/State Departments of Women and Child Development and National/State Commissions for Women. The Plans will specifically including the following:–

- (i) Measurable goals to be achieved by 2010.
- (ii) Identification and commitment of resources.
- (iii) Responsibilities for implementation of action points.
- (iv) Structures and mechanisms to ensure efficient monitoring, review and gender impact assessment of action points and policies.
- (v) Introduction of a gender perspective in the budgeting process.

10.2. In order to support better planning and programme formulation and adequate allocation of resources, Gender Development Indices (GDI) will be developed by networking with specialised agencies. These could be analysed and studied in depth. Gender auditing and development of evaluation mechanisms will also be undertaken along side.

10.3. Collection of gender disaggregated data by all primary data collecting agencies of the Central and State Governments as well as Research and Academic Institutions in the Public and Private Sectors will be undertaken. Data and information gaps in vital areas reflecting the status of women will be sought to be filled in by these immediately. All Ministries/Corporations/Banks and financial institutions etc will be advised to collect, collate, disseminate and maintain/publish data related to programmes and benefits on a gender disaggregated basis. This will help in meaningful planning and evaluation of policies.

Institutional Mechanisms

11.1. Institutional mechanisms, to promote the advancement of women, which exist at the Central and State levels, will be strengthened.

These will be through interventions as may be appropriate and will relate to, among others, provision of adequate resources, training and advocacy skills to effectively influence macro–policies, legislation, programmes *etc.* to achieve the empowerment of women.

11.2. National and State Councils will be formed to oversee the operationalisation of the Policy on a regular basis. The National Council will be headed by the Prime Minister and the State Councils by the Chief Ministers and be broad in composition having representatives from the concerned Departments/Ministries, National and State Commissions for Women, Social Welfare Boards, representatives of Non–Government Organisations, Women's Organisations, Corporate Sector, Trade Unions, financing institutions, academics, experts and social activists *etc.* These bodies will review the progress made in implementing the Policy twice a year. The National Development Council will also be informed of the progress of the programme undertaken under the policy from time to time for advice and comments.

11.3. National and State Resource Centres on women will be established with mandates for collection and dissemination of information, undertaking research work, conducting surveys, implementing training and awareness generation programmes, *etc.* These Centers will link up with Women's Studies Centres and other research and academic institutions through suitable information networking systems.

11.4. While institutions at the district level will be strengthened, at the grass–roots, women will be helped by Government through its programmes to organise and strengthen into Self–Help Groups (SHGs) at the Anganwadi/Village/Town level. The women's groups will be helped to institutionalise themselves into registered societies and to federate at the Panchyat/Municipal level. These societies will bring about synergistic implementation of all the social and economic development programmes by drawing resources made available through Government and Non–Government channels, including banks and financial institutions and by establishing a close Interface with the Panchayats/ Municipalities.

Resource Management

12.1. Availability of adequate financial, human and market resources to implement the Policy will be managed by concerned Departments, financial credit institutions and banks, private sector, civil society and other connected institutions. This process will include:

(a) Assessment of benefits flowing to women and resource allocation to the programmes relating to them through an exercise of gender budgeting. Appropriate changes in policies will be made to optimise benefits to women under these schemes;

(b) Adequate resource allocation to develop and promote the policy outlined earlier based on (a) above by concerned Departments.

(c) Developing synergy between personnel of Health, Rural Development, Education and Women and Child Development Department at field level and other village level functionaries'

(d) Meeting credit needs by banks and financial credit institutions through suitable policy initiatives and development of new institutions in coordination with the Department of Women and Child Development.

12.2. The strategy of Women's Component Plan adopted in the Ninth Plan of ensuring that not less than 30% of benefits/funds flow to women from all Ministries and Departments will be implemented effectively so that the needs and interests of women and girls are addressed by all concerned sectors. The Department of Women and Child Development being the nodal Ministry will monitor and review the progress of the implementation of the Component Plan from time to time, in terms of both quality and quantity in collabouration with the Planning Commission.

12.3. Efforts will be made to channelise private sector investments too, to support programmes and projects for advancement of women

Legislation

13.1. The existing legislative structure will be reviewed and additional legislative measures taken by identified departments to implement the Policy. This will also involve a review of all existing laws including personal, customary and tribal laws, subordinate legislation, related rules as well as executive and administrative regulations to eliminate all gender discriminatory references. The process will be planned over a time period 2000–2003. The specific measures required would be evolved through a consultation process involving civil society, National Commission for Women and Department of Women and Child Development. In appropriate cases the consultation process would be widened to include other stakeholders too.

13.2. Effective implementation of legislation would be promoted by involving civil society and community. Appropriate changes in legislation will be undertaken, if necessary.

13.3. In addition, following other specific measures will be taken to implement the legislation effectively.

(a) Strict enforcement of all relevant legal provisions and speedy redressal of grievances will be ensured, with a special focus on violence and gender related atrocities.

(b) Measures to prevent and punish sexual harassment at the place of work, protection for women workers in the organised/ unorganised sector and strict enforcement of relevant laws such as Equal Remuneration Act and Minimum Wages Act will be undertaken.

(c) Crimes against women, their incidence, prevention, investigation, detection and prosecution will be regularly reviewed at all Crime Review fora and Conferences at the Central, State and District levels. Recognised, local, voluntary organisations will be authorised to lodge Complaints and facilitate registration, investigations and legal proceedings related to violence and atrocities against girls and women.

(d) Women's Cells in Police Stations, Encourage Women Police Stations Family Courts, Mahila Courts, Counselling Centers, Legal Aid Centers and Nyaya Panchayats will be strengthened and expanded to eliminate violence and atrocities against women.

(e) Widespread dissemination of information on all aspects of legal rights, human rights and other entitlements of women, through specially designed legal literacy programmes and rights information programmes will be done.

Gender Sensitisation

14.1. Training of personnel of executive, legislative and judicial wings of the State, with a special focus on policy and programme framers, implementation and development agencies, law enforcement machinery and the judiciary, as well as non–governmental organisations will be undertaken. Other measures will include:

(a) Promoting societal awareness to gender issues and women's human rights.

(b) Review of curriculum and educational materials to include gender education and human rights issues.

(c) Removal of all references derogatory to the dignity of women from all public documents and legal instruments.

(d) Use of different forms of mass media to communicate social messages relating to women's equality and empowerment.

Panchayati Raj Institutions

15.1. The 73rd and 74th Amendments (1993) to the Indian Constitution have served as a breakthrough towards ensuring equal access and increased participation in political power structure for women. The PRIs will play a central role in the process of enhancing women's participation in public life. The PRIs and the local self Governments will be actively involved in the implementation and execution of the National Policy for Women at the grassroots level.

Partnership with the Voluntary Sector Organisations

16.1. The involvement of voluntary organisations, associations, federations, trade unions, non–governmental organisations, women's organisations, as well as institutions dealing with education, training and research will be ensured in the formulation, implementation, monitoring and review of all policies and programmes affecting women. Towards this end, they will be provided with appropriate support related to resources and capacity building and facilitated to participate actively in the process of the empowerment of women.

International Cooperation

17.1. The Policy will aim at implementation of international obligations/commitments in all sectors on empowerment of women such as the Convention on All Forms of Discrimination Against Women (CEDAW), Convention on the Rights of the Child (CRC), International Conference on Population and Development (ICPD+5) and other such instruments. International, regional and sub–regional cooperation towards the empowerment of women will continue to be encouraged through sharing of experiences, exchange of ideas and technology, networking with institutions and organisations and through bilateral and multi–lateral partnerships.

10

The Effects of Globalisation on Women in Developing Nations

Within the past two decades, globalisation has created a tremendous impact on the lives of women in developing nations. Globalisation can be defined as a complex economic, political, cultural, and geographic process in which the mobility of capital, organisations, ideas, discourses, and peoples has taken a global or transnational form. With the establishment of international free trade policies, such as North America Free Trade Agreement (NAFTA) and GATT, transnational corporations are using the profit motive to guide their factories toward developing nations in search of "cheap" female labour. Corporations prefer female labor over male labor because women are considered to be "docile" workers, who are willing to obey production demands at any price. In developing nations, certain types of work, such as garment assembly, is considered to be an extension of female household roles. Therefore, cultural influences in developing nations also impacts employment stratification.

Bringing a high demand of employment opportunities for women in developing nations creates an instantaneous change within the social structure of these societies. Although the demand for female employment brings about an array of opportunities and a sense of independence, the glass ceiling continues to exist with the "feminisation of poverty". Researchers in the fields of Sociology, Anthropology, and Economics have collected empirical data that shows the consequences of globalisation on the lives of women and their families in developing nations. Given these circumstances and the empirical evidence collected in the various studies, does globalisation have an overall positive or negative impact on the live of women in developing nations?

Economic Globalisation

The world economic market depends on the flow of imports and exports between developed and developing nations. Throughout history, developing nations are faced with the lack of capital for the internal development of their country. Deficient funds also puts limitations on the amount of imports transferred from developed to developing nations. In order to stabilise the flow of international capital, the World Bank and International Monetary Fund (IMF) enforce structural adjustment loans (SALs) in developing nations.

The amount of power and influence over the World Bank and IMF depends on the amount of capital being invested into the World Bank. The United States has an extremely large amount of capital invested into the World Bank, and is therefore a major instrument in determining the actions and procedures taken by the IMF and World Bank.

The IMF creates "one sided structural adjustments involving the destruction of real economic activity as well as attempts to construct new forms of production bit without a corresponding destruction of financial capital and without a reconstruction of international financial flows". Structural adjustments are mainly the privatisation of exports in developing nations. SALs were first exercised in African and Latin American countries "as a result of the debt crisis of the early 1980s". Corporations and the World Bank wanted to prevent the future loss of capital from overseas investments. They decided to work collectively with foreign governments to develop a World Market that would ensure high productivity rates and profit gains from developing nations. Investors felt that developing nations were incapable of surviving in the World Market without the aid of developed nations.

As a result, several industries (i.e.: agriculture and clothing) in developing countries were privatised by corporations (such as Nabisco and Ann Taylor). Privatisation, which causes a dependence on imports from developed nations because the loans from the World

Bank, is used to support export factories and can not be distributed to support local firms that don't have an international affiliation.

Structural adjustments also involve "cuts in public expenditure, reductions in public sector employment, higher prices for food and other crops, and reductions in the role of government intervention in the economy". Rather than allowing developing nations to spend the loans on healthcare, education, and other "quality of life" improvement projects, the World Bank and IMF are primarily concerned with debt repayment and creating profits for corporations in developed countries. Structural adjustments cause a cyclic pattern of dependence of developing nations upon the World Bank for monetary funding. SALs allow transnational corporations the freedom to enter into developing nations and take advantage of the labor force, while stripping these countries of the chance to become autonomous. Desperate for loans from the World Bank, mainly to pay off debts and buy imported goods, developing nations are willing to sell off vital aspects of their country (land, resources, and labor) to the World Market.

Capitalism motivates corporations towards countries that provide the most labour or resources at the cheapest cost. Corporations have changed the employment structure in developing nations. Prior to development, men and women relied on agricultural production as their main source of occupation. Upon entering these nations, corporations have created a sectoral shift in the labor force from the agricultural sector, to working in assembly production. Empirical evidence shows that there has been a significant decline in male agricultural work "from 62% to 14%... and a similar decline in agriculture for women". Despite this trend, assembly production is dominated entirely by a female labour force, with the exception of managers and foremen.

Corporations desire female labour for assembly production because women will "work in labour-intensive industries at wages lower than men would accept, and in conditions that unions would not permit". Females are attracted to assembly production because of the lack of opportunities for female employment in other industries (aside from the informal sector). The main reason for this lack of employment is gender employment segregation, which subjects women to inferior employment positions than those held by men. When comparing occupations, "nearly two-thirds of women in manufacturing are categorised as laborers, operators and production workers while only a few can be found in the administrative and managerial positions predominantly held by men". Corporations are reinforcing women's subordinate economic position in society by offering them inferior employment positions and wages that sustain this position.

During the 1960s Fairchild Camera and Instrument Corporation "was among the earliest corporations to expand their production overseas to Hong Kong". Other corporations followed this overseas trend, taking their export production plants to other developing countries such as: Mexico, South Korea, Hong Kong, the Philippines, India, Bangladesh, Malaysia, Honduras, Guatemala, and several other developing nations. Capitalist competition among various corporations sparked their interest in cheap labour overseas, which enables them to gain higher profits from cheaper production costs. Corporations are required to pay American Workers, at least, minimum wage (which varies according to state).

A female assembly line worker in the U.S. would probably earn "between $3.10- $5.00 an hour," whereas, a female assembly worker in a developing nation, doing the same work, would earn $3.10-$5.00 for the entire day's work. Despite these numbers, "wages earned in export factories are also usually higher than what they could earn as wage laborers in alternative low-skilled female occupations, such as farm labour, and domestic service...". These wages allow women and their families to provide more household items (i.e. television), than alternative occupation wages.

Therefore, the increase in factory wages over other forms of employment is a major influence on young females for choosing factory employment over the alternatives. This huge variation in the amount of wages earned between developed nations and developing nations has also created competition in developing nations over which country will work for the lowest wage. Corporations realise that inhabitants of developing countries are living under poverty-stricken conditions and are desperate for employment. While thousands of factory workers are living in poverty, multinational corporate leaders would rather "place their own profit and growth ahead of the needs of their host countries". Rather than bringing their production factories to countries that need the most economic assistance, corporations are merely concerned with which country can allow the corporation to make the highest profit from their labor and resources.

Most corporations insist that the wages distributed to the female factory workers in developing nations are enough for them to support themselves and their families. Some researchers have found that, "the minimum wage in most East Asian and Latin American countries comes nowhere near to covering basic living costs". Corporations have argued that the cost of living is cheaper in developing nations; therefore the lower wages allow developing families to survive on a subsistence level income. Medical benefits and educational assistance for children are not offered in work packages. Factory workers have to finance these needs from their weekly wages. What type of data source are the corporate analysts who are making these claims using? Are they looking at the average cost of food, clothing, healthcare, and education in their assessment?

Gloria Scott, head of the World Bank's Women and Development Program, claims that "our job is to help eliminate poverty in developing nations ... and it is not our responsibility if the multinationals come in and offer such low wages". This statement shows the extent to which the World Bank is willing to go to help developing nations. From this statement, it appears that they are unable to make the correlation between low wages and poverty. The officials at the World Bank are not as naïve at former statement made by Gloria Scott. They are aware of the fact that low wages contributes to poverty and continuous loans will further the debt of developing nations to the World Bank. The World Bank is not working towards the needs of developing nations. They are only concerned with corporate investments and how production costs in developing nations affect the economies of developed nations.

Offshore sourcing enables corporations to avoid the wage, health, safety, and environmental policies of developed nations. The United Nations Industrial Development Organisation (UNIDO) and the U.S. Agency for International Development (AID) work closely with the IMF and World Bank to ensure that developing countries base their economies on the reliance of corporations for employment and survival in the World Market. Foreign governments drop "protective trade barriers... and...offers tax incentives" to investors in order to attract corporations and their factories to developing countries. Subcontracting arrangements are available to corporations, which allow corporations that don't want to own their own factory, the opportunity to establish production contracts with local firms.

Throughout the developing world, "there are over one million people employed in industrial free trade zones (FTZs)". Free Trade Zones (FTZs) are areas within developing nations where there is "customs free import of raw materials, components and equipment, tax holidays of up to 20 yrs and government subsidisation of operating costs". Workers are treated like prisoners entering a penitentiary with high walls topped with barbed wire and a special police force that searches anyone leaving or entering the FTZ. Employees and supervisors are the only ones permitted with FTZs. If anyone is caught trespassing, they are subject to arrest and/or physical punishment by the police. The conditions within the zone are not publicly disclosed due to the lack of humanitarian treatment towards workers.

The lack of protective tariffs allows corporations to take advantage of female workers. Aside from low wages, women are also subjected to work in hazardous conditions that can cause health problems. The film entitled, The Hidden Face of Globalisation (2003), discusses the effects of globalisation and free trade on women in Bangladesh. All of the garment workers are young women who work long, tedious hours in order to support their families. Lengthy work hours and pressures to meet work quotas have caused nervous breakdowns in several female factory workers. Workers in textile factories are exposed to dust and lint which can cause lung disease. Electronic factory workers are exposed to carcinogenic chemicals without proper ventilation or tools to handle the dangerous materials. The Hidden Face of Globalisation (2003) also states that factory workers are rarely given breaks during the day and cannot afford to take sick days. Corporations, such as Sears and JCPenny, employ local subcontractors in developing nations that "show little concern for the health of their employees". Corporate leaders in the U.S. are using the "out of sight, out of mind" policy in regards to their factory workers. The corporate leaders use local subcontractors to carry out their "dirty work" and expedite the necessary force required to make profits from factory production.

The Hidden Face of Globalisation (2003) also shows how female factory workers in FTZs are treated in terms of maintaining quota deadlines. The women are constantly verbally and physically abused in order to keep up with production demands from corporations. One woman in the film claimed that even though she was sick she had to continue working. Women are dying from working under such hazardous conditions. In Taiwan, "12 women died from inhaling toxic fumes at a Philco-Ford plant".

If corporations use portions of their profit to renovate factories and make them safer for workers, their production rates and the quality of goods produced might increase. A healthier work environment might also alleviate the physical abuse that some workers are exposed to because of slow production rates. Free trade zones make it difficult for workers to unionise in order to attain their basic rights because of the lack protective social and economic policies. Since the governments of developing nations are restricted from creating trade regulation laws in free trade zones, workers have the arduous task of negotiating with the corporations that entered into their country in order to gain social and economic justice.

Unfortunately, corporations have made unionisation in free trade zones an almost unattainable task. The Jamaicans in the film Life or Debt (2001) also work in garment factories which are located in free trade zones. The conditions are similar to those in Bangladesh because workers who want to unionise are fired from their jobs. The film also mentioned that workers who try to begin a radical movement are blacklisted and cannot work in other factories.

Other researchers have found that although "working conditions, and job security in the export factories are inferior to those in the developed countries, they are comparable if not superior to those found in women's (and even men's) jobs in most other sectors of these still poor, underdeveloped local economies". Women working in larger, modern factories have better opportunities for unionisation.

They are more capable than smaller factory workers to organise a political demonstration, such as a strike, to negotiate more rights. It is important to understand that when analysing the economic conditions in developing nations, entirely Western views of social justice is liable to skew the data presented about working conditions and wages. Although women are subjected to certain terms and conditions, they are a significant improvement from traditional and alternative employment opportunities in these nations. The introduction of factory employment has improved the economic status for several families, even in the slightest way, as compared to other forms of employment.

Regardless of the advantage of earning more capital in manufacturing industries, "the wages earned are often insufficient to support a family". Based on the literature, females hold a secondary status compared to males in the household and work environment. Therefore, although women in export factories are likely to be paid higher wages than women who are farm workers, the wages are not enough to keep them from depending on the financial support of males in their family.

Economically, the denial of union rights contributes to poverty in developing nations and reinforces the imperialistic domination of developed nations over developing nations. Clearly then, structural adjustments are instruments of capitalistic imperialism over developing countries. They are not meant to develop the economies of developing nations. The dependency theory states that the "intrusion of Western capitalism destroys the self-sufficiency of Third World economies, loots them of resources, and blocks the ripening of diversified capitalist development". The inability of female factory workers to generate enough capital to support themselves and their families shows that until wages increase and better working conditions are available, the economies of developing nations will continue to exist in poverty.

How can developing nations end this cycle of debt repayment and cease the amount of poverty within each nation? Idealistically, the solution to this matter would include workers being paid higher wages, the enactment of trade taxes, and the ability for each developing nation to produce a stable internal economy that does not rely solely on imports. Realistically, the world market is designed in terms of "winners and losers." Developed nations are not going to allow developing nations to become economically independent because their goods and services are important assets to the wealthy economies of developed nations. Reducing the amount of interest owed to the World Bank is probably one of the first steps that should be taken to reducing poverty and the amount of debts owed to the World Bank.

Developing nations can also alleviate social and economic problems by imposing taxes on corporations for using their goods and services. This next step might be more of a challenge to achieve because of the corporate profit motive. The IMF, World Bank, and corporations have imposed a false consciousness over the governments of developing nations and their workers. Economically, developing nations are forced to believe that they must accept the ban on restrictive trade laws and compete with other nations in offering the cheapest labor. If developing nations enact a standard trade tax or wage system, dependent on the specific country's GNP and GDP, developing nations would receive an increase in revenue that might help them to create a stable economy.

Even with the imposition of higher wages and taxes, developed nations would still be paying an extremely discounted rate for the production of their goods-compared to the cost of employment in developed countries. If the IMF and World Bank negotiate a set total for the amount of debt each country owes, less the interest rate, developing nations would be able to pay off their debt. They can use the increased wage and tax revenue to manage import payments and promote social programs such as: healthcare, education, retirement plans and environmental protection. The debt issue is a major obstacle in the path of developing nations to improve their economies. With the alleviation of the debt cycle, developing nations will be able to improve the quality of life in their countries.

Production rates and working conditions are other concerns for factory workers. Corporations assume that orders can be produced in a short time span. They only take into consideration the amount of sales they are making on their merchandise. Rush orders are expected to arrive in perfect quality and condition, within the short time frame given. Are corporate leaders aware of the amount of hours needed in order to produce a rush shipment? Do corporate leaders equate factory workers with machines? Workers are "burnt out" from the pressure to meet their deadlines. Slaving in a factory for long hours without sleep has literally forced young women into retirement mostly due to health related injuries.

Creating a ventilated work environment with proper lightening is just the beginning. Advanced technological equipment and the necessary equipment to handle hazardous goods can also decrease work related injury, while increasing the rate of production. Corporations should track and forecast their sales more carefully, in order to space out their factory orders and ensure the required delivery rate. If rush orders are necessary, factory foremen might consider hiring temporary or part-time workers to meet the quota. A rational means of increasing production would entail hiring more workers, rather than enforcing longer work hours to complete the quota. The addition of temporary workers can relieve the pressure from full time workers to meet their deadlines. Therefore, healthier working conditions would exist in the factory and a new class of temporary/part-time workers would become an addition to the developing nations' economies. Given these alternatives, corporations can increase their production rates while assisting with the development of developing nations.

Despite these alternatives, a major problem in terms of production cost is libel to occur. Corporations might continue to scout from country to country in search of the cheapest labour and taxes on exports. Setting a standard price per industry might help to alleviate this unfair form of competition. What about FTZs? Since FTZs are a major source of corporate attraction to developing nations, they should continue to exist with the enforcement of taxes and policies to ensure the rights of workers and the nation's economy. The zones should be changed to "discounted trade zones" and only allow corporations to work there for a limited time and then move their production to regular export factories. Workers with the least experience should work in DTZs and promoted to regular export factories upon accelerated experience and skill level. Temporary and part -time workers can also be added to these zones to accommodate large shipments and rush orders. The temporary workforce might consist of young women looking for employment who have other responsibilities that prevent them from working full-time or older women who have surpassed the desirable age for factory employment but still want to contribute to the finances within the household. Clearly, economic globalisation has the potential to create a variety of changes within the social structure of developing nations. In what ways has economic globalisation contributed to the cultural changes within developing nations?

Cultural Globalisation

The culture of female employment in developing nations is based on "formal labour, housework, and informal-sector production". Only a small proportion of women work in export factories compared to the entire female population. Most work in agriculture, perform housework, or are employed in the informal sector. Females in these nations are limited in society by patriarchal control. These societies claim that female labour is an extension of their household chores. This ideology is "interwoven in the capitalist economy to justify women's subordination on the global assembly line, in the home and informal sector". Regardless of which sector of employment women are working in, they are given limited access to resources and authority over their work.

Informal sector work "provides the intermediate link between formal waged labour and unpaid house work in that it...is unprotected waged labour...that enables...the survival and maintenance of ..families". Employment opportunities within the informal sector are also stratified according to gender. Like the formal sector, males hold supervisory positions, while females are simply subcontracted workers. Women perform informal assembly work in their homes (done by most women) or factories as methods of survival. Working in the home allows women "to care for their children...and to retain control over the profits of their labor". Most women who choose this option are housewives who do not receive enough money from their husbands to pay for the basic necessities for their family's survival (i.e. food and clothing). These women cannot seek formal sector employment due to their family responsibilities within the household. Informal/ domestic jobs also provide a survival strategy for women dealing with husbands who don't want to contribute enough of their wages to provide for the families.

Although women may feel a sense of empowerment, their wages are substantially low in comparison to their male counterparts. Also, "women have the smallest shops, are the least able to compete in the informal-sector and are subject to more government inspections than men". The glass ceiling also exists in developing nations. Women are given a "taste" of independence that does not allow them to ascend to the same managerial positions as men. The fact that male supervisors believe that garment assembly is an extension of "female work" at home, causes supervisors to stigmatise all women as labors rather promote them to managers. They are confined to these positions because of gender roles and expectations. However, "unemployed...men refused to participate in their wives' informal work because they felt they could be called away at any time for a waged job". This double standard causes women in developing nations to develop a double role of survival. The informal-sector enables women to maintain these roles without the dependence of her husband's assistance.

There are other household issues that occur in relation to wages and survival. As mentioned earlier, several women seek informal jobs because their husbands are not contributing enough of their wages to ensure the family's survival. These men "simply reduce the amount of money they transfer to their wives so as to be able to maintain their preexisting level of alcohol and tobacco consumption". Why do men appear to be disconnected with their responsibilities to maintain the household? Alcohol and tobacco consumption usually leads to domestic arguments and is associated with domestic violence against women and children... because the men would often beat up the women and children to demand money for drinks". Men's addiction to alcohol and tobacco leads them to resort to using the money allocated towards household expenses after they have spent the money set aside for personal expenses. Does socialisation play an important role in this situation? Since gender expectations allocated women as caregivers and domestic workers, do men feel detached from household responsibilities? Does the media play a role in the male consumption of alcohol and tobacco? Men may use these devises as a form of relaxation from a long day at work. If males spend more time with their families they might develop a closer bond to them that might limit their alcohol and tobacco intake.

Unfortunately, this alternative is a challenge to achieve. Several males would rather desert their families than give up alcohol or tobacco. Although this reduces the expenses within the household, females hold a subordinate position in society and are forced to depend on a man for adequate survival. The "number of women headed households relying on insufficient and unstable remittances is reported to have grown". Family abandonment by males can be another reason for the advancement of poverty in developing nations. The unequal gender wages and limited access to resources puts women in a disadvantaged position towards the survival of the families.

Another problem that exists among women in developing nations is that "unpaid domestic tasks are private rather than social and because they are both unpaid and private, there is no social system of incentives, of rewards and penalties, to encourage change. Women whose daily lives are centered around housework are solely dependent on their husbands for financial support. They do not have access to the public sector that will enable them to enter the market. The lack of assistance towards women who perform housework, places them in a vulnerable position in relation to their husbands. They might feel obligated to their husbands for financial needs and possibly withstand cases of abuse in order to provide for their families.

In Malay Islamic societies, men are given authority over their wives because "women are believed to be particularly weak in spiritual essence...a condition which makes women susceptible to irrational and disruptive behaviour". The motif of female weakness transcends through Malay society. Are females themselves weak or do social institutions promote female weakness? Females who are deserted by their husbands appear to be weak because they are unable to provide the basic necessities to their family. Their inability to meet their children's needs is a result of the lack of social services and employment opportunities available to women. Why are men being paid more and given more opportunities if family responsibilities are assigned to women? In this instance, aren't the males exhibiting irrational and disruptive behavior by ignoring their familial responsibilities?

Women are showing their strength by taking responsibility for their family after their husbands leave. Women in the informal sector are also showing their strength by taking on assembly employment, while managing their familial responsibilities. The governments of developing nations are denying women the opportunities to expand their strength to their fullest potential. If men are afraid that giving women opportunities for advancement would decrease male power, they have already done so by disassociating themselves from the family unit. Men might feel that buying tobacco, alcohol, or abandoning their families are forms of domination over women, but females have found ways to support their families. Either through support networks or informal employment, women are using their strength to overcome obstacles. What if governments in developing nations developed a social services system to further assist the survival of families?

A welfare system, like the on in the United States, is nonexistent in developing nations because of the lack of capital devoted to public expenditure. The implementation of a welfare system would give women financial support, healthcare, and access to employment. Women working in the informal sector have an advantage over domestic workers because they are able to earn an income to contribute to the survival of their family. Do support networks also cater to women who perform domestic household work? Clearly women who perform this type of work are dependent on their husbands for financial security, since they are unable to provide a source of revenue.

How are these women able to support their families if their husbands spend a large portion of their income on alcohol and tobacco? What about the domestic workers who are abandoned by their husbands? The implementation of a welfare system would enable these women to recover from these scenarios and support their families. Corporations, the IMF and World Bank fail to investigate the social effects of economic globalisation on the cultures in developing nations. Do they believe that economic effects will not change the culture within these nations? If the quality of life in developing nations deteriorates due to the lack of social services, will that also have an adverse effect on the market? The health of labourers in developing nations is already withering away without the necessary access to healthcare or other facilities. Corporations are oblivious to the fact that children in developing nations are the future labourers.

If they are denied the basic necessities in life, how many of them will survive to adulthood? Although families in developing nations tend to be large, mainly due to the lack of birth control usage, there might be a significant decline in the number of family members do to illness or malnutrition. The women working in export factories are already exhibiting the adverse effects of the lack of healthcare. If their children are the next victims, who will carry out the future labour in factories? Corporations will lose money due to the decline in labor to produce merchandise for the World Market. Knowing the dangers that are associated with export factories, why are so many young women still attracted to this form of labour?

According to the literature, females' subordinate status in developing society shows a correlation with their motivation toward factory employment. Young, school aged females are socialised to be passive and obedient in the classroom. In contrast, boys are encouraged to be leaders in the classroom and in class projects. In May lay cultures, males and females have to take an exam to proceed from primary to secondary school. Males who pass the exam, usually attend vocational or technical to prepare for industrial jobs. Unfortunately for young women, "form three is the end of their school career...corporations take advantage of this by encouraging school trips to the local FTZ after students have sat for their Form Three exams".

From this study, it is apparent that females are kept in a subordinate position in society by the incorporation of assembly production into their young lives. Although a few females passed the Form Three exam and went on to further their education, "for most girls, however, Form Three is the end of their school career". Girls who move on to higher levels of education are also motivated towards factory production but often become dissatisfied with "work conditions and... look for better employment opportunities elsewhere". From this evidence, it appears that women with more educational opportunities have more options for earning a living than females with a limited educational background. Why are more females than males likely to fail the Form Three exams?

Based on the literature, young girls are given household chores and are required to assist with childcare, whereas boys, spend their "free time... on extracurricular school activities". Young females have to perform domestic chores in the house such as: cleaning and cooking, in addition to attending school and doing homework. Therefore, "their gradually increasing participation in these socially reproductive activities interferes with their... performance in school". Several females are unable to maintain a balance between household and school work responsibilities. Upholding strong family bonds become a major goal in a female's life and it eventually causes her to lose focus on school. In contrast, males are relieved from these responsibilities and use their free time towards the benefit of their education. The exam itself is tailored towards males. In several cases in the literature, the courses necessary to pass the exam are: "carpentry, agriculture, and domestic science. Females usually do not enroll in the first two courses because they are considered "masculine" subjects. Domestic science is also not taken because females are assumed to learn domestic responsibilities from their mothers and other roles performed at home. Therefore, females usually drop out of school because of this educational disadvantage.

In addition to household responsibilities and educational disadvantages, "the presence of the FTZ just down the road from the school also exerts an indirect influence on the poor performance of females students in secondary education". Females from poor families feel obligated to helping with the household finances and often choose to work in the FTZ as a means of survival. In comparison, young men, who "are engaged in wage employment ... ... often resist making a regular contribution to the family budget because of their privileged status at home".

As mentioned before, males are more likely than females to earn higher wages. Why is women's work considered a means of survival, while males' work is considered to be privileged? Again, there is a pattern of household dependence on females and the lack of financial responsibility on the behalf of males in the household. The "family economy ideology" seen among poor families, reinforces patriarchal values which state that women should hold a limited/ restricted position in society. Young women in Taiwan also end their educational career at an early age and are "socialised to be filial and to pay back the debt they incurred to their parents for brining them up". Females have to repay their debt before getting married, which usually occurs at an early age. Therefore, since females are considered to be "short-term members 'of the family, parents did not 'waste time in schooling them". This is a clear example of the lack of opportunities to females in Taiwan. Not only do most young women lack the educational background to advance in society, they are also considered to be less important to the family unit than males because of marital factors. Treating females as subordinates to males within the family unit transcends throughout other institutions within society (especially education and employment).

Females are also unable to advance because they relinquish their wages as a means of supporting the family. Retaining a portion of their wages would allow females to have more authority over their personal spending. However, research performed in Java shows that young men were motivated towards factory employment based on "individual social and economic reasons, not for the betterment of the family economy". Factory work in Java is considered to be a "higher status" job in comparison to agricultural labour. Women prefer working in factories than on farms because it frees them from the restrictions of familial control. Compared with agricultural work, several females felt that factory was easier and provided a better income. Factory work also brought females "into contact with males and females from other villages, which often led to romances and gave them some earnings of their own. Female workers enjoyed earning their own wages because it gave them the freedom to purchase "clothing, consumer goods for the household, and their wages were also made accessible to their parents for life-cycle events (birth, death, marriage,...)". Their low wages caused females to be somewhat dependent on their families, while allowing them the independence of attaining certain goods or tasks. Javanese female factory workers also have more autonomy over choosing their own spouse as opposed to traditional arranged marriages. Therefore, the remittance of wages, according to the literature, varies from one culture to another where some females are more autonomous than others.

Working in export factories also has several other cultural effects on women's lives in developing nations. Sexual harassment "is another hazard of factory work, especially for women who are out late at night working the graveyard shift". According to the literature, women in the Bataan Export Processing Zone in the Philippines are faced with common encounters of harassment from male supervisors. Workers are "often told to lay down or be laid off". Women often feel that they have to given in to their supervisors sexual advances in order to keep their jobs. Some women began to wonder "what they've gotten themselves into". Women wanted to know whether or not independence and earning their own wages was worth being subjected to unwanted sexual advances.

Another effect of women working in factories is that "westernised dress and changed lifestyles... often cause women to be ...rejected by their families and find it hard to reassimilate when they can no longer find employment on the assembly line". Factory workers exhibit a different lifestyle compared to informal and agriculture workers. Although factory workers are still bound to domestic responsibilities, working in an FTZ or other export factories introduces western cultural values such as dating and delaying marriage. When factory workers can no longer find work on the assembly line, it is difficult for them to make the transition back into mainstream society and incorporate the same values they tried to escape from by working in export factories.

Another effect of export factories surrounds "the issue of women workers morality which is debated by several women's groups, politicians, and community leaders in several Asian countries". Female factory workers are thought to be sexually explicit-especially those who don't live at home. Female workers "are often scorned by men as unsuitable marriage partners". Female workers also spend most of their youth working in factories -the age that most women in developing societies get married. Female workers are usually faced with competition over husbands once they leave the assembly line. Based on this data, factory work appears to be a temporary form of independence for young women in developing nations. Although some women enjoy the freedom of delaying marriage, they soon realise that this form of independence might actually be a burden because finding a husband later in life is not as easy as in their youth. As mentioned earlier, dependence on a husband for survival is common among developing nations. Even though female factory workers are able to gain limited independence and autonomy over their expenditures, they have to return to mainstream society and get married in order to survive.

Corporations target young female workers without thinking about the cultural changes that they create within developing societies. Based on the literature, it appears that these females live a "westernised fantasy" by working in export factories. Corporations are imposing ethnocentric values (independence both financial and socially) upon factory workers, without consideration for the implications that result from these value adjustments. The fact that female workers who leave the factories are forced to look for husbands in order to survive in society, makes it seem as though the efforts of these women to gain their independence were merely a waste of time. Corporations might be using the independence factor to lure young women into their factories. Nevertheless, females are still subjected to a subordinate status in society once they leave the export factories. How can women reclaim this form of independence without depending on the males in developing nations for support?

Political Globalisation

Women in various communities throughout developing nations have created self help groups that "might provide a springboard to transformation if...women were redirected toward women's strategic gender needs as well as toward their practical gender needs". Although women cannot prevent their husbands from leaving, they have joined together to address the problems in the public service sector, including: "housing, schools, nurseries, transport, social security, and hospitals". As mentioned earlier, the SALs require cuts in public expenditure. Therefore, poor women and children are unable to gain adequate access to the resources mentioned above. Women and children are suffering from the results of this inequality, as well as the effects of economic globalisation. Since women are becoming the heads of households, shouldn't the government acknowledge this form of social change and give them more access to resources?

Community support groups were somewhat successful in their attempts to implement prohibition in India. They've managed to reduce the amount of women being abused by their husbands over the consumption of alcohol. It is important to remember that "the degree to which survival and transformation strategies can be successful depends heavily on what happens to the international financial system". Women will continue to work in the informal sector, with or without the help of their husbands, to support their families. The only way for women to gain access to increased wages or social services is to reform the system that maintains their subordinate position.

Joining together and forming support groups is a step in the right direction towards achieving more rights for women. Breaking through inequalities is the next step in the process towards achieving more rights for women in society. Starting at the local level is important for women in developing nations because it enables more workers to join forces and create an awareness of women's needs throughout their country. These women share common backgrounds such as: abuse, poverty, and lack of adequate wages and resources. Creating support groups unites women towards a common goal in achieving more rights. The governments within developing nations should become aware that while males are being given more rights, wages, and access to resources, they are using these rights frivolously. Women are responsible for most of the household necessities and should be compensated in order to meet these needs.

During the U.N.'s Decade for Women (1976-85), women's groups from across international boundaries came together to discuss the impact of development on women in developing countries. Three goals that derived out of The Decade in order to reduce women's oppressed position in developing nations are: "Equality which was seen primarily as a feminist issue coming from Western industrialised countries, Peace which was included at the request of the Eastern Socialist bloc and Development which was perceived as key to the Third World countries of the South". Feminism is the main foundation of these goals, which essentially want to address and resolve the pressing issue of domination over the lives of women around the world.

The U.N. Decade sparked the "development of global feminism... where women of the North and South the diversity and commonality of our lives and about how to 'develop a global perspective with each of our movements' on all the issues that affect women". The organisations that attended The Decade discussed the male bias in development that fails to consider women's needs. Women are not considered in development projects because of the patriarchal "persistence in looking at women only in their roles as mothers, 'rather than as active agents,' workers, and managers of resources". An example of this scenario exists in Peru, where women are unable to access water for their daily chores because the male who has sole access to the water pump, works in the fields during the day. If a woman was in charge of the pump, women in the village would have adequate access to the water needed to complete their daily chores. Giving women power over their daily chores would advance their positions in society.

The literature also states that there are two long term goal of feminism: "1) the achievement of women's equality, dignity, and freedom of choice through women's power to control their own lives within and outside the home and 2) the removal of all forms of inequality and oppression through the creation of a more just social and economic order, nationally and internationally. In regards to formal and informal employment, women's work should be rewarded with wages and benefits that would enable them to support themselves and their family. Creating a just social and economic order will allow more women to further their education and to obtain managerial and technical positions. Allowing women who have worked in a certain industry to be promoted to managerial or higher level employment would also enable them to earn more wages to support their families. As mentioned earlier, females are the main providers for their families since males tend to spend their money on other means. Realising this cultural factor and allocating higher paying jobs to females, would release their dependency on males for financial support. Although The U.N. Decade established these essential goals to end the subordination of women, individual NGOs and grassroots organisations are tailored towards addressing specific issues surrounding development.

Transnational solidarity networks, which are comprised of: "unions, movements, NGOs of local women working in ... export processing zones... as well as middle-class activists from the country and transnational NGO movements," are formed when individual organisations work together with other organisations towards a common issue. Women Working Worldwide, The Clean Clothes Campaign, Label Behind the Label, and DAWN (Development Alternatives with Women for a New Era) are examples of NGOs that are working to protect the rights for factory workers and strive to improve factory conditions.

These NGOs incorporate "consumer education as a part of their advocacy network..." in order to raise public awareness about the inequalities that exist in developing nations. Educating consumers might encourage them to support these NGOs or petition corporations for their inhumane practices against women in developing countries.

As mentioned earlier, the informal sector continues to play an important role in the survival of women in developing nations. The "Self-Employed Women's Association (SEWA) in India was one of the first organisations to define the various informal activities of women, such as vegetable vending, ragpicking and producing goods at home for sale as work". SEWA has been successful in unionising informal workers in India and establishing a university to train women to become leaders. SEWA continues to empower women in India, allowing them to maintain control over various aspects of their daily lives. Another issue facing women in developing nations is the privatisation of healthcare. As mentioned earlier privatisation "has greatly reduced government funded primary care, thus limiting the access... of healthcare to women...". The Centre for Enquiry into Health and Allied Themes (CEHAT) in India conducts research on women's health in India and provides health services to poor communities. Health Watch, which derived out of CEHAT, strives toward a "more woman centered approach to reproduction and eliminated the quotas that local health practitioners had to meet for population control". At the population conference in Cairo, the declaration emphasised that "the need to empower women and protect their human rights is the best strategy of population control". Giving women more employment opportunities and power over their reproductive health will enable women to make more decisions in terms of family planning.

The environmental movement is another cause that has derived out of development. Deforestation and desertification caused by the increased need of natural resources in globalisation has created several obstacles in the lives of women in developing nations. For women "in the Third World, destruction of the environment means that women have to spend more time every day to gather wood for fuel, fodder for cattle, and fetch drinking water". Spending more time on these chores results in less time spent on production in the informal sector. Therefore, women are not able to produce enough goods to ensure a sustainable income or maintain rural land development. The Fundacion Ecuatoriana de Tecnologia Approproda, CENDA, and activists in Greenbelt, Kenya are focusing their attention on the environmental justice movement. Their goals include reforestation and the development of rural farming communities. The redevelopment of land will enable women to increase their production and possibly their household income.

The Central American Network of Women in Solidarity with Maquila Workers (The Network) "is made up of autonomous women's organisations from: Guatemala, Honduras, Nicaragua, and El Salvador" that strive towards the empowerment of women in Central America. Women in garment factories usually produce clothing in a "piecemeal" manner. Therefore, women cannot individually assemble one article of clothing. A Honduran organisation in The Network organised a workshop that provided women with the basic skills to sew their own clothes. These workshops are essential economic components to women because they allow women to sew their own clothing for their large families.

The Network also seeks to improve the wage and working conditions for women in all sectors of the economy in Central America. Their methods for improvement include "negation, lobbying, media campaigns, and electronically disseminated action alerts". The network also maintains records of human rights violations and other labour conditions of their research in factories. The Network uses careful tactics while lobbying so that they don't urge factories to the point of relocation. This "greatly limits The Network's ability to engage in the kinds of political maneuvering that have been successful for other transnational advocacy networks, such as international boycotts...". According to the literature, the Honduran Factory KIMI allowed member of The Network and other organisations to monitor the assembly production of the highly publicised Kathy Lee line of clothing. The Network used the media to gain attention to this factory and was successful in their attempts to monitor the factory conditions. Kathy Lee was in a position where relocation was not an option because if she did, the media would expose the conditions in the new factory. Therefore, NGOs have a significant impact of the lives of women in developing nations and offer women a form of support and protection against unfair conditions.

Conclusion

Globalisation has reduced the ability of women... in developing nations...to find paid work that offers security and dignity. Although women's roles in the labour force have changed from traditional agricultural and domestic roles, to manufacturing and assembly production, the overall effect of globalisation has proven to be negative. There are empirical claims of women gaining more autonomy over their own wages and a feeling of independence from traditional gender roles in society-especially in marriage and childrearing. Women are also becoming the breadwinners in most households because of the lack of male responsibility in the household. Young daughters are financially supporting their parents and fellow siblings, while mothers (married or single) are seeking informal work to provide for their children.

Globalisation has changed the intra household responsibilities for males and females, where females are given more responsibility over the survival of the family. Males are no longer the providers yet they have more opportunities for financial and social advancement in society. Although female responsibilities have increase, SALs implement by the IMF are gender biased towards males. They fail to include females in managerial and upper level positions. The limited advanced of women in the formal sector shows a great disregard for their social and economic responsibilities within developing nations. Female labour is not rewarded in relation to the impact they have on society. Therefore, women's work continues to be stigmatised as inferior, in comparison to males work, regardless of their increased responsibilities in society.

The establishment of various NGOs around the globe and the collaborative efforts of these organisations have improved the lives of women in developing nations. The U.N. Decade recognised the importance of female labor in developing nations and the fact that economic policies fail to address the needs of females. Representatives from NGOs agreed that global feminism should be established to reduce the inequality facing women in these nations and to improve the advancement of women in society.

As a result of The U.N. Decade, NGOs in throughout the developing world have reached out to women to meet their needs in farming, environmental protection, healthcare, domestic issues, employment conditions, and to reduce the financial strains in their everyday lives. The collective organisation of women's groups throughout the world has also generated the attention of the media, which is necessary in educating the general public about the current issues facing women in developing nations. The continued efforts of these groups and the economic realisation of the importance women's work will eventually create greater social awareness about the inequalities facing women in these nations.

The economic policies and structural adjustments associated with globalisation create the most negative impact on women in the developing world. The denial of social and economic rights is the most inhumane aspect associated with the formal and informal sectors. Economists and policy makers who implement these adjustments need to consider the impact of the current policies on women's lives and the inequalities that exist between men and women. Enabling the advancement of female opportunities and guaranteeing female workers more rights will increase the quality of life and create a more sustainable living standard for women and their families in the developing world. Without these changes, women will continue to suffer in their subordinate positions within the economic market.

11

Gender Budgeting and Women Component Plan

The National Common Minimum Program lays down empowerment of women politically, educationally and legally as one of the six basic principles. To provide an impetus to this objective, the Finance Minister in the budget speech for 2004-05 highlighted the perceived need for budget data to be presented in a manner that highlights the gender sensitiveness of the budgetary allocations. This was followed by a more emphatic commitment in the budget speech of 2005-06, wherein the budgetary allocations under 10 demands for grants estimated at Rs. 14379 crore were highlighted in a separate statement as a part of the Gender Budgeting exercise. The 2006-07 Budget

Speech revealed an estimated allocation of Rs.28, 737 cr. for benefit of women under 24 demands for grants in 18 Ministries and Departments.

There are a number of gender specific barriers, which prevent women for gaining access to their rightful share in the flow of public goods and services. Unless the felt needs of women are incorporated and mainstreamed in the planning and development process it is apprehended that the fruits of economic growth are likely to completely bypass a significant section of the country's population which does not augur well for the future growth of the economy. This calls for a focused priority in the Eleventh plan for the strengthening, expansion and universalisation of Gender Budgeting in all its aspects.

Gender Budgeting

Gender Budgeting is defined as the application of gender mainstreaming in the budgetary process. It encompasses incorporating a gender perspective at all levels and stages of the budgetary process and paves the way for translating gender commitments to budgetary commitments and carrying out an assessment of the budget to establish its gender differential impact.

In other words Gender Budgeting looks at Government budget from a gender perspective to assess how it addresses the needs of women not only in traditional areas like health, education etc but also in so called 'gender neutral' sectors like Transport , Power, Telecommunications, Defence etc. It does not seek to create a separate budget but seeks to put in place affirmative action for meeting women's specific needs, thus bringing into effect gender responsive Budgeting.

The ultimate objective of gender budgeting is to transform and transcend traditional perceptions and mind sets towards women and awaken a gender sensitive consciousness which will not only enable women to come into the mainstream but also give them their due recognition as equal citizens of the country.

Budgeting for Gender Equity: A step forward in Gender Mainstreaming

The Ministry of Women and Child Development (MWCD) in 2004-05 adopted the mission statement of 'Budgeting for Gender Equity'. In 2005-06 the task was to carry forward this exercise of universalising gender budgeting exercises in the Centre and the States. Several initiatives have been undertaken by MWCD to operationalise Gender Budgeting. A strategic framework of activities to implement "Budgeting for Gender. Equity" disseminated to all Departments identifies areas for gender mainstreaming including quantification of allocation of resources for women in Union/ State/ Local

Budgets, gender audit of polices of Governments, impact assessment of various schemes, analysing programmes and strategies, institutionalising generation and collection of gender disaggregated data, consultations and capacity building etc. Further, guidelines for gender sensitive review of public expenditure and policy were framed in the form of checklists both for beneficiary oriented sectors (such as Health, Rural Development,

Human Resource Development, Labour, Drinking Water, Textiles, Agriculture etc) and for mainstream sectors that may appear "gender neutral" like defence, power, telecom, transport etc.

The Ministry has conducted several workshops and training programmes to disseminate the tools of gender budgeting and has advocated that a review may be undertaken with respect to (1) Gender Based Profile of Public expenditure (2) Beneficiary needs assessment (3) Impact Analysis (4) Participative Budgeting and (5) Spatial Mapping. The MWCD has requested Ministries to set up Gender Budgeting Cells to undertake review of the public expenditure and policy guide and undertake collection of gender disaggregated data, conduct gender based impact analysis, and beneficiary needs assessment and beneficiary incidence analysis. As a result of these efforts 43 Ministries/ Departments have set up Gender Budget Cells as a nodal agency for all gender responsive budgeting initiatives.

Women's Component Plan (WCP)

The WCP was the first major initiative taken by the Government to address women related issues and requirements on a systematic basis involving the inputs from major Ministries/ Departments. The Women's Component Plan (WCP) involved efforts to ensure that not less than 30 per cent of funds/benefits were earmarked for women under the various schemes. However, performance on the WCP has been disappointing and the Mid Term Appraisal of the Tenth Plan notes that while "the Department of Education has confirmed a flow of funds of 42.37 per cent of the gross budgetary support to the WCP, the Ministry of Labour, which had reported flow of 33.5 per cent of its budget to the WCP in the Ninth Plan, has reported flow of funds of only 5 per cent of its budget during first three years of Tenth Plan." Several Ministries and/or Departments, which had earlier reported on the WCP in their sectoral budgets, have stopped doing so.

It also noted that there are some Ministries and Departments, which have the potential to go beyond 30 per cent of funds under WCP as well as devise and administer women related programmes. These include Education, Health, Family Welfare, Environment and

Forests, Rural Development, Agriculture, Labour, Urban Affairs, Drinking Water Supply, Tribal Affairs, Social Justice and Empowerment, and possibly others. It also pointed out that the Ministries and Departments "that have defaulted in providing WCP allocations or whose WCP is less than 30 per cent of their budgets are advised to immediately take the necessary steps to make amends."

Taking the essence and intent of the Mid term appraisal of the Tenth plan, WCP would need to be extended to all Ministries and Departments and not confined to the realm of some Ministries and Departments which have historically been perceived as "women-related". Simultaneously the implementation process of Gender Budgeting needs to be institutionalised and universalised in all the Ministries/ Departments at the Centre and States.

Recommendations

CP to continue as a bridging mechanism to ensure that the momentum of flow of funds to women related programs is sustained. WCP will require to be strengthened and to cover all sectors and schemes and all programmes both in the Centre and the States. Hitherto the emphasis of WCP has been on women related and women specific Ministries/ schemes. However, as women comprise nearly 50% of the population in the country, it is inevitable that all schemes and programs of the Government, irrespective of the sector, will impinge on women in one way or another. As such it is firmly believed that there is no sector /program / scheme that does not have gender implications. Hence the strong recommendation of the Sub Group is to extend the concept of WCP to all Ministries/ Sectors in the Centre and the States.

At least 30 per cent of the funds for all schemes to be earmarked for women beneficiaries. For this purpose the Ministries should identify women related schemes or engender existing schemes so that women can get the benefits under such schemes. The essential earmarking of 30% funds for women under the WCP for all Ministries at the Centre and the States is, at the very least, a good exercise as it forces the policy makers to start thinking on the lines of gendered-impact of policies. This commitment of resources is both vital and necessary.

Beneficiary incidence is an important part of WCP. It should be ensured that at least 30 per cent of the beneficiaries should be women.

PRIs should be intensively involved to ensure 30% earmarking for women. As per the Seventy Third Constitutional Amendment, 29 subjects have been transferred to the panchayats. The schemes falling under these subjects could be looked into by the Panchayats to ensure implementation of WCP.

To ensure that funds actually reach the women, a 'non-lapsable pool' of women's fund could be created in every State and also at the Centre. If there is under-utilisation of funds allocated for women specific programmes/schemes under any Ministry (Central or State), the balance amount of funds should be transferred to this pool.

Funds from this non-lapsable pool should be transferred to MWCD for utilising the same in women related programmes/ projects.

At present, WCP treats women as one homogenous group but in reality, there are layers of discrimination even within women,. Thus some women are more vulnerable than others. For example, a dalit woman will be doubly discriminated and a differently-abled dalit woman will be even more vulnerable. Thus WCP needs to factor in this intersectionality-framework while addressing issues of most vulnerable women, like dalit women, adivasi women, HIV positive women, sex-workers, etc.

Planning Commission should take quarterly meetings to review the progress of WCP. It should mandatorily obtain the information on WCP from Ministries/ States as a part of the Annual Plan exercise. The proposals submitted by the Ministries/Departments and the States should document the progress/review of the WCP during the current/previous year and the steps proposed to be taken during the forthcoming year. Revised proforma need to be devised which should be simple and user-friendly in order to collect information on WCP.

Gender Budgeting

With the objective of gender mainstreaming as the ultimate aim, Gender Budgeting seeks to truly empower woman in every respect and enable her to realise her full potential in all spheres political, economic, social, cultural and civil. Towards this end Gender Budgeting helps ensure better access of women to health and education facilities, vocational training, employment opportunity and social security etc. for women. Setting up functional Gender Budgeting Cells in all Ministries/ Departments in the Centre and the States with a view to mainstream gender concerns in all areas of Government is therefore vital and needs to be taken up on a priority basis.

Gender Budgeting cannot be restricted only to government programmes and schemes. If it is to be to be truly successful and beneficial to women, the process has to permeate and penetrate to all sectors (government and non government), policies and strategies and reach out to all sections of the governance and the community. Only then can gender budgeting completely fulfill its objective of truly empowering women keeping in view this macro vision of gender budgeting the recommendations for the Eleventh plan are as follows.

Important National Macro-economic Policies to be Engendered

Policies of the Government form the genesis for programs and schemes providing the direction and describing the components of inputs that go into them. They determine the quantum of flow of the funds to different schemes, its components and also spatial spread of the programme. Unless the policies are engendered, it cannot be hoped that the programs and the schemes that emerge from this will be gender sensitive. Therefore, it is very essential that all policies of the Government from its very inception and formulation stage be thoroughly examined from a gender perspective. The following paragraphs indicate the various possibilities and potential of engendering some important national polices.

The fiscal and monetary policies will need to be analysed from a gender perspective as both have tremendous potential to have malefic or benign influence on the lives of women. Indirect taxation impinges heavily on women as the tax incidence, by and large, affects important items of sustenance which are generally highly price inelastic and even a small price rise in such items will have a negative impact on women; again the subsidy needs a re-look to ensure that withdrawal of subsidies do not adversely impinge on women.

For example, withdrawal of subsidy on kerosene with no other alternative fuel options will result in the woman wasting valuable productive time in gathering firewood, twigs etc and in the process also face health hazards. Thus the ramifications of indirect taxes are quite significant as far as women's well being is considered. The gender affirmative role of direct taxation could be further enhanced through various incentives like reduction in stamp duties for women if assets are registered in their name, lowering of income tax slabs for women etc.

Monetary policy has to be viewed from a gender angle, especially in the case of credit and loan facilities and easy access of women to financial instruments and attractive saving options. In this context the spread of private micro credit lending instruments needs to be carefully regulated to ensure that women and SHGs are not exploited through high interest rates.

Agricultural policies are of prime importance in gender budgeting exercises as there is a growing feminisation of agriculture in recent years with out migration of men moving to urban areas in search of work. It is estimated that 75% of all female workers and 85% of all rural female workers are in agriculture. Women constitute 40% of the agriculture force and this percentage is rising. The number of women headed households in the agricultural sector is also increasing. The prosperity of agriculture therefore will largely depend on how effectively these women are empowered.

Enhancing women's' rights to land, providing infrastructure support to women farmers and advancing legal support on existing laws are some of the policy interventions needed. However, critical problems persist. The lack of formal titles to women on the land they cultivate is a big drawback. This adversely affects their access to credit, inputs and marketing outlets. It also reinforces the woman's position as unpaid farm labour which reduces their incentives to invest in the land. It further excludes them from receiving services of agricultural extension services, new production techniques etc. The lack of appropriate women friendly tools and agricultural implements is another drawback. Also the farmers' cooperatives basically comprise of men and therefore disadvantageous to women in terms of mind set and location and services profile. The agricultural policy will therefore need to be reviewed to provide a gender friendly perspective.

Policies for the Non farm sector and information is another highly important area that has to seriously reviewed keeping in view the gender perspective. As women tend to remain in the rural sector they also undertake non-farm activities, which significantly contributed to the family's income. In times of agricultural stress, it is these non-farm activities of women that support the family. Therefore, the requirements of women in this sector needs to be identified and appropriate support facilities in terms of access to raw materials, micro credit, skill development, training, market linkages etc. have to be ensured.

Poverty alleviation programs should essentially focus on women as they are economically more disadvantaged than men and chronically poor. These alleviation programs should be geared and designed to meet women's needs with strengthening of SHGs, easy access to cheap credit, equal wages for equal work and a judicious mix of cash and non cash in the wages etc. With the advent of mega poverty alleviation schemes like the National Rural Employment Guarantee Scheme, more and more women are coming forward to work. It is important that the work place should be made safe from harassment and woman friendly with adequate provision of sanitation, drinking water and crèche facilities.

The existing public distribution system has failed to deliver the required food grains to the vulnerable groups on time in the requisite quality and quantity. The persisting problems of under weight, malnutrition, anemia are primary causes for early mortality, morbidity, high rates of MMR etc. There is urgent need to review and streamline the policy and strategy of PDS to ensure easy and timely distribution of food grains to women. The institution of food grain banks and managing the same by women SHGs could be considered to enable uninterrupted supply of food grains even in times of drought or other natural/ man-made disasters.

Public policy with respect to migration is another area for consideration. Due to extreme poverty or seasonal farm work, women are forced to migrate to semi urban areas. There are large numbers of social and economic consequences, which these women face such as exploitation in work place, wages differentials, low paid work etc. Also their access to safe housing, food, sanitation and health remain precarious. A very alarming feature of unregulated migration is the trafficking of young girls and women by duping, luring or kidnapping them. Such women are forced into prostitution, bonded labour or slavery. These social aspects need to be looked into in greater detail while reviewing the Migration policy.

The possibilities of gender differentials for social security insurance schemes is another area that need to be examined, as there is an urgent need for low cost and gender friendly insurance systems that cater to the specific life cycle needs of women. It must be acknowledged that a safety net /social security in the informal sector is almost non existent. As women comprise a large proportion of the informal sector, this implies that they are excluded from the insurance framework and therefore not protected against social, medical or economic emergencies. More importantly, it is absolutely necessary to put in place a well designed Health Insurance scheme (which can operate under the aegis of the National Rural Health Mission) for women in view of their inability to access medical facilities. Also pensions policy needs a relook in view of the large number of widow population in the country.

Environmental concerns also warrant gender mainstreaming. Providing alternative sources of fuel for women especially in rural areas reduces both her drudgery with collection of firewood and exposure to pollutants; switching from fossil fuel to non conventional fuel based systems such as green fuels(bio-mass), solar power, hydel power etc. should be stressed. Women's SHGs should be encouraged to be actively involved in Watershed Committees, Joint Forest Management Committees etc. There is a double advantage from this exercise, as on the one hand environment preservation issues will be addressed and on the other women will be empowered.

Disaster management policy should become gender sensitive as experiences have shown that women are most affected by disasters whether manmade or natural. The tendency for trafficking, sale of women and children is quite common in these extenuating circumstances. The emergency response systems in the event of such disasters should have well thought out gender relief measures to cater to afflicted women and children without any delay.

Media policy needs to be gender proactive. There is a need to encourage media to project positive images and balanced portrayal of women and girls to enable attitudinal changes. The media policy should also help in generating awareness on gender issues and concerns so that the process of societal reorientation towards creating a gender just society gets widely disseminated.

Research and Development should also be geared with a view to identify technological needs of women and develop and adapt technology especially to reduce the drudgery of women, facilitating her health and also income generating activities. The Information Technology Policy should also be women oriented imparting skills and strengthening the knowledge base of girls and women in the field of computer software and hardware especially in rural areas. Dissemination of information in local languages on socio-economic and legal issues concerning women would encourage better awareness and instill confidence. Information Technology Kiosks need to be opened for women which would facilitate the Self Help Groups in using internet facilities to purchase raw material designing and marketing of their products.

The above is an illustrative list of engendering national policies. Similar gender perspectives and mainstreaming has to be built into all policies whether they are economic, social or political in nature as Gender Budgeting cannot be seen in isolation from the overall socio-economic-political scenario. The successful impact of these policies on women implies the successful implementation of Gender Budgeting.

Intersectoral Convergence for Important Gender Development Indices/Parameters

While the gender sensitisation of policies, programmes and schemes go a long way in empowering women, it is human development indicators, which reflect the ultimate and true empowerment of women in the country. In a way, these indicators are the outcomes of the gender budgeting, yet in their own sphere they are also the process inputs for gender budgeting.

Unfortunately, the basic parameters of health (declining sex ratio, IMR, MMR, immunisation levels, morbidity, mortality, anemia etc.), nutrition (Mal-Nutrition, under weight, anemia etc.), education, (literacy levels, poor enrolment, drop out etc) employment and training (unorganised, unpaid sectors, discrimination in wages, poor skill development, mainly in drudgery areas of occupations such as agriculture, construction) reflect the continuing dismal status of women in the country.

While individual sectoral policies, be it health, education, employment etc. will be separately engendered, cross cutting holistic intersectoral policies also need to be converged effectively with a gender perspective, if Human Development Indicies are to improve. Therefore along with sectoral polices, intersectoral polices too need to be gendered defined.

Review of and Effective Implementation of All Legislations and Laws with a Gender Perspective to Eliminate All forms of Discrimination and Violence Against women

The laws and legalisation are the framework that provide women her rights as equal citizens of the country. There are over 42 women specific and related legislations. Some women specific legislations include the Immoral Traffic (Prevention) Act 1956, Maternity Benefit Act 1961, Dowry Prohibition Act 1961, Protection of women from Domestic Violence Act 2005 etc which seek to protect the women from sexual exploitation and other violence and abuse; women related legislations which have economic implications include the Factories Act 1948, Minimum Wages Act 1948, Equal

Remuneration Act, 1976 etc, many of which have provisions for providing economic justice and fair wages to women ; there are other Acts which are Protection oriented such as Pre conception and Prenatal Diagnostic Technique (Regulation and Prevention) Act 1994, Child Marriage Restraint Act 1929; and those with Social implications like Family Courts Act 1984, Hindu Succession 1956, Indian Divorce Act 1969.

Thus while there are a plethora of Acts existing for the protection and socio-economic equality of women, it is only through their effective implementation that women receive the intended benefits. However, gaps still remain and it is essential that specific laws are brought into effect which provide adequate safeguards and protection to women. One such very important Act is the Compulsory Registration of Marriage Act, which will protect the marital rights of the women and ensure her rightful share in the husband's property. A review of the legislations is also required to bring about conformity in the laws. In this context, it may be noted that necessary provisions of Indian Penal Code be brought in harmony with the provisions of the women related Acts so that there is no dichotomy between the different legislations.

Mainstreaming and Sensitising Gender Concerns in Various Organs such as Police, Legislation, Judiciary and Trade Unions

While the planning process and public expenditure in terms of programs and schemes are sought to be included in Gender Budgeting, yet without gender sensitivity of important organs such as police, judiciary etc the implementation will not be successful. This is especially true of such schemes which have a strong element of protection or are rights based. For example, if the woman is not given her due share of property or other assets as per law it is essential that these agencies help and support her in getting her share without much delay or harassment. This can happen only if gender sensitivity is inculcated in such bodies, and they are made aware of the laws, polices, programs and other initiatives for women. It is also important that justice delivery is quick with the enforcement machinery being responsive and gender sensitive to women's needs especially in cases of domestic violence and personal assault. In addition, trade unions also need to be sensitised to play an active role protecting women's rights/interests. A very effective method of ensuring that gender concerns are not lost sight of in such bodies is the induction of larger number of women at different levels.

This will encourage women to actively participate in power sharing and active participation in decision-making. Efforts should be made to provide coaching facilities and support services so that women can compete along with men both at entry and to facilitate upward mobility of women in these institutions. The setting up of "women" police stations, women's help desk in every police station, and increasing the strength of women police to 30% of the total force has been reiterated a number of times by the Ministry of Women and Child Development in a number of forums. The Ministry of Home Affairs should take requisite steps to fulfill their obligations towards gender budgeting by 'engendering the police force'.

Gender Mainstreaming to be Extended to Corporate Sector and other Civil Society Organisations

While so far the focus of gender budgeting has been on public expenditure of Government only, an increasing quantum of funds is being invested by the corporate sector in their businesses as well as in fulfilling their corporate social responsibility. The development of the corporate sector as an employer has grown tremendously in the wake of liberalisation and globalisation, especially with it's entry in those sectors which were hitherto the domain of the Government. Therefore the time has come to apply the strategy of Gender Budgeting to the private sector. There is a three fold responsibility that rests with the corporate sector, one of extending the scope of their employment opportunities to more and more women, provide them with level playing fields, equal wages and promotion opportunities; two, to support skill building, training ,vocational courses etc; and thirdly, to fulfill their social obligations towards women employees in terms of extending maternity benefits, protection from occupational hazards and sexual harassment, provision of facilities like crèches, toilets, sanitation and hygiene, allowing formation of women's associations, legal protection *etc.*

The civil society organisations whether NGOs, or other community based organisations are partnering government in formulation and implementation of government policies and programs. Thus their voice and views have an important bearing on shaping economic or social issues pertaining to women. They have to function as 'watch dogs' ensuring that Gender budgeting and mainstreaming is actually taking place right at the grass root levels and helping in implementing gender concerns effectively.

Estimation of Value Addition by Women in the Unorganised, Informal and Rural non farm Sector and Systemised Mechanism in Place to Monetise the Labour, Efforts and Output and Include the Same in the GDP

Informal farm work and non farm work where women are increasingly employed are mostly non monetised and therefore cannot be captured in the national accounting system. Despite the sizeable value addition to the national economy, on account of home based and other non farm and informal activities, the contribution of women's work continues to be invisible. Women also spend considerable time in collecting fuel, fodder, and water and on care related activities, which is neither aid or recognised as an economic activity. The statistical invisibility of such unpaid work implies that the economic system is missing out on a substantial part of the income generated and value added. The Eleventh Plan should ensure that the National Income includes these activities in their accounting system so that it forms a part of the GDP.

Gender Outcome Assessment

Gender outcome assessment and evaluation is of utmost importance for ensuring the success of Gender Budgeting. For this it is necessary that the gender fund flow into schemes are properly and correctly assessed. The Finance Ministry has made it mandatory that Gender Outcomes form a part of the Outcome Budget prepared by every Ministry/ Department as part of the Budget documents. Some anomalies have been observed in allocations reflected in Union Budget 2005-06, under various programmes/schemes for women. In 2005-06 this exercise covered 10 Departments and the total magnitude of Gender Budget (i.e., women specific allocations) was recorded at 2.8% of total Union Government expenditure. In 2006-07, 24 Departments of the Union Government were included under this exercise and the magnitude of Gender Budget went up to 5.1% of total budget estimates. However, it has been observed that schemes which do not have a 100% womens' component found a mention as women specific schemes. Therefore the first step towards proper outcome assessment of Gender Budget is that each Ministry/ Department of both Centre and State should put in place a systematic and comprehensive monitoring and auditing mechanism for outcome assessment.

At present, the major task of the Gender budgeting Cells in the Ministries/Departments is limited to identification of schemes and computation of allocations meant for women. To bring a qualitative improvement in the functioning of the Cells and make Gender Budgeting exercises more meaningful and effective, the following approach can be followed by the Cells for extending gender outcomes.

- Assessing budget allocations and proposing for additional allocations for gender related schemes / components ;
- Analysing and reviewing policy, strategies, programmes and schemes from the perspective of women as also improving the status of women, identifying constraints and taking into view their needs and requirements
- Identify constraints in flow of funds to women through expenditure tracking studies institutionalise generation, collection and compilation of gender disaggregated data through various mechanisms right form the grass root level and ensure that this should be an inbuilt part of the programme/ scheme.
- Identify data gaps and design the future steps for building gender disaggregated data
- Monitoring of spending and service delivery
- Assessing the extent to which women are benefiting under the schemes and programs of the Ministry

- Assessing beneficiary incidence
- Identification of areas where existing schemes can be further engendered and Initiating new initiatives, innovative ideas and schemes for gender benefit. In addition to the above, which will primarily be the responsibility of the individual sectoral Ministries/ Departments, the Planning Commission and the Finance Ministry should enable assessment of national level gender outcome assessment through:
- Spatial mapping of gender gaps and resource gaps by Planning Commission
- Gender audit of public expenditure, programmes and policies
- There is a need to collect gender disaggregated data at national, state and district levels. Standardisation of data is also necessary to facilitate comparison not only at national but also international levels. The data should flow on a regular basis and should be compiled, collected and analysed periodically.

Training and Capacity Building

MWCD being the nodal Ministry for Gender Budget should have a full fledged Unit for Gender Budgeting with appropriate staff and infrastructural facilities. At present, there is no staff allotted for Gender Budgeting.

As the MWCD undertakes all coordination, orientation and sensitisation exercises for Gender Budgeting at Centre and States, it is very essential that adequate staff be provided for the unit. It is recommended that the Gender Budgeting unit should comprise of the following officers who have a strong base in formulation, evaluation, project appraisal, monitoring etc of economic strategies, policies and programmes etc.

The capacity of the Gender Budgeting Cells that have been set up in various Departments and Ministries too need to be strengthened, especially as the Cells will have a large number of activities to carry out. For this purpose it is suggested that each Gender Budgeting Cell should comprise of officers who have a strong base in formulation, evaluation project appraisal, monitoring etc of economic strategies, policies and programmes.

Setting up of Regional Resource and Training Centers for Gender Budgeting (RRTCGB)

With the basic objective of building a core team of resource agencies and trainers to disseminate the tools, strategy and process of Gender Budgeting throughout the country so as to enable a wider outreach and to decentralise the technical support and capacity building activities, there is a need to set up Regional Resource and Training Centers for Gender Budgeting (RRTCGB). Institutions/ centers which have the requisite Infrastructure and expertise in the related disciplines of gender budgeting and gender related issues need to be identified in different parts of the country. Such centres should have experience in promotional activities such as outreach, advocacy and in facilitating networking and linkages through convergence and with sound financial capability. To enable such training programs and capacity building will require adequate funding under a new separate head of account titled 'Training and Capacity building in Gender budgeting'.

Preparation of Training Manuals

Detailed training manuals will need to be prepared which can be used by the Trainers. These manuals will give the approach and the methodology to be taken in the engendering policies, schemes, programmes and assessing their gender outcomes.

Gender budgeting cannot be the sole responsibility of any one Ministry or any one sector. It is only through the commitment and efforts of all sectors of the Government, be it at the Centre or in the States, the Private Sector and Civil Society, can the objective of redressing the inequalities faced by women be achieved, thus establishing the true essence and spirit of Gender Budgeting in empowering women holistically.

12

Education and Economic Development

According to 1992-93 figures, only 9.2% of the households in India were female-headed. However, approximately 35% of the households below the poverty line were found to be female-headed.

Education

Though it is gradually rising, the female literacy rate in India is lower than the male literacy rate. Compared to boys, far fewer girls are enrolled in the schools, and many of them drop out. According to the National Sample Survey Data of 1997, only the states of Kerala and Mizoram have approached universal female literacy rates. According to majority of the scholars, the major factor behind the improved social and economic status of women in Kerala is literacy.

Under Non-Formal Education programme, about 40% of the centers in states and 10% of the centers in UTs are exclusively reserved for females. As of 2000, about 0.3 million NFE centers were catering to about 7.42 million children, out of which about 0.12 million were exclusively for girls. In urban India, girls are nearly at par with the boys in terms of education. However, in rural India girls continue to be less educated than the boys.

According to a 1998 report by U.S. Department of Commerce, the chief barrier to female education in India are inadequate school facilities (such as sanitary facilities), shortage of female teachers and gender bias in curriculum (majority of the female characters being depicted as weak and helpless).

Workforce Participation

Contrary to the common perception, a large per cent of women in India work. The National data collection agencies accept the fact that there is a serious under-estimation of women's contribution as workers. However, there are far fewer women in the paid workforce than there are men. In urban India Women have impressive number in the workforce. As an example at software industry 30% of the workforce is female. They are at par with their male counter parts in terms of wages, position at the work place.

In rural India, agriculture and allied industrial sectors employ as much as 89.5% of the total female labour.In overall farm production, women's average contribution is estimated at 55% to 66% of the total labour. According to a 1991 World Bank report, women accounted for 94% of total employment in dairy production in India. Women constitute 51% of the total employed in forest-based small-scale enterprises.

One of the most famous female business success stories is the Shri Mahila Griha Udyog Lijjat Papad. In 2006, Kiran Mazumdar-Shaw, who started Biocon one of India's first biotech companies, was rated India's richest woman. Lalita Gupte and Kalpana Morparia (both were the only businesswomen in India who made the list of the Forbes World's Most Powerful Women), run India's second-largest bank, ICICI Bank.

Land and Property Rights

In most Indian families , women do not own any property in their own names, and do not get a share of parental property. Due to weak enforcement of laws protecting them, women continue to have little access to land and property. In fact, some of the laws discriminate against women, when it comes to land and property rights.

The Hindu personal laws of mid-1956s (applied to Hindus, Buddhists, Sikhs and Jains) gave women rights to inheritance. However, the sons had an independent share in the ancestral property, while the daughters' shares were based on the share received by their father. Hence, a father could effectively disinherit a daughter by renouncing his share of the ancestral property, but the son will continue to have a share in his own right. Additionally, married daughters, even those facing marital harassment, had no residential rights in the ancestral home. After amendment of Hindu laws in 2005, now women in have been provided the same status as that of men.

In 1986, the Supreme Court of India ruled that Shah Bano, an old divorced Muslim woman was eligible for maintenance money. However, the decision was vociferously opposed by fundamentalist Muslim leaders, who alleged that the court was interfering in their personal law. The Union Government subsequently passed the Muslim Women's (Protection of Rights Upon Divorce) Act. Similarly, the Christian women have struggled over years for equal rights of divorce and succession. In 1994, all the churches, jointly with women's organisations, drew up a draft law called the Christian Marriage and Matrimonial Causes Bill. However, the government has still not amended the relevant laws.

Crimes against Women

Police records show high incidence of crimes against women in India. The National Crime Records Bureau reported in 1998 that the growth rate of crimes against women would be higher than the population growth rate by 2010.Earlier; many cases were not registered with the police due to the social stigma attached to rape and molestation cases. Official statistics show that there has been a dramatic increase in the number of reported crimes against women.

Sexual Harassment

Half of the total number of crimes against women reported in 1990 related to molestation and harassment at the workplace. Eve teasing is a euphemism used for sexual harassment or molestation of women by men. Many activists blame the rising incidents of sexual harassment against women on the influence of "Western culture". In 1987, The Indecent Representation of Women (Prohibition) Act was passed to prohibit indecent representation of women through advertisements or in publications, writings, paintings, figures or in any other manner.

In 1997, in a landmark judgement, the Supreme Court of India took a strong stand against sexual harassment of women in the workplace. The Court also laid down detailed guidelines for prevention and redressal of grievances. The National Commission for Women subsequently elaborated these guidelines into a Code of Conduct for employers.

Dowry

In 1961, the Government of India passed the Dowry Prohibition Act,making the dowry demands in wedding arrangements illegal. However, many cases of dowry-related domestic violence, suicides and murders have been reported. In the 1980s, numerous such cases were reported. In 1985, the Dowry Prohibition (maintenance of lists of presents to the bride and bridegroom) rules were framed. According to these rules, a signed list of presents given at the time of the marriage to the bride and the bridegroom should be maintained. The list should contain a brief description of each present, its approximate value, the name of whoever has given the present and his/her relationship to the person. However, such rules are hardly enforced.

A 1997 report claimed that at least 5,000 women die each year because of dowry deaths, and at least a dozen die each day in 'kitchen fires' thought to be intentional. The term for this is "bride burning" and is criticised within India itself. Amongst the urban educated, such dowry abuse has reduced considerably.

Child Marriage

Child marriage has been traditionally prevalent in India and continues to this day. Historically, young girls would live with their parents till they reached puberty. In the past, the child widows were condemned to a life of great agony, shaving heads, living in isolation, and shunned by the society. Although child marriage was outlawed in 1860, it is still a common practice. According to UNICEF's "State of the World's Children-2009" report, 47% of India's women aged 20-24 were married before the legal age of 18, with 56% in rural areas. The report also showed that 40% of the world's child marriages occur in India.

Female Infanticides and Sex Selective Abortions

India has a highly masculine sex ratio, the chief reason being that many women die before reaching adulthood. Tribal societies in India have a less masculine sex ratio than all other caste groups. This, in spite of the fact that tribal communities have far lower levels of income, literacy and health facilities. It is therefore suggested by many experts, that the highly masculine sex ratio in India can be attributed to female infanticides and sex-selective abortions. All medical tests that can be used to determine the sex of the child have been banned in India, due to incidents of these tests being used to get rid of unwanted female children before birth. Female infanticide (killing of girl infants) is still prevalent in some rural areas. The abuse of the dowry tradition has been one of the main reasons for sex-selective abortions and female infanticides in India.

Domestic Violence

The incidents of domestic violence are higher among the lower Socio-Economic Classes (SECs).The Protection of Women from Domestic Violence Act, 2005 came into force on October 26, 2006.

Trafficking

The Immoral Traffic (Prevention) Act was passed in 1956. However many cases of trafficking of young girls and women have been reported. These women are either forced into prostitution, domestic work or child labor.

Other Concerns

Health

The average female life expectancy today in India is low compared to many countries, but it has shown gradual improvement over the years. In many families, especially rural ones, the girls and women face nutritional discrimination within the family, and are anaemic and malnourished. The maternal mortality in India is the second highest in the world. Only 42% of births in the country are supervised by health professionals. Most women deliver with help from women in the family who often lack the skills and resources to save the mother's life if it is in danger. According to UNDP Human Development Report (1997), 88% of pregnant women (age 15-49) were found to be suffering from anemia.

Family Planning

The average woman in rural areas of India has little or no control over her reproductivity. Women, particularly women in rural areas, do not have access to safe and self-controlled methods of contraception. The public health system emphasises permanent methods like sterilisation, or long-term methods like IUDs that do not need follow-up. Sterilisation accounts for more than 75% of total contraception, with female sterilisation accounting for almost 95% of all sterilisations.

13

Women Empowerment through Micro Finance: A Boon for Development

Empowerment implies expansion of assets and capabilities of people to influence control and hold accountable institution that affects their lives. Empowerment is the process of enabling or authorising an individual to think, behave take action and control work in an autonomous way. It is the state of feelings of self-empowered to take control of one's own destiny. It includes both controls over resources (Physical, Human, Intellectual and Financial) and over ideology (Belief, values and attitudes). Empowerment can be viewed as a means of creating a social environment in which one can take decisions and make choice either individually or collectively for social transformation. It strength innate ability by way of acquiring knowledge power and experience.

Empowerment is a multi-dimensional social process that helps people gain control over their own lives communities and in their society, by acting on issues that they define as important. Empowerment occurs within sociological psychological economic spheres and at various levels, such as individual, group and community and challenges our assumptions about status quo, asymmetrical power relationship and social dynamics. Empowering women puts the spotlight on education and employment which are an essential element to sustainable development.

Empowerment: Focus on Poor Women

In India, the trickle down effects of macroeconomic policies have failed to resolve the problem of gender inequality. Women have been the vulnerable section of society and constitute a sizeable segment of the poverty-struck population. Women face gender specific barriers to access education health, employment etc. Micro finance deals with women below the poverty line. Micro loans are available solely and entirely to this target group of women. There are several reason for this: Among the poor , the poor women are most disadvantaged they are characterised by lack of education and access of resources, both of which is required to help them work their way out of poverty and for upward economic and social mobility. The problem is more acute for women in countries like India, despite the fact that women's labour makes a critical contribution to the economy. This is due to the low social status and lack of access to key resources. Evidence shows that groups of women are better customers than men, the better managers of resources. If loans are routed through women benefits of loans are spread wider among the household.

Since women's empowerment is the key to socio economic development of the community; bringing women into the mainstream of national development has been a major concern of government. The ministry of rural development has special components for women in its programmes. Funds are earmarked as "Women's component" to ensure flow of adequate resources for the same. Besides Swarnagayanti Grameen Swarazgar Yojona (SGSY), Ministry of Rural Development is implementing other scheme having women's component .They are the Indira Awas Yojona (IAJ), National Social Assistance Programme (NSAP), Restructured Rural Sanitation Programme, Accelerated Rural Water Supply programme (ARWSP) the (erstwhile) Integrated Rural Development Programme (IRDP), the (erstwhile) Development of Women and Children in Rural Areas (DWCRA) and the Jowahar Rozgar Yojana (JRY).

Concept and Features of Microfinance

The term micro finance is of recent origin and is commonly used in addressing issues related to poverty alleviation, financial support to micro entrepreneurs, gender development etc. There is, however, no statutory definition of microfinance. The taskforce on supportitative policy and Regulatory Framework for Microfinance has defined microfinance as "Provision of thrift, credit and other financial services and products of very small amounts to the poor in rural, semi-urban or urban areas for enabling them to raise their income levels and improve living standards". The term "Micro" literally means "small". But the task force has not defined any amount. However as per Micro Credit Special Cell of the Reserve Bank Of India, the borrowal amounts upto the limit of Rs.25000/ could be considered as micro credit products and this amount could be gradually increased up to Rs.40000/ over a period of time which roughly equals to $500 a standard for South Asia as per international perceptions.

The term microfinance, sometimes is used interchangeably with the term micro credit. However while micro credit refers to purveyance of loans in small quantities, the term microfinance has a broader meaning covering in its ambit other financial services like saving, insurance etc. as well.

The mantra "Microfinance" is banking through groups. The essential features of the approach are to provide financial services through the groups of individuals, formed either in joint liability or co-obligation mode. The other dimensions of the microfinance approach are:

- Savings/Thrift precedes credit
- Credit is linked with savings/thrift
- Absence of subsidies
- Group plays an important role in credit appraisal, monitoring and recovery.

Basically groups can be of two types:

Self Help Groups (SHGs): The group in this case does financial intermediation on behalf of the formal institution. This is the predominant model followed in India.

Grameen Groups: In this model, financial assistance is provided to the individual in a group by the formal institution on the strength of group's assurance. In other words, individual loans are provided on the strength of joint liability/co obligation. This microfinance model was initiated by Bangladesh Grameen Bank and is being used by some of the Microfinance Institutions (MFIs) in our country.

Women's Empowerment and Micro Finance: Different Paradigms

Concern with women's access to credit and assumptions about contributions to women's empowerment are not new. From the early 1970s women's movements in a number of countries became increasingly interested in the degree to which women were able to access poverty-focused credit programmes and credit cooperatives. In India organisations like Self- Employed Women's Association (SEWA) among others with origins and affiliations in the Indian labour and women's movements identified credit as a major constraint in their work with informal sector women workers.

The problem of women's access to credit was given particular emphasis at the first International Women's Conference in Mexico in 1975 as part of the emerging awareness of the importance of women's productive role both for national economies, and for women's rights. This led to the setting up of the Women's World Banking network and production of manuals for women's credit provision. Other women's organisations world-wide set up credit and savings components both as a way of increasing women's incomes and bringing women together to address wider gender issues. From the mid-1980s there was a mushrooming of donor, government and NGO-sponsored credit programmes in the wake of the 1985 Nairobi women's conference.

The 1980s and 1990s also saw development and rapid expansion of large minimalist poverty targeted micro-finance institutions and networks like Grameen Bank, ACCION and Finca among others. In these organisations and others evidence of significantly higher female repayment rates led to increasing emphasis on targeting women as an efficiency strategy to increase credit recovery. A number of donors also saw female-targeted financially sustainable micro-finance as a means of marrying internal demands for increased efficiency because of declining budgets with demands of the increasingly vocal gender lobbies.

The trend was further reinforced by the Micro Credit Summit Campaign starting in 1997 which had 'reaching and empowering women' as it's second key goal after poverty reduction (RESULTS

1997). Micro-finance for women has recently been seen as a key strategy in meeting not only Millennium Goal 3 on gender equality, but also poverty Reduction, Health, HIV/AIDS and other goals.

Feminist Empowerment Paradigm

The feminist empowerment paradigm did not originate as a Northern imposition, but is firmly rooted in the development of some of the earliest micro-finance programmes in the South, including SEWA in India. It currently underlies the gender policies of many NGOs and the perspectives of some of the consultants and researchers looking at gender impact of micro-finance programmes.

Here the underlying concerns are gender equality and women's human rights. Women's empowerment is seen as an integral and inseparable part of a wider process of social transformation. The main target group is poor women and women capable of providing alternative female role models for change. Increasing attention has also been paid to men's role in challenging gender inequality.

Micro-finance is promoted as an entry point in the context of a wider strategy for women's economic and socio-political empowerment which focuses on gender awareness and feminist organisation. As developed by Chen in her proposals for a sub sector approach to micro credit, based partly on SEWA's strategy and promoted by UNIFEM, microfinance must be:

Part of a sectoral strategy for change which identifies opportunities, constraints and bottlenecks within industries which if addressed can raise returns and prospects for large numbers of women. Possible strategies include linking women to existing services and infrastructure, developing new technology such as labour-saving food processing, building information networks, shifting to new markets, policy level changes to overcome legislative barriers and unionisation.

Based on participatory principles to build up incremental knowledge of industries and enable women to develop their strategies for change. Economic empowerment is however defined in more than individualist terms to include issues such as property rights, changes intra-household relations and transformation of the macroeconomic context. Many organisations go further than interventions at the industry level to include gender-specific strategies for social and political empowerment. Some programmes have developed very effective means for integrating gender awareness into programmes and for organising women and men to challenge and change gender discrimination. Some also have legal rights support for women and engage in gender advocacy. These interventions to increase social and political empowerment are seen as essential prerequisites for economic empowerment.

Poverty Reduction Paradigm

The poverty alleviation paradigm underlies many NGO integrated poverty-targeted community development programmes. Poverty alleviation here is defined in broader terms than market incomes to encompass increasing capacities and choices and decreasing the vulnerability of poor people. The main focus of programmes as a whole is on developing sustainable livelihoods, community development and social service provision like literacy, healthcare and infrastructure development. There is not only a concern with reaching the poor, but also the poorest.

Policy debates have focused particularly on the importance of small savings and loan provision for consumption as well as production, group formation and the possible justification for some level of subsidy for programmes working with particular client groups or in particular contexts. Some programmes have developed effective methodologies for poverty targeting and/or operating in remote areas. Such strategies have recently become a focus of interest from some donors and also the Microcredit Summit Campaign.

Here gender lobbies have argued for targeting women because of higher levels of female poverty and women's responsibility for household well-being. However although gender inequality is recognised as an issue, the focus is on assistance to households and there is a tendency to see gender issues as cultural and hence not subject to outside intervention.

Although term 'empowerment' is frequently used in general terms, often synonymous with a multi-dimensional definition of poverty alleviation, the term 'women's empowerment' is often considered best avoided as being too controversial and political. The assumption is that increasing women's access to micro-finance will enable women to make a greater contribution to household income and this, together with other interventions to increase household well-being, will translate into improved well-being for women and enable women to bring about wider changes in gender inequality.

Financial Sustainability Paradigm

The financial self-sustainability paradigm (also referred to as the financial systems approach or sustainability approach) underlies the models of microfinance promoted since the mid-1990s by most donor agencies and the Best Practice guidelines promoted in publications by USAID, World Bank, UNDP and CGAP.

The ultimate aim is large programmes which are profitable and fully self-supporting in competition with other private sector banking institutions and able to raise funds from international financial markets rather than relying on funds from development agencies. The main target group, despite claims to reach the poorest, is the 'bankable poor': small entrepreneurs and farmers. This emphasis on financial sustainability is seen as necessary to create institutions which reach significant numbers of poor people in the context of declining aid budgets and opposition to welfare and redistribution in macro-economic policy.

Policy discussions have focused particularly on setting of interest rates to cover costs, separation of micro-finance from other interventions to enable separate accounting and programme expansion to increase outreach and economies of scale, reduction of transaction costs and ways of using groups to decrease costs of delivery. Recent guidelines for CGAP funding and best practice focus on production of a 'financial sustainability index' which charts progress of programmes in covering costs from incomes.

Within this paradigm gender lobbies have been able to argue for targeting women on the grounds of high female repayment rates and the need to stimulate women's economic activity as a hitherto underutilised resource for economic growth. They have had some success in ensuring that considerations of female targeting are integrated into conditions of micro-finance delivery and programme evaluation.

Alongside this focus on female targeting, the term 'empowerment' is frequently used in promotional literature. Definitions of empowerment are in individualist terms with the ultimate aim being the expansion of individual choice or capacity for Self-reliance. It is assumed that increasing women's access to micro-finance services will in itself lead to individual economic empowerment through enabling women's decisions about savings and credit use, enabling women to set up micro-enterprise, increasing incomes under their control. It is then assumed that this increased economic empowerment will lead to increased well-being of women and also to social and political empowerment.

These paradigms do not correspond systematically to any one organisational model of micro-finance. Micro-finance providers with the same organisational form eg. village bank, Grameen model or cooperative model may have very different gender policies and/or emphases and strategies for poverty alleviation. The three paradigms represent different 'discourses' each with its own relatively consistent internal logic in relating aims to policies, based on different underlying understandings of development. They are not only different, but often seen as 'incompatible discourses' in uneasy tension and with continually contested degrees of dominance. In many programmes and donor agencies there is considerable disagreement, lack of communication and/or personal animosity and promoted by different stakeholders within organisations between staff involved in micro-finance (generally firm followers of financial self-sustainability), staff concerned with human development (generally with more sympathy for the poverty alleviation paradigm and emphasising participation and integrated development) gender lobbies (generally incorporating at least some elements of the feminist empowerment paradigm). What is of concern in current debates is the way in which the use of apparently similar terminology of empowerment, participation and sustainability conceals radical differences in policy priorities. Although women's empowerment may be a stated aim in the rhetoric of official gender policy and program promotion, in practice it becomes subsumed in and marginalised by concerns of financial sustainability and/or poverty alleviation.

Micro Finance Instrument for Women's Empowerment

Micro Finance is emerging as a powerful instrument for poverty alleviation in the new economy. In India, micro finance scene is dominated by Self Help Groups (SHGs) Bank Linkage Programme, aimed at providing a cost effective mechanism for providing financial services to the "unreached poor". Based on the philosophy of peer pressure and group savings as collateral substitute, the SHG programme has been successful in not only in meeting peculiar needs of the rural poor, but also in strengthening collective self-help capacities of the poor at the local level, leading to their empowerment.

Micro Finance for the poor and women has received extensive recognition as a strategy for poverty reduction and for economic empowerment. Increasingly in the last five years , there is questioning of whether micro credit is most effective approach to economic empowerment of poorest and, among them, women in particular. Development practiti ners in India and developing countries often argue that the exaggerated focus on micro finance as a solution for the poor has led to neglect by the state and public institutions in addressing employment and livelihood needs of the poor. Credit for empowerment is about organising people, particularly around credit and building capacities to manage money. The focus is on getting the poor to mobilise their own funds, building their capacities and empowering them to leverage external credit. Perception women is that learning to manage money and rotate funds builds women's capacities and confidence to intervene in local governance beyond the limited goals of ensuring access to credit. Further, it combines the goals of financial sustainability with that of creating community owned institutions.

Before 1990's, credit schemes for rural women were almost negligible. The concept of women's credit was born on the insistence by women oriented studies that highlighted the discrimination and struggle of women in having the access of credit. However, there is a perceptible gap in financing genuine credit needs of the poor especially women in the rural sector.

There are certain misconception about the poor people that they need loan at subsidised rate of interest on soft terms, they lack education, skill, capacity to save, credit worthiness and therefore are not bankable. Nevertheless, the experience of several SHGs reveal that rural poor are actually efficient managers of credit and finance. Availability of timely and adequate credit is essential for them to undertake any economic activity rather than credit subsidy.

The Government measures have attempted to help the poor by implementing different poverty alleviation programmes but with little success. Since most of them are target based involving lengthy procedures for loan disbursement, high transaction costs, and lack of supervision and monitoring. Since the credit requirements of the rural poor cannot be adopted on project lending app roach as it is in the case of organised sector, there emerged the need for an informal credit supply through SHGs. The rural poor with the assistance from NGOs have demonstrated their potential for self help to secure economic and financial strength. Various case studies show that there is a positive correlation between credit availability and women's empowerment.

Problem and Challenges

Surveys have shown that many elements contribute to make it more Difficult for women empowerment through micro businesses. These elements are:

- Lack of knowledge of the market and potential profitability, thus making the choice of business difficult.
- Inadequate book-keeping.
- Employment of too many relatives which increases social pressure to share benefits.
- Setting prices arbitrarily.
- Lack of capital.
- High interest rates.
- Inventory and inflation accounting is never undertaken.
- Credit policies that can gradually ruin their business (many customers cannot pay cash; on the other hand, suppliers are very harsh towards women).

Other shortcomings includes,

1. **Burden of meeting:** Time consuming meetings, in particular in programmes based on group lending, and time consuming income generating activities without reduction of traditional responsibilities increase women's work and time burden.
2. **New Pressures:** By using social capital, in-group lending/ group collateral programmes, additional stresses and pressures are introduced, which might increase vulnerability and reflect disempowerment.
3. **Reinforcement of traditional gender roles:** lack of economic empowerment: Micro finance assists women to perform traditional roles better and women thus remain trapped in low productivity sectors, not moving from the group of survival enterprises to micro-enterprises. There are evidence of men withdrawing their contributions to certain types of household expenditures.

Challenging Economic Empowerment

However impact on incomes is widely variable. Studies which consider income levels find that for the majority of borrowers income increases are small, and in some cases negative. All the evidence suggests that most women invest in existing activities which are low profit and insecure and/or in their husband's activities. In many programmes and contexts it is only in a minority of cases that women can develop lucrative activities of their own through credit and savings alone. It is clear that women's choices about activity and their ability to increase incomes are seriously constrained by gender inequalities in access to other resources for investment, responsibility for household subsistence expenditure, lack of time because of unpaid domestic work and low levels of mobility, constraints on sexuality and sexual violence which limit access to markets in many cultures.

These gender constraints are in addition to market constraints on expansion of the informal sector and resource and skill constraints on the ability of poor men as well as women to move up from survival activities to expanding businesses. There are signs, particularly in some urban markets like Harare and Lusaka, that the **rapid** expansion of micro-finance programmes may be contributing to market saturation in 'female' activities and hence declining profits.

Challenging well being and Intra Household Relation

There have undoubtedly been women whose status in the household has improved, particularly where they have become successful entrepreneurs. Even where income impacts have been small, or men have used the loan, the fact that micro-finance programmes have thought women worth targeting and women bring an asset into the household may give some women more negotiating power. Savings provide women with a means of building up an asset base. Women themselves also often value the opportunity to be seen to be making a greater contribution to household well-being giving them greater confidence and sense of self-worth.

However women's contribution to increased income going into households does not ensure that women necessarily benefit or that there is any challenge to gender inequalities within the household. Women's expenditure patterns may replicate rather than counter gender inequalities and continue to disadvantage girls. Without substitute care for small children, the elderly and disabled, and provision of services to reduce domestic work many programmes reported adverse effects of women's outside work on children and the elderly. Daughters in particular may be withdrawn from school to assist their mothers.

Although in some contexts women may be seeking to increase their influence within joint decision-making processes rather than independent control over income (Kabeer 1998), neither of these outcomes can be assumed. Women's perceptions of value and self-worth are not necessarily translated into actual well-being benefits or change in gender relations in the household (Sen 1990, Kandiyoti 1999). Worryingly, in response to women's increased incomes evidence indicates that men may be withdrawing more of their own contribution for their own luxury expenditure. Men are often very enthusiastic about women's credit programmes, and other income generation out programmes, for this reason because their wives no longer 'nag' them for money (Mayoux 1999).

Small increases in access to income and influence may therefore be at the cost of heavier work loads, increased stress and women's health. Although in many cases women's increased contribution to household well-being has improved domestic relations, in other cases it intensifies tensions.

Challenging Social and Political Empowerment

There have been positive changes in household and community perceptions of women's productive role, as well as changes at the individual level. In societies like Sudan and Bangladesh where women's role has been very circumscribed and women previously had little opportunity to meet women outside their immediate family there have sometimes been significant changes. It is likely that changes at the individual, household and community levels are interlinked and that individual women who gain respect in their households then act as role models for others leading to a wider process of change in community perceptions and male willingness to accept change.

Micro-finance has also been strategically used by some NGOs as an entry point for wider social and political mobilisation of women around gender issues. For example SEWA in India, CODEC in Bangladesh and CIPCRE in Cameroon, indicate the potential of micro-finance to form a basis for organisation against other issues like domestic violence, male alcohol abuse and dowry. However there is no necessary link between women's individual economic empowerment and/or participation in micro-finance groups and social and political empowerment. These changes are not an automatic consequence of microfinance per se. As noted above, women's increased productive role has also often had it costs.

In most programmes there is little attempt to link micro-finance with wider social and political activity. In the absence of specific measures to encourage this there is little evidence of any significant contribution of micro-finance. Micro-finance groups may put severe strains on women's existing networks if repayment becomes a problem. There is evidence to the contrary that micro-finance and income-earning may take women away from other social and political activities.

The evidence therefore indicates that contributions of micro-finance per se to women's empowerment cannot be assumed and current complacency in this regard is misplaced. In many cases contextual constraints at all levels have prevented women from accessing programmes, increasing or controlling incomes or challenging subordination. Where women are not able to significantly increase incomes under their control or negotiate changes in intra-household and community gender inequalities, women may become dependent on loans to continue in very low-paid occupations with heavier workloads and enjoying little benefit.

For some women micro-finance has been positively disempowering, as indicated by some of the cases shown above which are far from isolated examples:

- Credit (i.e. debt) may lead to severe impoverishment, abandonment and put serious strains on networks with other women.
- Pressure to save may mean women forgoing their own necessary consumption.
- The contribution of micro-finance alone appears to be most limited for the poorest and most disadvantaged women.

All the evidence suggests the poorest women are the most likely to be explicitly excluded by programmes and also peer groups where repayment is the prime consideration and/or where the main emphasis of programmes is on existing micro-entrepreneurs. It also suggests that even where they get access to credit they are particularly vulnerable to falling further into debt.

Conclusions and Suggestions

Numerous traditional and informal system of credit that were already in existence before micro finance came into vogue. Viability of micro finance needs to be understood from a dimension that is far broader- in looking at its long-term aspects too .very little attention has been given to empowerment questions or ways in which both empowerment and sustainability aims may be accommodated. Failure to take into account impact on income also has potentially adverse implications for both repayment and outreach, and hence also for financial sustainability. An effort is made here to present some of these aspects to complete the picture.

A conclusion that emerges from this account is that micro finance can contribute to solving the problems of inadequate housing and urban services as an integral part of poverty alleviation programmes. The challenge lies in finding the level of flexibility in the credit instrument that could make it match the multiple credit requirements of the low income borrower without imposing unbearably high cost of monitoring its end use upon the lenders. A promising solution is to provide multipurpose lone or composite credit for income generation, housing improvement and consumption support. Consumption loan is found to be especially important during the gestation period between commencing a new economic activity and deriving positive income. Careful research on demand for financing and savings behavior of the potential borrowers and their participation in determing the mix of multi-purpose loans are essential in making the concept work. The organisations involved in micro credit initiatives should take account of the fact that:

- Credit is important for development but cannot by itself enable very poor women to overcome their poverty.
- Making credit available to women does not automatically mean they have control over its use and over any income they might generate from micro enterprises.
- In situations of chronic poverty it is more important to provide saving services than to offer credit.
- A useful indicator of the tangible impact of micro credit schemes is the number of additional proposals and demands presented by local villagers to public authorities.

Nevertheless ensuring that the micro-finance sector continues to move forward in relation to gender equality and women's empowerment will require a long-term strategic process of the same order as the one in relation to poverty if gender is not to continue to 'evaporate' in a combination of complacency and resistance within donor agencies and the micro-finance sector. This will involve:

- Ongoing exchange of experience and innovation between practitioners

- Constant awareness and questioning of 'bad practice' lobbying donors for sufficient funding for empowerment strategies bringing together the different players in the sector to develop coherent policies and for gender advocacy.

India is the country where a collaborative model between banks, NGOs, MFIs and Women's organisations is furthest advanced. It therefore serves as a good starting point to look at what we know so far about 'Best Practice' in relation to micro-finance for women's empowerment and how different institutions can work together.

It is clear that gender strategies in micro finance need to look beyond just increasing women's access to savings and credit and organising self help groups to look strategically at how programmes can actively promote gender equality and women's empowerment. Moreover the focus should be on developing a diversified micro finance sector where different type of organisations, NGO, MFIs and formal sector banks all should have gender policies adapted to the needs of their particular target groups/institutional roles and capacities and collaborate and work together to make a significant contribution to gender equality and pro-poor development.

Bibliography

Acker, J. *Class Questions: Feminist Answers*. Rowman & Littlefield Publishers, Inc., 2006.

Alber, Jens, and Guy Standing. Social dumping, catch-up, or convergence? Europe in comparative global context. Journal of European Social Policy 10 (2):99-119, 2000.

Amaury de Riencourt; Woman and Power in History, Ind. Ed., 1989, Sterling Publishers Pt. Ltd. New Delhi, 2003.

Appleton, S. Problems of measuring poverty over time: the case of Uganda. IDS Bulletin 27 (1):43-55, 1996.

Baulch, B. Neglected Trade-offs in Poverty Measurement. IDS Bulletin 27 (1):36-42, 1996.

Begum, Dr. O.P. Women Rights and Rural Employment. Kurukshetra Journal, Pub. Divn. M.o I & B, Govt. of India, New Delhi, 2000.

Bhattacharya, D., and M. Rahman. Female Employment under Export-Propelled Industrialization: Prospect for Internalizing Global Opportunities in Bangladesh's Apparels Sector. Geneve: UNRISD mimeo, 1998.

Bunch, Charlotte and Roxanna Carrillo. "Feminist Perspectives on Women in Development." Pp. 70-82 in *Persistent Inequalities: Women & World Development* Irene Tinker, editor. New York: Oxford University Press, 1990.

Charmes, Jacques. Informal Sector, Poverty and Gender: A Review of Emperical Evidence, Background paper for the World Development Report. Washington, D.C.: World Bank, 2001.

Chen, M., J. Sebstad, and L. O'Connell. Counting the invisible workforce: the case of homebased workers. World Development 27 (3):603-610, 1999.

Connell, R.W. *Gender: Short Introduction*. Polity Press, 2002.

Cornia, Giovanni Andrea. An Economic Policy for Growth and Social Progress. UNRISD News (24):3-4, 2001.

Cornia, Giovanni Andrea. Preliminary comments on the paper 'Social Policy in a Development Context'. Paper read at UNRISD Conference on Social Policy in a Development Context, 23-24 September, at Stockholm, 2000.

Croll, Elisabeth. Social Welfare Refom: Trends and Tensions. The China Quarterly 159:684-699, 1999.

Davin, Delia. The Impact of Export-Oriented Manufacturing on Chine Women Workers. Geneva: UNRISD mimeo, 2001.

Davis, N.Y. Gender & Nations. Sage Publications, 1997.

Deacon, Bob. Eastern Europe WelfareSates: The Impact of the Politics of Globalization. Journal of European Social Policy 10 (2):146-161, 2001.

Deacon, Bob. Globalization and Social Policy, Occasional Paper 5. Geneva: UNRISD, 2000.

Desai, Manisha. "Transnational Solidarity: Women's Agency, Structural Adjustment, and Globalization." pp. 15-33 in *Women's Activism and Globalization: Linking Local Struggles and Transnational Politics,* edited by Nancy A. Naples and Manisha Desai. New York: Routledge, 2002.

Elson, D., and N. Cagatay. The Social Content of Macroeconomic Policies. World Development 28 (7), 2000.

Elson, Diane: "From Survival Strategies to Transformation Strategies: Women's Needs and Structural Adjustments." Pp. 26 48 in *Unequal Burden: Economic Crises, Persistent Poverty and Women's Work.* Lourdes Beneria and Shelley Feldman, editors. Boulder, CO: West view Press, 1992.

Elson, Diane. Gender Justice, Human Rights and Neo-liberal Economic Policies. Geneva: UNRISD mimeo, 2001.

Elson, Diane. Labor Markets as Gendered Institutions: Equality, Efficiency, and Empowerment Issues. World Development 27 (3), 1999.

Escobar, A. Encountering Development: The Making and Unmaking of the Third World.

Esping-Andersen, G., ed. Welfare States in Transition: National Adaptations in Global Economies. London and Geneva: Sage/ UNRISD, 1996.

Fuettes, Annette and Barbara Ehenreich. *Women & the Global Factory* Boston: South End Press, 1998.

GFONT *Search for Alternatives* . GEFONT/KAD Study Report on Women Workers Issues, 2003.

GFONT: Woman Participation in Nepali Labour Movement (Study Report) GFONT. Nepal, 2001.

Gupta, Prof. V.S. Nation Building and Empowerment of Women, Employment News, 11–17, Aug. 2001, New Delhi, 2001.

Harper, Charles. & Leicht, Kevin. *Exploring Social Change: America and the World*, 4th ed. Upper Saddle River, N.J: Prentice Hall, 2002.

Hart, G. Clothes for next to nothing: Rethinking global competition. South African Labour Bulletin 9 (6):41-7, 1995.

Hart, Gillian. Reworking Apartheid Legacies:Global Competition, Gender, and Social Wages in South Africa, 1980-2000. Geneva: UNRISD mimeo, 2001.

Lewis, G. 'Race', Gender, Social Welfare: Encounters in a Postcolonial Society. Polity Press, 2000.

Lim, Linda. "Women's Work in Export Factories: The Politics of a Cause." Pp. 101-122 *Persistent Inequalities: Women and World Development*. Irene Tinker, editor. Oxford: Oxford University Press, 1990.

Loomba, A. *Colonialism/ Postcolonialism: The New Critical Idiom*. Routledge, 2005.

Maurya, Dr. O.P. Occupation Pattern of Employment of Women in India and the World. Employment News, 11–17 August, 2001, New Delhi, 2001.

Mendez, Jennifer Bickham. "Creating Alternatives from a Gender Perspective: Transnational Organizing for Maquila Workers' Rights in Central America."Pp. 121-141 in *Women's Activism and Globalization: Linking Local Struggles and Transnational Politics,* edited by Nancy A. Naples and Manisha Desai. New York: Routledge, 2002.

Moghadam V.M. Globalising Women: Transforming Feminist Networks. The Johns Hopkins University Press, 2005.

Moghadam, Valentine M. "Gender and Globalization: Female Labor and Women's Mobilization." *Journal of World Systems Research* 2: 367-388, 1999.

Mohanty, C.T. Feminism Without Borders: Decolonising Theory, Practicing Solidarity. Duke University Press, 2003.

Nepal Human Development Report, Poverty Reduction and Governance. UNDP, Nepal, 2001.

Ong, A. Colonialism and Modernity: Feminist Re-presentations of Women in non-Western Societies. Inscriptions 3 (4):79-9, 1988.

Orloff, Ann Shola. Women's Employment and Welfare Regimes. Globalization, Export-Oriented Employment for Women and Social Policy, 2001.

Pattanaik, B.K. Women Welfare and Social Development, Yojana, Nov. 2000, New Delhi, 2000.

Perrons, D. Globalisation and Social Change: People and Places in a Divided World, 2004.

Rana, B. and Navin Singh: *Mother Sister Daughter: Nepal's Press on Women*, Sancharika Samuha, Nepal, 2005.

Rao, N.J. Usha.; Women in a Developing Society, Ashish Publishing House, New Delhi, 1985.

Schultz, T. Paul. "Women's Changing Participation in the Labor Force: A World Perspective." *Economic Development and Cultural Change* 38 (3): 457- 487, 1990.

Tzannatos, Zafiris. "Women and Labor Market Changes in the Global Economy: Growth Helps, Inequalities Hurt, and Public Policy Matters" *World Development*, 3: 551-569, 1999.

Wade, Robert, and Frank Veneroso The Asian Crisis: The High-Debt Model Versus the Wall Street-Treasury-IMF Complex. New Left Review 288:3-23, 1998.

Wade, Robert. Is Globalization Making World Income Distribution More Equal, Working Paper Series No. 01-01. London: LSE Development Studies Institute, 2001.

Ward, Katharine. *Women Workers and Global Restructuring.* New York: Cornell University Press, 1990.

Wolf, Diane L. "Daughters, Decisions and Domination: An Empirical and Conceptual Critique of Household Strategies." Pp. 118-132 in *The Women, Gender and Development Reader*, edited by Nalini Visvanathan. Atlantic- Highlands, NJ: Zed Books, 1997.